RIVALS!

On the cover: Boston Red Sox catcher Jason Varitek and New York Yankees third baseman Alex Rodriguez exchange pleasantries during a game at Fenway Park on July 24, 2004. This tiff began when Rodriguez was hit on the arm by pitcher Bronson Arroyo and it quickly escalated into a full-scale brawl that saw both dugouts empty. Varitek and Rodriguez both were given four game suspensions for their actions.

For Sharon

RIVALS!

The Ten Greatest American Sports
Rivalries of the 20th Century

Richard O. Davies

WILEY-BLACKWELL

A John Wiley & Sons, Ltd., Publication

This edition first published 2010
© 2010 Richard O. Davies

Blackwell Publishing was acquired by John Wiley & Sons in February 2007.
Blackwell's publishing program has been merged with Wiley's global Scientific,
Technical, and Medical business to form Wiley-Blackwell.

Registered Office
John Wiley & Sons Ltd, The Atrium, Southern Gate, Chichester, West Sussex,
PO19 8SQ, United Kingdom

Editorial Offices
350 Main Street, Malden, MA 02148-5020, USA
9600 Garsington Road, Oxford, OX4 2DQ, UK
The Atrium, Southern Gate, Chichester, West Sussex, PO19 8SQ, UK

For details of our global editorial offices, for customer services, and for information
about how to apply for permission to reuse the copyright material in this book
please see our website at www.wiley.com/wiley-blackwell.

The right of Richard O. Davies to be identified as the author of this work has been
asserted in accordance with the UK Copyright, Designs and Patents Act 1988.

Library of Congress Cataloging-in-Publication Data is available for this book
Davies, Richard O., 1937–
  Rivals! : the ten greatest American sports rivalries of the 20th century /
Richard O. Davies.
    p. cm.
  Includes bibliographical references and index.
  ISBN 978-1-4051-7765-8 (hardcover : alk. paper) – ISBN 978-1-4051-7764-1
(pbk. : alk. paper) 1. Sports rivalries–United States–History. 2. Sports–United
States–History. I. Title.
  GV583.D389 2010
  796.0973–dc22
                                                                    2009050933

A catalogue record for this book is available from the British Library.

Set in 10/12.5pt Galliard by Graphicraft Limited, Hong Kong
Printed in Singapore by Ho Printing Singapore Pte Ltd

01   2010

Contents

List of Figures

Preface

This book examines what I consider the ten greatest sports rivalries of the past century or more. Sports constitute an important part of American popular culture, and big games and big matches between top teams and athletes add to the excitement and pleasure of millions of American sports fans. I have chosen ten rivalries that illuminate and highlight some of the great moments of American sports from the late 19th century to the present. None of my selections will be a surprise because they have been identified many times and in numerous places. Although many contemporary sports fans are emotionally involved in the fates of their special teams, and become especially focused during rivalry week, I have learned from teaching sports history to many bright college students that they have little understanding of the underlying events and traditions that have made prominent sports rivalries so compelling. This book is intended to provide that historical dimension, hopefully without slighting events that resonate in recent memory.

There are no great secrets as to what constitutes a good rivalry. Both participants must win their share of the contests, and competitive fires must burn brightly. Big upsets and unusual plays – such as the improvised multilateral game-winning miracle by California that concluded with the ball carrier plowing through the Stanford Band on the final play of the Big Game in 1982 – add to the richness of rivalry mythology. Great team rivalries are built by skilled athletes and leading coaches who face off, season after season, in high-pressure games, creating vivid traditions that flourish with the passing years.

Rivalries between individual athletes, however, are much shorter and several special factors must coalesce for a significant personal rivalry to take shape. Sometimes they emerge when a young challenger rises to take on a seasoned veteran who has been at the top of his or her sport, and has a large bag of tricks to draw upon to hold off the upstart. Compelling individual rivalries also benefit from the contrasts in personalities and a fierce determination on the part of both athletes to prevail. Rivalries between individuals normally last for only a few years, which is what makes the rivalry between two of the best women tennis players of all time so fascinating. It began in 1973, and when their string of 80 tournament matches had run its course in 1988, Martina Navratilova held a scant 43–37 edge on Chris Evert. Each woman claimed 18 Grand Slam singles titles. The sharp contrast in personalities and playing styles added to the drama. No wonder journalist Bud Palmer called it the "Rivalry of the Century."

The competition between two of the world's greatest golfers, Arnold Palmer and Jack Nicklaus, lasted for a decade. Like Navratilova and Evert, they competed with everything they could muster, but nonetheless remained cordial despite the intense competition. Palmer's exuberant style and blue-collar upbringing attracted new fans to golf and gave the game unprecedented popularity. When a new player on the tour who was ten years Palmer's junior burst onto the scene with his cerebral and artfully calibrated approach to the game, the contrast made for an instant rivalry that saw millions of fans take sides in this spirited competition that played out at several major tournaments.

Cordiality is a word that cannot be applied to the malevolence that pervaded the four year war between boxers Joe Frazier and Muhammad Ali. Neither man liked the other and made no effort to hide that fact. Their raw personal feelings were on full display during their three high-stakes matches. The intensity of these bouts and the courage both men exhibited produced the greatest individual rivalry in boxing history. Thanks to the emerging satellite communications technology, millions of fight fans around the world were able to watch.

In contrast to these individual match-ups, team rivalries can last for long periods of time. The seven team rivalries described here have existed for many decades, five for more than a century. During these long rivalries, both pairs of teams have had their many ups and downs, but are all sparked by the presence of great athletes, legendary coaches or managers, high-profile team owners, and large contingents of fans passionate about their team.

The great majority of America's most identifiable rivalries exist in college football. Tradition is an essential ingredient, and the 135 year history of the Yale–Harvard rivalry is filled with great stories of the days of yore. These two great universities played their first "foot-ball match" in 1875 and they are still going at it. This series produced more than just a timeless football rivalry; the Bulldogs and Crimson essentially created the template for college football. Well into the 1900s, their game was often a showdown that carried national title implications. For almost 50 years, the pervasive influence of Yale's Walter Camp was evident, first as a star player, then as the formulator of the essential rules of the game, and ultimately as a master strategist, teacher, and publicist. Contemporary Americans pay little attention to this storied Ivy League rivalry because it no longer influences national rankings and bowl games, but for nearly a half-century these two giants of East Coast football often vied for the national championship. Yale claims 15 national titles, Harvard eight. To understand the history of the rivalry is to appreciate the rich heritage of college football.

The other college football rivalry I've selected became a major autumn sporting event in the 1920s and remains so today. The outcome of the Ohio State–Michigan game has been crucial to determining the Big Ten champion, obtaining major bowl invitations, and, on several occasions, to deciding a national championship. The series has been marked by the presence of an endless parade of All-Americans, eight Heisman Trophy winners, and a host of famous coaches. The series began in 1897, became a major attraction after the First World War, and ever since the 1930s has been played in late November before enormous crowds in two of the biggest stadiums in college football. The ritual and excitement stirred by this Big Game convey the deep and powerful emotions evoked by major college football.

College basketball rivalries generally do not create the same high level of emotional involvement as football. Longer schedules and postseason tournaments mean that two games, and sometimes three, are played between the same two teams. This frequency of games tends to dissipate somewhat the intensity of the rivalry. The autumn football contest is infused with much greater pageantry and media interest than basketball games between the same schools. The one college basketball rivalry that defies these generalizations is, of course, North Carolina–Duke. A convergence of several factors in the years after the Second World War helped produce college basketball's undisputed greatest rivalry. Since that time, both teams have routinely enjoyed lofty national rankings and have figured prominently in many a National Collegiate Athletic Association tournament. The Tar Heels boast of five NCAA championships, the Blue Devils three. The intensity of the rivalry became white hot during the 1950s and remains so today.

Surprisingly, the National Football League has only one enduring rivalry. The Green Bay Packers and the Chicago Bears first met in 1921 and have played each year since 1923. As the 2009 season began, the Bears held a ten game edge in this special rivalry between teams representing an enormous metropolis and a small blue-collar town, home to several meatpacking and paper processing plants. It is a very special rivalry that gives us valuable insight into the history of what has become the most dominant professional sport in contemporary America. Because of constant changes in leagues, conference affiliations, club ownership, and franchise locations, most professional football rivalries take shape and flourish for a few years when two teams are in the hunt for championships, but then fade when personnel and coaching changes undercut the dynamics that are so essential to the making of a lasting rivalry. Frequent player movement from one team to another has further eroded the potential for enduring NFL rivalries.

Professional basketball has seen several leagues and innumerable franchises come and go since the Second World War, thereby short-circuiting the potential for lasting rivalries. That is what makes the rivalry between the Boston Celtics and the Los Angeles Lakers so significant. The host cities are located on two oceans some 2,600 air miles distant, which puts to rest the generalization that proximity is a major factor in creating lasting rivalries. Their rivalry has featured great players, great coaches, great fans, and many a compelling championship series. Together these two teams have won half of all National Basketball Association championships and they have squared off in the finals on 11 separate occasions.

The two baseball rivalries I've selected (Giants–Dodgers and Red Sox–Yankees) are those that most experts routinely identify as the best. Both are deeply connected to the early history of professional baseball. The Giants and Dodgers have been playing since the early years of the National League, and their cumulative record as of the start of the 2009 season stood at a virtual dead heat (Giants 1,160, Dodgers 1,139). This rivalry began on the East Coast and did not miss a beat when the two teams moved to California for the 1958 season. It has sparked many a classic game, played by some of baseball's greatest players and managed by such legendary characters as John J. McGraw, Wilbert Robinson, Leo Durocher, and Tommy Lasorda. The Red Sox have a long way to go to catch up with the Yankees in head-to-head games (Yankees 1,126, Red Sox 940), but the location of these two pre-eminent teams in the northeastern corridor has produced a delightful co-mingling of their extremely loyal fans, who are important components in the cultural mix that keeps this rivalry at the top of the national sports consciousness.

Ever since Red Sox owner Harry Frazee sold superstar Babe Ruth to the Yankees after the 1919 season, the rivalry took on a special quality. What eventually was called the "Curse of the Bambino" might have helped some disconsolate Red Sox fans explain away the spate of Yankee American League pennants (39) and World Series titles (26) while their team could claim only four pennants between 1920 and 2004. In that year, the Red Sox finally exorcised the "Curse" in dramatic fashion, overcoming a 3–0 Yankee margin in the American League Championship Series and then rolling to a 4–0 romp over the St Louis Cardinals to capture their first World Series title since 1918.

In picking the "ten greatest" rivalries, I had little trouble except for deciding which compelling college football rivalries had to be excluded. Whenever a friend or colleague learned of my project, I was immediately asked whether or not I was going to include their alma mater. Every college or university that plays football, it seems, has a special rival, sometimes more than one. Because I live in Reno and teach at the University of Nevada, I have been asked many times how I could dare exclude the relatively brief UNLV–Nevada rivalry that has been the source of considerable ill will, replete with bitter political overtones and marked by general down-and-dirty acrimony. The same can probably be said for most great in-state rivalries where proximity and local issues are embroiled in the deep emotions that become attached to an athletic contest: Indiana–Purdue, Arizona–Arizona State, Stanford–California, Florida–Florida State, Iowa–Iowa State, Oregon–Oregon State, Idaho–Boise State, Virginia–Virginia Tech, Brigham Young–Utah, Mississippi State–Ole Miss, and Texas–Texas A&M are among many such notable rivalries. There are also great football rivalries that are conducted across contiguous state lines, such as Oklahoma–Texas, Colorado–Nebraska, Tennessee–Kentucky, Florida–Georgia, and Ohio State–Michigan. And, as I have learned from impassioned friends, the rivalries between such small colleges as Williams–Amherst and DePauw–Wabash can generate their own very special brand of alumni enthusiasm.

One of my personal favorite football rivalries is that between my alma mater, the University of Missouri, and neighboring Kansas University. This rivalry is one of the nation's oldest, having begun in 1891, and has had its share of great games and memorable upsets, not to mention some very nasty moments, perhaps because its roots are embedded in the violence of the border warfare conducted across state lines between the slavery and anti-slavery guerrilla gangs before the Civil War. The two schools cannot even agree on the overall head-to-head record due to a forfeit of a crucial game in 1960 that saw the Jayhawks upset the undefeated Tigers 23–7 in Columbia and ruin hopes for their only national championship. An ineligible Kansas player produced a forfeit, but only long after the season had ended. Official Kansas records still defiantly show that game as a victory, but so do Missouri's. So the series stands either 55–53–9 in favor of the Jayhawks or tied at 54–54–9 if you accept the Tigers' version of history. Evoking memories of Border Ruffians, Quantrill's Raiders, and Bleeding Kansas, this heated rivalry was long appropriately called the "Border War." However, in 2005 a sanitized new appellation was imposed by a corporate banking sponsor, which insisted it be changed to the more politically correct "Border Showdown." Former KU coach Don Fambrough was appalled by the change: "It's a goddam war and they started it!" he fumed.

The Auburn–Alabama rivalry was the most difficult to exclude. It is a game played by two great state universities located just 100 miles apart in the heart of a state obsessed with football. To be in Tuscaloosa, as I have been, during game week is an unforgettable experience. I ultimately selected Ohio State–Michigan because the Tigers–Crimson Tide series was interrupted by a 40 year hiatus. After the 1907 game ended in a 6–6 tie and resulted in an unseemly brawl involving players and spectators, university officials called off the 1908 game. Various disagreements and downright cantankerousness prevented the game from being played again until 1948. Even then, university officials opted to do so only after the Alabama state legislature passed a resolution urging resumption of play, with the unofficial message being that budget appropriations might be imperiled.

Many people have identified the "Civil War" between the military academies at West Point and Annapolis as one of the most important football rivalries. No doubt it is. "Although Army–Navy does not decide national championships anymore," John Feinstein writes, "it is played by teams who try to crush each other for three hours, then stand at attention together when the game is over. It is the tradition and the uniqueness of the scene inside the stadium that makes the rivalry unique. After all, it is the only college football game played each year that is attended by the entire student body of both schools." This celebrated series has been closely contested, with Navy holding a narrow 53–49 margin (with seven ties) at the end of 2008. Many a future military leader played in these games, including two giants of the Second World War: West Point halfback General Dwight D. Eisenhower and Annapolis fullback Admiral William "Bull" Halsey.

Notre Dame has developed several traditional games – Michigan, Purdue, Southern California, Navy – but none reaches the highest level. Navy and Notre Dame have played each year since 1927, but on the eve of the 2009 season, the record was a lopsided 71–10–1 in favor of the Irish. It might be a traditional game, but it is not much of a rivalry. USC and Notre Dame began their series in 1926, making it football's greatest intersectional rivalry. Despite many a memorable game, the overall intensity has been diluted because it has no conference affiliation. I am certain that most Trojan fans would, if given the choice, prefer to beat cross-town UCLA than the Irish.

I am certain that many fans will disagree with some of my selections, and I know that some dissent is inevitable because of the emotions that great rivalries evoke. Be that as it may, the reader will have to agree that the underlying narratives of the ten rivalries I have selected provide a colorful prism through which to examine and appreciate the important role that rivalries have played in making sports an integral part of our everyday lives.

Acknowledgments

Many friends, colleagues, and students contributed to this book. Senior Editor Peter Coveney of Wiley-Blackwell Publishing has been supportive from the inception of the project and I have benefitted from his guidance and learned from his vast experience in the world of academic publishing. Editorial Assistant Galen Smith has taken care of myriad details during the final stages of production and her efforts kept me on track and helped me avoid pitfalls. Officials at several universities were helpful on specific rivalries: Stephen Conn of Yale University, Matt Bowers of University of North Carolina, and Thomas Harkins of Duke University. I appreciate very much the research assistance provided by graduate students Katherine Robinson, Kimberly Esse, and Lindsay Martin. Jayme Hoy read various drafts and provided important research assistance. Dr Tom Bittker, MD, provided perspective on Ohio State–Michigan derived from his role as a former student sports editor of the *Michigan Daily.* Dee Kille (University of Nevada), Joe Amato (Southwest Minnesota State), and Charles Alexander (Ohio University) responded generously to my requests for assistance. I am especially indebted to long-time friend Frank Mitchell (University of Southern California), who not only made many helpful suggestions that improved the narrative, but also provided welcome words of encouragement at critical times during the writing process. If errors remain, they are my responsibility. I am fortunate to be a member of a Department of History where the words *collegiality* and *professionalism* have special resonance. I gratefully acknowledge the encouragement and support of my colleagues. Several years ago, two special friends established the John and Marie Noble Endowment for Historical Research at the University of Nevada. I gratefully acknowledge the financial support their Endowment provided for this book.

This book was completed during my 50th year as a member of the professoriate. I cannot think of a better career choice that I could have made. During that half-century I have benefitted from the many courtesies extended to me by students, faculty colleagues, and administrators. To those many individuals who have helped me along the way, I can only say a heartfelt "Thank you!" This book is dedicated to Sharon, whose life with me began during our courtship days watching our Missouri Tigers battle the Kansas Jayhawks on field and court in one of the greatest and most enduring of all college sports rivalries.

Richard O. Davies
University of Nevada, Reno

1 Fight Fiercely

Harvard and Yale Create the First Great Football Rivalry

Gentlemen, you are now going to play football against Harvard. Never again in your life will you do anything as important. (Yale Coach Tad Jones, November 1923)

When he arrived on the Harvard campus in the fall of 1876, 18-year-old Theodore Roosevelt would have given most anything to become a member of the football team. But he was still a gangly youngster whose physical development had been slowed by childhood illnesses. The vigorous and robust man – cowboy, military hero, and outdoorsman – that Americans would admire as their 26th president had yet to emerge. Slender and awkward, slow afoot, and afflicted with severe myopia that required eyeglasses, young Roosevelt was definitely not football material. That November, however, he accompanied classmates to New Haven to cheer on the Crimson in the second football game ever played against Yale. What he witnessed was a hard-fought game, resembling English rugby, that was dominated by the Blues. Keenly disappointed by the loss, he wrote his parents, "I am sorry to say we were beaten, principally because our opponents played very foul."

Perhaps memories of that game – when the Yale men "played very foul" – were in the back of his mind in 1905, when he summoned the football coaches from Harvard, Yale, and Princeton – college football's indisputable "Big Three" at the time – to the White House to discuss the issue of excessive violence that had contributed to innumerable injuries and several deaths. Roosevelt had often contemplated the issue of unsportsmanlike behavior by football players and the high number of serious injuries. Even though the dangerous "flying wedge" formation had been made illegal in 1894 after just two years of mayhem, the "mass momentum" strategies that had become popular during football's formative years remained in vogue. Players competed in a crude game where slugging, biting, kicking, and other forms of raw violence were commonplace and helmets and protective padding were not commonly worn. Newspaper accounts of college games often included a "hospital report." It was no surprise that many college administrators and faculty advocated abolishing the game. In 1893, President Grover Cleveland banned the game at the two military academies due to excessive numbers of injuries that kept cadets and midshipmen from drill and class.

The more Roosevelt learned about the game, however, the more conflicted he seemed. He was, after all, among the enthusiastic advocates of "muscular Christianity," a set of religious and social teachings that sought to create future male leaders by emphasizing programs that would test their courage, build physical strength, and develop high moral character. As one of the movement's prominent early proponents, Henry Ward Beecher, put it, "Give to the young men in our cities the means to physical vigor and health, separated from the temptations of vice."

Roosevelt believed a vigorous life was important in developing young men for future leadership roles. As a frail teenager, he had "built his body" with a stout regimen of weightlifting, calisthenics, boxing, and long hikes in the outdoors. That experience led him in 1902 to publish an article entitled "The American Boy" in which he urged parents to emphasize both the physical and moral development of their youngsters by providing opportunities for exercise and the playing of games in which they would be challenged physically and psychologically. "Now, the chances are he won't be much of a man unless he is a good deal of a boy. He must not be a coward or a weakling, a bully, a shirk, or a prig. He must work hard and play hard. He must be clean-minded and clean-lived, and able to hold his own under all circumstances and against all comers." With an eye to the development of America's future soldiers, statesmen, and business executives, he wrote, "A boy needs both physical and moral courage," that would prepare him for the challenges of adulthood when he would be "in the arena." What better way to accomplish this than on the football field? "In short, in life, as in a foot-ball game, the fundamental principle is, Hit the line hard; don't foul and don't shirk, but hit the line hard."

A persistent myth grew out of that October White House meeting in 1905, to which President Roosevelt summoned, among others, William Reid and Walter Camp, the head football men from Harvard and Yale. It was widely perceived – and the myth has endured in some quarters – that Roosevelt threatened to abolish football unless ways were found to reduce the number of serious injuries. That widely held view, however, could not have been further from the truth. Rather, Roosevelt was fearful that unless substantial reforms were introduced to reduce violent mass momentum play, college administrators and faculty would ban the game from their campuses. TR knew that prominent university faculty members were advocating abolition, including the distinguished University of Chicago professor Shailer Mathews, who had condemned the game as "a social obsession – this boy-killing, man-mutilating, education-prostituting, gladiatorial sport." For years, Roosevelt had fretted that the president of his own alma mater, Charles Eliot, would succeed in his campaign to convince the Board of Overseers to abolish football. Having learned of many instances of unsportsmanlike tactics, Roosevelt wanted to save the good by getting rid of the bad – in this case, by eliminating the foul play of the "muckers."

Two broken noses during that pivotal season helped focus the president's attention. The first belonged to his son Theodore, Jr, who, at a mere 150 pounds, had bravely held his position at the center of the Harvard junior varsity line against a larger and stronger Yale team in a very physical contest. In return for his courageous play "Teedie" received a powerful blow to the face that required reconstructive nose surgery. Harvard rooters felt that the Bulldogs had singled out the president's son for special treatment, but standard strategy at the time was to concentrate powerful attacks upon the weakest spot along the opponent's line. At 150 pounds, the president's son seemed an inviting target. In November, during what had already become known simply as "The Game," Yale's James Quill flew through the air and smacked Harvard freshman Francis Burr in the face with a vicious forearm just as he was about to catch a punt. Most of the 43,000 fans who witnessed this blow in the open field were shocked as a torrent of blood spurted in the air from a shattered nose. The ensuing media coverage was heavy.

These events led to a major national conference in December at which representatives of more than 100 universities discussed the problems that threatened college football. The eventual result was a series of rules changes and administrative reforms that promised to reduce Saturday afternoon mayhem. Among the innovations announced was legalization of the forward pass (with several limiting conditions that would slowly be eliminated over the next two decades), and changes in blocking and tackling rules designed to encourage the use of deceptive running plays that moved the game away from pushing and shoving (and slugging) in the middle of the line. Behind Roosevelt's involvement in this effort, there undoubtedly remained lingering memories of his undergraduate days when Yale played "foul."

Yale and the Invention of Football

Up to this point, Yale had dominated college football. The Blues also enjoyed a lopsided 23–4 advantage in the annual contest with Harvard. This was a depressing statistic that good Harvard men could not abide. The Harvard–Yale football rivalry had grown naturally: the two universities had viewed each other as academic rivals for two centuries. Harvard was founded in 1636 to prepare ministers for the Massachusetts theocracy that the Bay Colony's early settlers envisioned, but doctrinal disputes within the New England faithful led to the creation of Yale in 1701 with a mission to educate Congregational ministers who would not be influenced by the unsettling "liberal" tendencies critics believed were being taught at Harvard. It was only fitting that these two educational rivals would meet in the first known intercollegiate athletic contest in August of 1852. This historic event, however, was not football, but rather a crew race held on Lake Winnipesaukee in New Hampshire. The Harvard eight-oar shell defeated two Yale crews, with presidential candidate Franklin Pierce among the spectators.

Nineteenth-century college students engaged in many hazing and interclass competitions that were often violent. One of these activities included kicking and running with an inflated ball. Despite the bruises and bloodletting, these activities grew in popularity, and by the early 1870s Harvard students had taken to playing an informal game not much different from today's rugby. Yale students, however, favored a different game that was akin to today's soccer, in which the ball could be kicked, but not carried. Yale students created an informal association to play teams from Princeton, Rutgers, and Columbia, and for several years they invited Harvard to join in the competition. Disputes over acceptable rules precluded such an event. Harvard, exhibiting certitude (Yale students called it arrogance) that its rules were superior, insisted that Yale adopt its rules. Consequently, Harvard's first intercollegiate games played under the "Boston Rules" – that featured running with the ball and tackling – were with McGill and Tufts. Eventually the Yale students agreed to meet on Harvard's terms (a concession duly interpreted as a victory in Cambridge) and on November 13, 1875, the two teams squared off at Hamilton Park in New Haven. An estimated crowd of 2,000 curious onlookers watched the Yale team, outfitted in blue shirts, attempting to adapt their play to unfamiliar rules. Wearing crimson shirts and brown knee breeches, the Harvard team dominated by a lopsided 4–0 score. The points were scored when a drop-kick after a touchdown went through the uprights (touchdowns during the early years did not register points, but merely permitted a team the opportunity to kick a one point goal) and three field goals that also counted for one point.

This initial game, informal and experimental as it was, nonetheless was a pivotal moment in the history of American sports. Observers from the several colleges that had initially opted for a free-flowing soccer-style format now decided that the more physical Harvard game was preferable. The following year, teams from Yale, Harvard, Princeton, and Columbia formed the Intercollegiate Football Association, and a major American sports institution was born.

Harvard students probably regretted their determination to require any contest be played by their rules because the Blues quickly adjusted and put together a juggernaut that became the preeminent college football program in America for the next three decades. Yale's domination of a game devised on the Harvard campus was virtually complete. Central to this remarkable period was Walter Camp. He grew up near the Yale campus and enrolled in the fall of 1876 at a time when Yale men were still smarting from their initial loss to Harvard. An all-round athlete, Camp became a big man on campus, pitching for the baseball team, rowing in the Yale shell, and running the hurdles on the track. He earned a position on the football team as a halfback and, at a time before eligibility limits were imposed, played for six years (four as an undergraduate and two as a medical student). He remained directly involved in Yale football until 1909 and, more than any other individual, exerted enormous influence not only upon Yale football, but also upon the structure of the game itself.

Camp's informal title of "Father of American Football" is not overstated. During this 34-year period, Yale won 95 percent of its games, losing only 14 times. After his playing days ended, Camp served as an advisor to the elected team captains who actually ran practices and supervised the team during games. Camp was the driving force behind Yale's domination of the game, and he also provided a formal structure to a complex game with his concisely written rules. A Harvard professor close to the game at the time is quoted by college football's leading historian, Ronald A.

Smith, as saying: "I knew him as a master of football, whose advice – if the Yale captain would listen to it – meant inevitable defeat to the college I loved best."

Elected team captain for his junior year, Camp became heavily involved in the annual negotiations with other representatives of the Big Three – from Princeton and Harvard – over the rapidly evolving rules by which the game was being played. Within a short period of time he emerged as a veritable czar of football rules and dominated this important endeavor until pushed aside in 1906 by a new generation of football coaches. In 1880, for reasons that remain unclear, he convinced the others to reduce the number of players from 15 to 11 and in that same year persuaded other schools to adopt a radical reform that would set American football apart from similar games.

Under existing rules, the ball was put in play by a "scrum" in which the ball was tossed into a melee of players who struggled to gain possession and then attempted to advance it toward the goal. The resulting helter-skelter nature of the game offended Camp's sense of order and discipline, and he proposed that a team should gain possession after a kickoff, punt, or recovered fumble, and that each play would begin with the ball being put in play by a player positioned on the line of "scrimmage." Initially, a lineman would tap the ball with his foot backward to a "quarterback," but within a few years the snap of the ball between the legs was introduced. When the 1881 game between Yale and Princeton curiously deteriorated into each team holding the ball for each half by simply downing it after the snap (both teams believing that by earning a 0–0 tie they would win the mythical national championship), Camp introduced the "down and distance" concept; to retain possession of the ball, the team was required to gain five yards in three "fairs" (attempts to advance the ball, soon to be called "downs"). The "down and distance" concept required that the field be lined, thus prompting an observer to suggest that the field of play looked like a "gridiron."

Camp's influence was also seen in making the scoring system more accurately reflect the nature of the new game. Initially the game emphasized scoring by kicking the ball through the uprights, but in 1883 his reformed scoring system was implemented, which awarded four points for advancing the ball across the goal line, with a safety counting two points, and a goal kicked after a touchdown two points. A goal kicked from the field (today's field goal) was credited with five points but the number of points subsequently was reduced to three over the next 20 years.

By the mid-1880s, Camp's leadership had produced a set of rules that established the foundation for today's American game of football, a game substantially different from the English games of soccer and rugby. The result was a much more controlled, less spontaneous, game than rugby or soccer. Spectators responded enthusiastically, and crowds upwards of 20,000 for "big games" became commonplace.

As early as 1879, Camp had introduced into the Yale system the running of interference (blocking) for the ball carrier, and, with the establishment of a line of "scrimmage," Camp began scripting offensive plays. Calling of signals soon followed. Camp assigned each offensive player a specific task on every play, with all 11 men expected to perform them in synchronized fashion – the correlation with the emerging assembly-line manufacturing system was not missed by sharp observers. Camp's changes fundamentally shaped the structure of the game, producing in effect a replication of innovations taking place in American industry in which organization, cooperation, specialization, and integration of many workers into the steady flow of the manufacturing process were being implemented in accordance with the ideas of manufacturing efficiency guru Frederick Winslow Taylor. In his public lectures and writings on football, Camp was given to using such business-like terms as "scientific football," "strategy and tactics," and "scientific planning." His objective was to create a game in which spontaneity and chance were reduced while emphasis was placed upon discipline and organized patterns of play. His game inevitably made the head coach central to the organization and strategies employed by a team, somewhat analogous to the duties of a corporate executive. It is not surprising that Camp's day job was as a manager of a New Haven clock factory (he had discovered medicine was not his calling) and that he often referred to the "work" that constituted the playing of Yale football. It was his ability to organize, plan, and implement his concepts that enabled Yale to operate one of the most efficient and successful football machines in the history of the game. Under Camp, college football became a metaphor for the emerging American industrial system of large factories and complex distribution systems.

When Camp pushed through the legalization of tackling below the waist in 1888, he did so with the specific intent of reducing the ability of ball carriers to evade tackles in open field, thereby encouraging the use of hard-hitting plays directed into the middle of the line. This led to intense hand-to-hand combat along the line of scrimmage. The ball carrier might be pushed through the line or even tossed over it by teammates.

In order to gain the necessary five yards, conventional strategy dictated the use of brute force at the point of attack in the line, and the game became one in which players often interlocked arms to provide protection for the ball carrier. This was the heyday of brutal "mass momentum" football, and Yale was its most accomplished practitioner.

Thanks to Camp's attention to detail, the annual game with Harvard became a one-sided affair, with the Blues winning consecutive games from 1880 until Harvard finally broke the tide with a 12–6 victory in 1890. In that memorable game, Harvard double-teamed Yale's great lineman "Pudge" Heffelfinger on every play. The game was marked by ferocious play at the line of scrimmage. Yale's 6'3", 210 pound behemoth was so exhausted at game's end that he had to be helped from the field of battle. Heffelfinger later said, "We went out there and murdered one another for 60 minutes. . . . The slaughter had been so fierce that it was a wonder any of us came out alive." Harvard's long-suffering fans thus thrilled to their team's first undefeated 11–0 record, which more than a half-century later prompted the Helms Foundation to formally award the Crimson the 1890 national championship.

Over the next three years, Harvard went into The Game with impressive winning records – twice undefeated – only to lose in hard-fought, close games. Adding to the frustration of Harvard supporters was the fact that the Crimson failed to score a single point against the Blues during that span. Spearheading the Yale team was a diminutive fireball, 140 pound Frank Hinkey. He and his teammates were the beneficiaries of Walter Camp's heavy emphasis on physical conditioning, and they blocked, tackled, and ran with intensity and proficiency. Hinkey was a quiet, reserved loner off the field, known to his teammates as "Silent Frank," but when on the gridiron he became a fiery cauldron of hostility. He asked for and gave no quarter. As one sportswriter observed of Hinkey, "When he tackled 'em, they stayed tackled," and "when he hit 'em on his blocking assignments, they stayed hit." Walter Camp's 1892 team, led by Frank Hinkey, was probably his best. That year, Yale enjoyed a season of superlatives, as the Bulldogs went undefeated, untied, and unscored against, overwhelming opponents by a combined score of 435–0.

Even Harvard's surprise unveiling of football's most fearsome play in 1892 could not prevent domination by Hinkey and the powerful Yale Eleven. The famous (or infamous) flying wedge play was designed by businessman and Harvard booster Lorin Deland, whose interest in military history had led to a fascination with Napoleon's strategy of concentrating force upon a single point of the enemy's defense. Deland devised a play that capitalized on a rule, then current, that permitted the kickoff team to tap the ball backward and take possession. Harvard practiced the play in secret throughout the fall, saving it to surprise Yale. With the score tied 0–0 as the second half began, Harvard faked a kick-off, and the kicker tapped the ball backward as two groups of linemen, starting 20 yards behind the fake kicker, began running at full speed to form a V-shaped formation, not unlike a flock of geese. The ball was tossed backwards to a running back as the wedge slammed into an isolated Yale defender. The play, which sparked enormous comment, only gained 20 yards because, as game reports indicated, a determined Frank Hinkey brought down the runner. The flying wedge failed to turn the tide of the lopsided series in Harvard's favor, as Yale went on to win the game 6–0, but its sheer brutal nature overshadowed the game's outcome. "What a grand play!" a *New York Times* writer exclaimed. "A half-ton of bone and muscle coming into collision with a man weighing 160 or 170 pounds!" The following season, most teams ran their own variation of the flying wedge, often beginning with the linemen starting their charge from several yards behind the line of scrimmage with the ball carrier surrounded by his teammates' human wedge.

Mayhem on the Gridiron: Football Imperiled

The flying wedge symbolized to the growing band of football critics the brutality of the game. Even the most ardent advocate of mass momentum play, Walter Camp, had to agree and the play was eliminated after just two seasons when he inserted a new rule for the 1894 season that required seven linemen to be set within a yard of the line of scrimmage before the snap. This negated the opportunity for blockers to pick up steam before reaching the line of scrimmage. That same year, the rules committee also made illegal the wearing of special belts outfitted with handles that running backs could grasp to be pulled forward by stout blockers.

The abolition of the flying wedge, however, failed to deter the growing level of violence that had come to characterize the Yale–Harvard game. That November, The Game was once again played at Hampden Field in Springfield, Massachusetts, a railroad center that provided a convenient destination for fans of both teams. Twenty-five thousand spectators,

many waving crimson or blue pennants, braved bitter weather to wit-
ness what became known as the "Springfield Massacre." After the teams
swapped touchdowns, the game deteriorated into little more than a semi-
organized brawl. A Harvard lineman jabbed his finger into the eye of Frank
Butterworth, producing blood and obscuring his vision. In retaliation, Frank
Hinkey reportedly jumped on the back of downed Harvard punt returner
Edgar Wrightington, knees first, breaking a collarbone. The game official,
Alex Moffat, was unable to keep the game under even a modicum of
control, and injuries piled up on both sides as Yale played cautiously in
the final minutes, protecting a 12–4 lead. The score of the game, however, was not the biggest story of the day, but rather the slugfest that
unfolded. At one point, Yale tackle Fred Murphy struck Bob Hallowell
after a play had ended, producing a bloody broken nose. The Crimson
thereupon piled on the perpetrator, who was carried unconscious off the
field on a stretcher and dumped unceremoniously along the sidelines.
Other players were assisted off the field, wobbling from blows they had
received to their unprotected heads. Several players were ejected and
the "hospital list" after the game revealed the carnage: Harvard had lost
three players to broken bones – Charlie Brewer's leg, Wrightington's
collar bone, and Hallowell's nose – while Yale had several men sent to
the hospital for concussions, including Murphy who remained in a coma
for several hours, to the point that false rumors floated around town that
he had died.

Recriminations flew, insults were swapped, and newspapers published
sensational accounts of the brutality of the game with an emphasis on
unsportsmanlike play by both sides. Harvard officials demanded that Yale
apologize for Hinkey's illegal hit, but received no satisfaction, and Crimson
fans took out their frustrations in letters-to-the-editor regarding referee
Alex Moffat's perceived incompetence. There was another casualty of
the "Bloodbath of Hampden Field" – the administrations at both schools
decided that the time had come to let emotions cool. It was agreed that
all athletic contests between the schools be suspended and that The Game
would not resume until two seasons had passed.

The "Springfield Massacre" gave Harvard President Charles Eliot
renewed incentive to pursue his campaign to abolish football. Denouncing the game as "unfit for colleges and schools," he fumed that football
had become "a spectacle more brutalizing than prize fighting, cock
fighting or bull fighting" because it "sets up the wrong kind of hero –
the man who uses his strength brutally, with a reckless disregard both of

the injuries he may suffer and of the injuries he may inflict on others." Despite his contention that "the game of foot-ball grows worse and worse as regards foul and violent play," Eliot was unsuccessful in persuading the Harvard Board of Overseers to abolish the game. That fact pleased Harvard alumnus Theodore Roosevelt, who wrote Walter Camp that he had become "utterly disgusted" with Eliot's anti-football crusade. Football, he maintained, taught young men that they had to be "manly" in order to succeed in the world after college. "I would a hundred fold rather keep the game as it is now, with the brutality, than give it up." At Yale, however, where victorious seasons were commonplace and the game was firmly entrenched in the campus culture, abolishing the sport was never given serious contemplation.

And so the Harvard–Yale football rivalry survived the crisis of 1894. Despite modest reforms and the introduction of protective padding, including a leather "head harness" that players could opt to wear (most initially refused as a demonstration of their manliness), the game remained a particularly violent one. In 1904, newspapers reported that 18 high school and college players had died from injuries. The controversial hit in The Game in November of 1905 by Yale's James Quill that leveled Francis Burr resulted in renewed furor over the game's ethics and rules. The result was that Walter Camp's obstinate opposition to opening up the game, including legalizing the forward pass, was overcome by a younger group of coaches who recognized that reform was essential to quiet those who would abolish the game as well as to make it more exciting for spectators.

Thus in 1906, the game took on a new look. A few innovative teams attempted forward passes, and players no longer could push, pull, or throw a ball carrier through or over would-be tacklers. The neutral zone was established, and the team in possession had to advance the ball ten yards to retain possession instead of five, thereby encouraging more creative plays away from the center of the line that might produce long gains. The game was evolving into one where speed, skill, and deception began to replace reliance upon sheer physical force. Fans were thrilled, and coaches responded by opening up their offenses with all sorts of new wrinkles.

Simultaneously, a vanguard of paid professional coaches now took control of the game away from the students – yet another nod to the managerial revolution that was reshaping American business. Walter Camp remained a national icon, but his influence had been diminished as the game moved away from his mass momentum style to one that was more open and dynamic – and definitely more exciting.

Camp's influence at Yale, however, remained strong. Throughout most of his tenure at Yale, he had exerted his authority by consulting with the team captains as an informal advisor, often dispatching his wife to practices to provide him with a direct report. In 1909, however, with his power on the rules committee stripped away and his business responsibilities increasing, Camp ended his active role as team advisor. He remained close to the game, however, by continuing to write extensively about football in prominent magazines and newspapers as well as selecting his annual All-American team, a practice he had begun in 1889. He remained active in this capacity until his death in 1925.

During his long association with the Yale football program, Camp also applied his business acumen to his role as Treasurer of the Yale Financial Union that oversaw the funding of all Yale athletic programs. He managed to quietly squirrel away monies that paid for the construction of the Yale Bowl, which opened in 1914 with a seating capacity of 70,000. The Yale Bowl, constructed with innovative engineering techniques utilizing structural steel and reinforced concrete, had more than twice the seating capacity of the neo-classical Harvard Stadium that had opened to public acclaim in 1903. The Yale Bowl, functional and enormous, established the template for construction of the many football stadiums that were built during the 1920s. Massive structures with permanent seating for 50,000 or more spectators appeared on flagship university campuses across the nation. These monuments to football as mass spectacle ironically led to the decline of Harvard and Yale as national honors contenders. The growing professionalism of this alleged amateur sport – which placed coaches under enormous pressure to produce winning teams in order to fill the new stadiums – can be traced to Walter Camp's pervasive influence in transforming what was once a simple game organized and played by college men into a highly structured economic enterprise of considerable size and influence.

Harvard as Football Factory

For a time, despite the size of their stadiums, with the attendant emphasis on winning teams, both Harvard and Yale administrators attempted to maintain a patina of innocent amateurism by resisting the hiring of professional coaches, adhering instead to the system of elected team captains operating the program. Out west, however, former Yale All-American end (1889) Amos Alonzo Stagg had established the prototype of the professional coach when he was named head coach and Director of the Department of Physical Culture at the newly established University of Chicago in 1892. In appointing Stagg, President William Rainey Harper established a pattern that would become all too familiar when he offered Stagg a lucrative position that included a tenured associate professorship and a lofty salary of $2,500. This munificent pay package exceeded those of most deans and senior professors. Harper believed that a great university required a winning football team. "The University of Chicago believes in football," he said. "We shall encourage it here." And Stagg delivered, developing a powerful team that enjoyed two decades near the top of the nation's college football heap between 1905 and 1925.

The idea of employing a professional coach was not part of the amateur athlete ethos that existed at elite eastern football schools. But the desire to maintain a winning program forced a change. By tradition, squad members elected an experienced senior to the position of captain who ran the team, sometimes receiving advice from a volunteer advisor who was a former player – someone like Camp – who desired to continue his involvement with the game. By the onset of the new century, however, the concept of paid professional coaches was catching on. The early success that Stagg enjoyed at Chicago, capped off in 1905, before 27,000 enthusiastic Chicago spectators, with a stirring 2–0 victory over the powerful Michigan team coached by another innovative professional coach, Fielding "Hurry Up" Yost, had gotten everyone's attention. Other professional coaches were also making their mark: Glenn "Pop" Warner at Cornell and the Carlisle Indian School, John Heisman at Georgia Tech, and Foster Sanford at Columbia and Rutgers.

A growing recognition that the complexity of football required more experience and technical knowledge than an elected senior captain might provide, even if assisted by alumni advisors, prompted disgruntled Harvard boosters – tired of enduring the annual embarrassment to Yale – to dig into their pocketbooks to fund the hiring of the Crimson's first professional coach in 1908. Percy Haughton had been named to Walter Camp's All-American second team in 1898 as a Harvard tackle, and, after coaching briefly at Cornell, had settled into a business career that returned him to Boston where he became a volunteer Harvard advisor-coach. When he accepted an offer to assume a full-time position as coach, it had become clear that Harvard was taking its football seriously. During his first season in 1908, Haughton established himself as a skilled tactician and strict disciplinarian. He whipped his charges into exceptional physical condition and introduced new formations and plays that challenged conventional coaching wisdom. He also developed the prototype of a corporate-style organization for a college football program, with himself as CEO. He built a staff of several assistants who specialized in different aspects of the game. Because his teams initially lacked the size of their opponents, Haughton relied upon speed and guile, introducing such innovations as a roving middle linebacker and the "mousetrap" block that permitted a defensive lineman to penetrate the line only to be leveled by a blocker from his blindside, thereby opening up a gaping hole in the defensive line. He put his backs in motion, used unbalanced offensive lines to confuse defenses, and introduced a five man defensive front (instead of the standard seven) with three or four linebackers. He even placed the quarterback under center to take a direct snap (in anticipation of the T formation), often faking in one direction before handing the ball off to a running back running a counter-trap play. One sports writer concluded, "Rivals chase will-o'-the-wisps, only to discover somebody else has the ball." Although Haughton had a reputation for stoic aloofness, before the first Yale game he fired up his team by wringing the neck of a stuffed toy bulldog during a pre-game oration, leading to widespread but unfounded rumors that he had actually strangled a live pooch. Such was the emotion generated by The Game.

After throttling the stuffed bulldog, Haughton demonstrated that he was not a conventional football man. At a time when substitutions were rare (a player who left the game could not return), he sent into the fray a left-footed drop-kicker, Vic Kennard, who had not appeared in a game before. Kennard's game-winning drop kick from the 25 yard line sailed through the uprights when the onrushing Yale linemen missed blocking the attempt as they threw themselves toward Kennard's right side. At a time when field goals counted four points, Haughton's deceptive play ended a six game losing streak to give Harvard a glorious upset victory.

Harvard football never enjoyed a greater span of time than the nine years Percy Haughton coached the Crimson. His teams went undefeated between 1911 and 1915, with only a scoreless tie with Yale in 1911 to tarnish the slate. Four straight wins (1912–15) over Yale created considerable buzz on the Harvard Yard and this streak included two lopsided routs: 36–0 in the Crimson's first visit to the Yale Bowl in 1914, and the worst defeat in Yale history the following year, a glorious 41–0 thumping at Harvard Stadium. That blowout prompted a *Boston Globe* reporter to gush, "Never before in a big game has the winning team played the better football in every department of the game or the loser been so hapless to stave off an overwhelming defeat." Haughton departed for military service in 1917, and following the war he returned to the business world briefly before taking the head coaching position at Columbia in 1923. Harvard fans were aghast that their former coach would sign on to coach a competitor, until they heard the details. The Lions, having endured many a losing season, agreed to pay Haughton a whopping $20,000. Unfortunately, Percy Haughton did not live long enough to enjoy his lofty salary, dying of a heart attack at the age of 48 in 1924.

Standoff: Yale and Harvard in an Era of Parity

After Walter Camp moved away from his role as football advisor in 1909, Yale continued for a time with the captain/voluntary field coach system, but the turnaround produced by Percy Haughton at Harvard demanded an equivalent response, leading to the appointment of Yale's first paid coach in 1913. The choice was Howard Jones, a star running back of the undefeated 1905–7 Yale teams that compiled a combined 28–0–2 record and claimed a national championship in 1907. Jones served as the unpaid graduate advisor in 1909 when Yale powered its way to a 12–1 record and another national championship (including a rare victory over Haughton, 8–0). However, Jones spent only one season on the Yale payroll: his team played through a lackluster 6–3–1 season, and he departed for the University of Iowa. Jones' departure indicated that the football pendulum was beginning to swing westward to large public universities that had plenty of money, were constructing large stadiums, and had ready access to large recruiting pools in which high academic achievement was not a major consideration. Jones ultimately ended up at the University of Southern California in 1926, where he coached until 1941, winning seven Pacific Coast Conference championships and five Rose Bowl contests, while laying claim to four national championships.

In 1916, Yale hired his brother Thomas "Tad" Jones, the All-American quarterback of the undefeated 1905–7 teams. After serving in the Great War, Tad Jones returned to New Haven in 1920 where he coached until 1927. His teams enjoyed undefeated seasons in 1923 and 1924, and he compiled an impressive career record of 60–15–4. His teams defeated Harvard in six of nine games, including a stirring 6–3 victory over the Crimson in 1916 before an overflow crowd estimated at 80,000 in the Yale Bowl. They watched James Neville score on a short run, which was the only touchdown the Bulldogs managed against a Haughton-coached team during his nine years at Cambridge.

Tad Jones also coached his team to one of the most memorable Yale victories in The Game. In 1923, his undefeated team traveled to Cambridge in hopes of capping an undefeated season, but a torrential downpour that began early on Friday continued throughout Saturday afternoon. One reporter said the field had become "two inches of slime," while legendary sports writer Grantland Rice called the field "a gridiron of seventeen lakes, five quagmires, and a water hazard." The game was highlighted by numerous fumbles and much slipping and sliding – and an astounding 54 punts. Yale sealed another national championship when the appropriately named Raymond "Ducky" Pond scooped up a first-quarter fumble and sloshed his way 63 yards for a touchdown.

For any rivalry to be sustained over a long period of time, both teams have to win their share of the games. Following the hiatus created by the First World War, the Harvard–Yale game took on increasing significance because the contests between two of the nation's oldest and most prestigious universities were usually hard-fought, close affairs. That both schools ended their season with this special game meant that bragging rights derived from a big win resonated wherever alumni from the two schools interacted until the next autumn adventure. The proximity of the two campuses added to the mix, as did the continued competition in all things academic. Success of alumni – in business, the professions, cultural affairs, and politics – meant that good-natured joshing and bragging about The Game occurred whenever Yale and Harvard alumni encountered each other. Over the years, important annual alumni events were built around The Game, and proud Blues and Crimsons routinely set aside the third Saturday in November on their calendars to renew their campus ties. Traditional game week luncheons, banquets, and receptions became part of the social scene, and with the advent of tailgating in the latter decades of the 20th century, game day outdoor parties near the stadium – with elaborate food, drink and festive decorations – took on an importance that made more than one observer conclude that the football game existed only as an excuse for elaborate and enthusiastic socializing.

The Pleasant Reality of De-Emphasis

In some respects, The Game took on even greater significance after both schools made the decision to abandon any pretense of fielding nationally competitive teams by agreeing to membership in the Ivy League. The realization that neither school could maintain both their lofty academic reputations and a nationally competitive football program began to settle in during the 1930s when both teams fell upon relatively hard times. Yale claimed a disputed national championship in 1927 with a 7–1 record, but neither university ever came close again. Between 1880 and 1927, however, Yale won the mythical national championship a resounding 15 times, while Harvard claimed a not-so-inconsequential eight. Harvard played in the only postseason game – the 1920 Rose Bowl, defeating Oregon 7–6 – but three years later both schools announced that they would no longer accept postseason bowl invitations. During the 1920s and 1930s the football spotlight moved away from the private eastern universities, never to return.

By the end of the 1920s, the stature of eastern football had greatly diminished, as the game became ever more important in the South, Midwest, and West. Private eastern schools continued playing a schedule not unlike they had always played, seldom moving beyond the narrow band of seaboard states from Maryland to Massachusetts to find opponents. The closest they came to playing nationally ranked teams would be the two military academies at West Point and Annapolis. New national powers, such as Michigan, Notre Dame, Ohio State, Louisiana State, and California never replaced such traditional opponents as Cornell, Dartmouth, Northeastern, Tufts, Maine, Connecticut, and Wesleyan on the Yale and Harvard autumn slates. Yale's last moment in the national football spotlight occurred when end Larry Kelley and running back Cliff Frank captured back-to-back Heisman trophies in 1936 and 1937, but the domination of the national media by New York City journalists and the preponderance of east coast voters likely skewed the selection process. Yale's other top player of that era typified the downward trajectory of the competitive quality of the program, when the talented but slightly built back Albie Booth, who weighed a mere 140 pounds, was the team's standout player between 1929 and 1931. In his final game, the popular "Little Boy Blue" became an instant campus hero when he drop-kicked a field goal in the waning minutes to beat Harvard 3–0.

The Great Depression had little discernable impact on the popularity of college football. Unlike professional baseball, once the economy bottomed out in 1933, good attendance not only returned, but also increased until the Second World War. Despite many outspoken critics who argued that football had lost its innocence due to recruiting scandals and academic dishonesty, by the mid-1930s the game seemed to be gaining in popularity. Many universities sought to become "big time" by hiring famous coaches and arming them with large budgets. A wave of new postseason bowl games designed to promote tourism added to the mix – the Orange, Cotton, and Sugar became the best known along with the older Rose, but several other fruit, flower, vegetable, and climate games were added to the postseason bowl mix, including the Celery, Salad, Flower, Grape, Orchid, Pineapple, and Sun. These were further supplemented by the East–West and North–South all-star games. The result was that during the 1930s many universities decided to make the leap into the ranks of nationally competitive football programs, although many would opt out of big time football during and shortly after World War II. For Yale, Harvard, and other eastern private schools with relatively small enrollments and traditionally high football expectations, the costs of continuing to compete with major state universities – with their much larger enrollments and aggressive booster organizations – became financially and philosophically too great to stay in the hunt for national gridiron honors.

In 1935, the Southeastern Conference decided to quit disguising its payments to athletes under such subterfuges as "leadership grants" and "general activity scholarships," and announced it would offer tuition, board and room stipends strictly on the basis of athletic ability. Although other conferences, such as the Southwest, Big Ten, and Pacific Coast, expressed shock at such a flouting of the amateur ideal, they knew full well that they were engaged in similar forms of subterfuge to funnel monies to football players. Many schools had long provided "jobs" on campus for athletes which were the butt of jokes: Governor Martin L. Davey of Ohio created a brief sensation in 1935 when he candidly noted that most members of the Ohio State football team – heralded as a preseason favorite for the national championship – were on the payroll of the Ohio Highway Department. In 1929, the Carnegie Report had exposed the ethical shortcomings of college football, and throughout the 1930s such prominent journalists as John Tunis and Paul Gallico wrote extensively of academic and financial dishonesty in college football programs. Following the Second World War, academic reformers sought to bring this era of excess to a close, but the so-called Sanity Code established by the National Collegiate Athletic Association in 1948 that attempted to eliminate all financial support for athletic participation lasted for less than two years before it was scuttled. Attendance boomed with the postwar economy – a record 104,000 attended the 1947 game between Southern California and Notre Dame in the Los Angeles Coliseum – and many teams routinely played before more than 70,000 spectators. The introduction in the early 1950s of two-platoon football added to the quality of play because players could now concentrate on developing only those skills required of their specialized positions. Unlimited substitution, however, meant that teams now had to field separate teams for offense, defense, and kicking, which consequently mandated the necessity of funding much larger squads – and budgets to support them.

All of these factors led to long and serious discussions about the viability of big-time football on many campuses. In 1939, the once-powerful University of Chicago had stunned the sports world when it dropped football, and, after the Second World War, many private institutions – including San Francisco, Villanova, Fordham, Washington University, Georgetown, and Western Reserve – dropped the game for financial reasons. This trend greatly affected the thinking on the campuses in Cambridge and New Haven. Several years of discussions led to the signing of the Ivy Group Accord in 1945 by eight prestigious private eastern institutions. The Accord affirmed the primacy of academic integrity and the importance of strictly controlling the cost and influence of football programs. Of this group, seven institutions made the decision to abandon any pretense of competing for national football honors – Dartmouth, Brown, Princeton, Columbia, Cornell, Yale, and Harvard; for a brief time, the University of Pennsylvania attempted to continue its effort to mount a nationally competitive program, but pressure from the other seven, and a power play in 1952 by the NCAA forced Penn to forgo a lucrative television contract with the DuMont network. The fighting Quakers had no choice but to fall into line. By 1956, the Ivy League had been formalized. It was no small thing for these fiercely independent private institutions to agree to bend to an external authority such as an athletic conference, but now they did so with gusto, agreeing to abolish spring football practice, curtail the size of coaching staffs, eliminate all financial aid based on athletic abilities, require the same admission standards for potential athletes as for non-athletes, forbid wealthy alumni to "sponsor" a needy student who could make tackles or throw the deep pass, and prohibit postseason bowl appearances.

For Yale and Harvard, the days of national football glory were over. Although there were the expected complaints, within a few years for the vast majority of students, faculty, and alumni, the new orientation provided a source of unique pride that a Nebraska or Alabama fan could scarcely comprehend. Football, still played with enthusiasm and at a respectable level, remained a part of campus life, but it was now merely one small part of a comprehensive educational experience. Winning seasons and conference championships remained worthwhile goals, but football was but one of many extracurricular activities that were open to the student body. In the long run, de-emphasizing football meant that a wide spectrum of intercollegiate sports was made available to students. When women students were admitted at a time that coincided with the advent of Title IX and the establishment of competitive women's sports programs, the Ivy institutions were in the forefront of sponsoring a large number of women's athletic programs. With their athletic budgets folded into the overall institutional budgets, Harvard and Yale offered a wide range of intercollegiate sports that numbered about 30, far more than many institutions compelled to allocate the bulk of their athletic budget to maintaining a Division I-A football program.

During his undergraduate years in the late 1940s, Harvard mathematics major Tom Lehrer aptly captured the spirit of the new approach to Harvard football with his enormously popular satirical song "Fight Fiercely, Harvard," which became a popular parody extolling the new Ivy League ethos.

Although administrators felt the sharp sting of alumni carping, over the years those sour notes dissipated and the institutions proceeded to retrofit their athletic programs. Costs were contained, the much-maligned term of "student-athlete" took on special meaning, and campus presidents were assured that their institutions would not be embarrassed by a recruiting or academic fraud scandal such as those that had long bedeviled administrators. Very quickly, a new spirit of competition among the eight Ivy schools emerged, and for more than half a century the same eight schools have competed on a more-or-less even playing field, with the level of competition remaining high but with the win-at-all-costs mentality absent.

"The Game" Flourishes

This new direction and philosophy meshed well with the continued quest for academic leadership that characterized Yale and Harvard between 1945 and the present. The restructuring of their football programs, if anything, served to intensify the rivalry between the two elite institutions. Significantly, almost eerily, the number of wins and losses has remained almost equal, and both schools have benefitted from long tenures by distinguished coaches. The quality of players has been evenly distributed, and a few have even enjoyed outstanding careers in the National Football League – running backs Chuck Mercein and Calvin Hill of Yale and end/punter Pat McInally and center Matt Birk of Harvard. Rather than talking about national rankings, bowl appearances, and the number of players drafted by the NFL, sports publicists have been able to report some of the nation's highest graduation rates and write about the number of players who moved on to outstanding careers in medicine, business, law, government, and other professions.

It is a difficult task to pick the single most compelling game from the more than 120 games that have been played in college football's longest running and most colorful rivalry. Harvard traditionalists might point to the big upset of 1908 that new Coach Percy Haughton engineered or perhaps the recent stirring comeback of 2005 when the Crimson rallied from an 18 point deficit in the third quarter to win a heart-thumping 30–24 victory that required three overtime periods. That distinction, however, has to belong to the 1968 game played before a raucous overflow Harvard Stadium crowd. The pre-game hype was extensive as both teams came into The Game undefeated and untied, a delightful situation that had not existed since the 1920s. The Game would decide the Ivy League championship.

Experts handicapped the game as one of contrasting strengths. Under head coach Carmen Cozza, Yale operated a potent offense that was led by two of its greatest offensive players of all time, running back Calvin Hill and quarterback Brian Dowling. Hill would go on to a distinguished professional career with the Dallas Cowboys, but it was Dowling who was the star performer. He had turned down scholarship offers from Ohio State and Notre Dame (and an estimated 100 other schools) to attend Yale. He had never lost a game as quarterback since the seventh grade. His sensational exploits in leading Yale to two previous undefeated

Figure 1.1 Many leading US figures played in the Harvard–Yale series. On a snowy November day in 1955, a future senator, tight end Ted Kennedy, is unable to haul in an overthrown pass in the end zone during his team's 21–7 loss to Yale. © Bettmann/CORBIS

seasons – running, passing, play-calling, improvising on broken plays – had resulted in his becoming a larger-than-life icon on the New Haven campus. The game was played as one of the most turbulent years in the nation's history was winding down. The stunning Tet Offensive by Ho Chi Minh's forces in Vietnam, the shocking retirement announcement by President Lyndon Johnson, the assassinations of Martin Luther King, Jr, and Robert F. Kennedy, massive anti-war protests, violence on the streets of Chicago during the Democratic convention, sustained angry demonstrations on college campuses, and a close presidential election had all contributed to a national mood of fear, anger and uncertainty. The mood on both campuses in 1968 was consumed by the times. At Yale, many students found a modicum of relief by following the daring exploits of Brian Dowling and rallying behind the Bulldogs. Dowling was even prominently featured in a cartoon strip in the *Yale Daily News* drawn by undergraduate Gary Trudeau ('70). "B. D." first appeared as a gangly quarterback barking signals in the huddle wearing jersey number 10 in a cartoon series entitled "Bull Tales." Later on, "B. D." would become a central figure in Trudeau's nationally syndicated Doonesbury cartoon strip, first as a hard-nosed political conservative with a football helmet firmly implanted on his head, later as a college football coach at academically anemic Walden University, and finally as a tragic and vulnerable American soldier who lost a leg in a roadside bombing in Iraq.

As the 1968 Big Game approached, it was clear that Harvard's offense was no match for the potent Bulldogs; it had sputtered and wheezed for much of the year. Coach John Yovicsin's strong defense, however, had frustrated opponents all season long, and it provided a formidable foil to the explosive Yale offense. Dubbed the "Boston Stranglers" by the media, a stout defense was clearly the strength of the Harvard team.

It was thus a scintillating offense against a stifling defense in The Game played on a crisp and clear New England day in mid-November. More than 40,000 spectators squeezed into Harvard Stadium. Scalpers had a field day and game officials estimated they could have sold 100,000 tickets for the match that would decide the Ivy championship. This was beyond question the biggest Big Game in decades, indicative of the new spirit that had coalesced around the Ivy League commitment to true amateur athletics.

From the opening kickoff it seemed as if the handicappers, who made Yale a seven point favorite, were right on the money. Dowling more than lived up to his reputation, leading Yale to a comfortable 22–6 lead

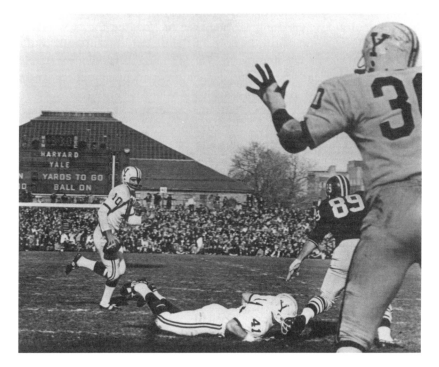

Figure 1.2 "B. D." is on the loose! Star Yale quarterback Brian Dowling (10) takes off on an option play against Harvard during the final quarter of his last game as a senior. In the forefront is overlooked receiver, Calvin Hill (30). Yale football experts believe Dowling and Hill to be the two best players ever to wear the Blue and White of the Bulldogs. Reproduced by permission of Sabby Frinzi and Yale University Athletic Department

heading in to half-time. Late in the first half, though, Yovicsin had removed quarterback George Lolich because the offense had gained only six yards. He inserted junior Frank Champi, who had taken only a few snaps all season. It seemed to be (and probably was) a desperate gamble, but it paid off. Champi immediately led Harvard on a long drive that ended with his first touchdown pass, but the extra point failed on a mishandled snap.

Midway through the third quarter, Champi engineered another touchdown drive, but Dowling rallied the Bulldogs to a seemingly commanding 29–13 lead when he scored on a 15 yard dash around end. Late in the fourth quarter, Dowling seemed poised to put the game away when he drove the Bulldogs deep into Harvard territory, but a fumble at the 14 yard line gave Harvard a slim glimmer of hope. Two timely Yale penalties, a 26 yard gain when Champi flipped a lateral in desperation to a tackle, a Champi touchdown pass to end Bruce Freeman, and a successful two point conversion (made on a second attempt thanks to a facemask penalty) pulled Harvard within eight points, 29–21. Just 42 seconds remained on the scoreboard clock. As if following a Hollywood script, Yale mishandled the onside kick, and Champi moved his team toward the end zone, aided by another facemask penalty. From the 20 yard line he threw two incomplete passes, but a draw play moved the ball to the six yard line. Champi was sacked on the next play but managed to call time out with three seconds left on the clock. A ferocious Yale rush spoiled the play sent in from Yovicsin, but a desperately improvising Champi managed to elude several pass rushers and found Vic Gatto open in the corner of the end zone: Yale 29, Harvard 27. On the extra point attempt, Champi again eluded the furious Yale rush, looked in vain for an open receiver, and finally threw a strike to end Pete Varney. Ecstatic Harvard fans swarmed the field and, as the *Harvard Alumni Magazine* later reported, "Strangers embraced, full professors danced, and the Yale people put their handkerchiefs to the use for which they were intended."

On Monday morning, the *Harvard Crimson* unveiled its most memorable headline: "Harvard Beats Yale, 29–29!"

Yale's dream of an undefeated season ended in shock. Brian Dowling's personal streak of 67 games without a loss extending back to his junior high school days in Cleveland came to a bitter end in his last collegiate game. Yale center Fred Morris later recalled, "We couldn't believe that it just happened. . . . We saw the Harvard fans going nuts. It was a stunning, speechless moment." Harvard coach John Yovicsin was equally shocked: "Never in my lifetime will I ever see another ending like that one," he gasped. "It just doesn't happen."

Even ten years later, at a reunion that brought the two teams together on the eve of another Big Game, Yale head coach Carmen Cozza could still not smile, telling the evening's master of ceremonies, broadcaster Curt Gowdy, "The score read 29–29, but I admit it was the worst loss of my career."

"We Hate Each Other's Guts"
The Dodgers and the Giants

We didn't like them and they didn't like us. (Bobby Thomson)

We didn't need pep talks when the Dodgers played the Giants. Grudges got carried not only from game to game but from year to year. It was like war all the time. (Maury Wills)

This is a tale of four cities. America's oldest and most enduring baseball rivalry can be traced back to the year 1883 when in New York, the nation's baseball capital, two ball clubs that would eventually assume the names of Dodgers and Giants were established. During this early period of professional baseball, both clubs endured multiple changes in ownership and relocations of their home ballparks where, on good days, they played before small crowds in ramshackle wooden stadiums. The Brooklyn club eventually landed in a rickety 10,000-seat wooden stadium at Washington Park, while in 1891 the Giants took up occupancy in the largest sports venue of the day, the 18,000-seat Polo Grounds under Coogan's Bluff on 157th Street and 8th Avenue.

One hundred and twenty years later, now relocated to California, the two franchises continue to compete against each other in two magnificent baseball parks before enthusiastic crowds. The rivalry has been incredibly close: as the two teams concluded the 2009 season, the Giants led the all-time series 1,163 to 1,145. In 11 seasons the teams have finished first and second, and on other occasions the team that had fallen out of contention would spoil the pennant hopes of the other with a late-season victory.

The roots of the intense rivalry between the Giants and Dodgers are deeply entwined with the history of New York City. One of the first recorded reports of a baseball game describes how the New York Baseball Club defeated a club from Brooklyn by a resounding 20 aces (runs) at

Elysian Fields in Hoboken, New Jersey, on October 21, 1845. Over the ensuing years, as baseball went through several stages of growth and refinement, teams representing the neighboring cities separated by the East River squared off amidst much excitement and controversy. (Until 1897 Brooklyn was a separate city, at which time it was absorbed as one of five boroughs within the metropolitan government of New York City.)

"Brooklyn is fast earning the title of the 'City' of Base Ball Clubs," a national sports-oriented newspaper reported in 1857. The early history of baseball is filled with the exploits of the Atlantics (a team comprised largely of German and Irish immigrant laborers engaged in ship building) and their local rivals the Eckfords and the Excelsiors, whose players were likewise drawn from the ranks of the working classes. In 1860, crowds that approached 20,000 watched the Atlantics and Excelsiors battle for the mythical Brooklyn championship. Two years later, 15,000 fans paid good money to see the two clubs play an important game on the same day that thousands of young men were dying in western Maryland at the Battle of Antietam. In 1860, the *Brooklyn Eagle* gave plaintive expression to the intense urban rivalry that already existed between Manhattan and the struggling city that had originally been named Breuckelen by Dutch settlers in 1646: "If we are not ahead of the big city in nothing else, we can beat her in baseball." When the Atlantics and the perennially powerful New York Mutuals met late in the season of 1870, a reporter noted, "No other games throughout the year arouse the same amount of excitement. The spectators feel as if they themselves were engaged in the strife and not merely lookers-on."

Creation of an Enduring Rivalry

In 1883, the New York Gothams became a new entry in the National League, while a new club was formed in Brooklyn to compete in the American Association, initially taking the storied name of Atlantics. In 1889, the two teams won their respective league championships and squared off in what proved to be a short-lived precursor to the World Series, a best-of-three series for the Dauvray Cup. Amidst a flurry of arguments, the New Yorkers won, but not before losing the first game 12–10. In commenting on the shock of losing that game, the *New York Times* lamented, "Defeat from any other quarter would be bad enough, but the stigma was intensified because Brooklyn made the mighty Giants lower their colors. The rivalry between New York and Brooklyn as regards baseball is unparalleled in the history of the national game."

In 1890, both clubs began to square off on a regular basis when the Brooklyn club moved to the National League. By this time the New York club had been renamed the Giants. According to legend, that occurred when reporters observed that several of the Gothams were markedly taller than their opponents, although another version has it that reporters overheard a delighted manager state that his team had "played like giants" during a particularly rewarding victory. Reporters also took note of the substantial number of Brooklyn players who had recently married in 1887 and gave them the moniker of Bridegrooms, but that name had a short honeymoon and was replaced by Trolley Dodgers in response to several unfortunate souls being run down by the street cars that roamed the maze of tracks criss-crossing the city. That colorful name, however, did not inspire, and in 1899 the Brooklyn club took on the moniker of Superbas, which at the time was the name of a popular high-wire acrobatic group that thrilled spectators in Europe and America.

Whatever their names, however, the quality of play by the two New York City entries in the National League was anything but gigantic or superb. Both teams struggled through inglorious losing seasons throughout much of the 1890s, although in 1894 the Giants won the league crown with a postseason victory over Baltimore, and Brooklyn won pennants in 1899 and 1900. The plight of the Giants could easily be found in the disruptive and contentious manner in which their universally despised owner, Andrew Freedman, ran the club. An unpleasant, pugnacious man who had made his bones as a political operative in the notoriously corrupt Democratic Party's Tammy Hall machine, Freedman alienated fans and players alike with his erratic management style and penny-pinching ways. In 1902, under intense criticism, Freedman apparently decided to get serious about setting his team on a winning (and more profitable) course when he lured 29-year-old John J. McGraw away from the Baltimore Orioles of the new American League to manage his team for the stupendous salary of $11,000 a year, the highest salary ever paid up to that time in baseball.

Muggsy Rules Gotham

From the time he arrived in July of 1902, John "Muggsy" McGraw dominated the sports world of New York City. His larger-than-life persona, coupled with the ten pennants and three World Series titles he accumulated until poor health forced his retirement in 1932, completely overshadowed the mostly mediocre teams that owner Charles Ebbets fielded in Brooklyn. The hard-charging McGraw led the Giants to the National League pennant in 1904, but because of his hatred of American League president Ban Johnson, McGraw refused to play the Boston Americans (or Pilgrims) in what should have been the second World Series. McGraw was a familiar and popular figure at local watering holes and on off-days could be seen at racetracks. His outgoing personality, coupled with his Irish heritage – and the success of his Giants – made him a favorite among the sporting crowd in New York. His popularity soared even higher in 1905 when his team won another National League pennant (while the inelegant Dodgers finished a distant 56 games behind their nominal cross-town rivals, winning just 48 games while losing 104). This time, new team owner John Brush made certain that his team participated in the World Series. When the Giants won the final game of the 1905 World Series, defeating the favored Philadelphia Athletics on the strength of Christy Mathewson's strong right arm, the outpouring of emotions at the Polo Grounds produced, according to a reporter for the *New York Times*, "a deafening, reverberating roar" that "lifted Manhattan's soil from its base."

The Superbas and Robins

Season after season, McGraw's Giants were usually in the thick of the pennant race. They dominated New York baseball, at least until the appearance of Babe Ruth in a Yankees uniform in 1920. The Giants won three consecutive pennants between 1911 and 1913, and another in 1917, although losing all four World Series. Meanwhile the Superbas struggled in near oblivion, saddled with an inept owner in Charlie Ebbets, whose lack of capital was accentuated by flawed decision-making. In 1913, Ebbets proudly presided over the opening of his much-ballyhooed, doubledecked stadium. Seeking to reduce land acquisition costs, Ebbets built his stadium on a minuscule four and a half acre site that forced architects to create a ballpark with short distances to the fences, a weirdly angled right field concrete fence, and just 25,000 seats (later an additional 7,000 seats were squeezed into the small confines). Although the lobby was spectacular, the ballpark became well known for its narrow aisles, cramped concession areas, and inadequate bathrooms. During the 1920s, with the arrival of the automobile age, it also lacked the necessary parking.

The numbing mediocrity of the Superbas did little to entice fans to the new ballpark. In 1914, Ebbets sought to improve the team's performance when he named Wilbert Robinson as manager. The rotund and jovial "Uncle Robbie" knew his baseball: a former catcher, he had served as pitching coach for John McGraw for many years. Loveable Robbie was rewarded when fans and reporters began calling the team the Robins in his honor, and the Suberbas faded into obscurity.

During the rest of Robinson's 18 year tenure, his teams remained the Robins, but when he departed in 1931, management revived the name of Dodgers and in 1937 changed the team's basic color from green to blue (later glorified by Tommy Lasorda as "Dodger Blue"). In 1916, Robinson won the everlasting affection of fans when the Robins, a preseason pick once again for the cellar, managed to edge out the Philadelphia Phillies and the Giants for the pennant. The Robins were arguably one of the least-compelling teams ever to play in the World Series. They lost four games to one to the Boston Red Sox, who were led by youthful pitcher Babe Ruth. In 1917, the Robins reverted to form, finishing well behind McGraw's pennant-winning Giants, but in 1920 Uncle Robbie once more led the Robins to the NL pennant, getting career performances from pitcher Burleigh Grimes and outfielder Zack Wheat while beating out the underperforming Giants team by seven games. Despite winning the pennant, the Robins lost the World Series to Cleveland five games to two. McGraw thereupon prodded his Giants to four consecutive pennants as the Robins faded. The Giants won two World Series titles, defeating the Yankees in 1921 and 1922, but lost to the surging Yankees in 1923 and the Walter Johnson-led Washington Senators in 1924.

The Dodgers Make Their Move

McGraw's final years featured a seemingly endless series of conflicts with his players and umpires (naturally). Meanwhile, the Dodgers remained mired in the second division, becoming best known for their mediocrity on the field and bizarre behavior off it. After McGraw's departure in 1932, the Giants continued their winning ways under their first new manager in three decades, star first baseman Bill Terry, who had won the 1933 World Series over the Senators, but had lost in 1936 and 1937 to the

Yankees. Meanwhile, the financially hard-pressed Dodgers continued to founder, finishing 25 games or more out of first place for three consecutive seasons under Uncle Robbie's successor Casey Stengel. Asked before the 1934 season about a possible challenge from across the East River, Terry, perhaps much too honestly, famously responded, "Is Brooklyn still in the league?" His question was answered during the final two days of the season when manager Casey Stengel's sixth-place team knocked the Giants out of the pennant with victories in the last two games of the season.

Such sarcasm as Terry's directed at the laughable Brooklyn "Bums" would soon disappear because the fortunes of the Dodgers improved dramatically with the arrival of two savvy baseball men, Larry MacPhail and Branch Rickey. MacPhail became General Manager in 1938. By the time he left for military service in 1942, MacPhail had made several bold personnel moves that transformed the Dodgers into a young and talented team led by the combative player-manager, shortstop Leo Durocher.

The aggressive Durocher instilled in the team his take-no-prisoners approach to the game. In his first season, the Dodgers finished third, but six games ahead of the Giants; in response, more than 1 million fans paid their way into Ebbets Field. As the winds of war began to swirl across the United States, the revitalized Dodgers won the 1941 National League pennant, only to be swept aside in five games in the World Series by the powerful Yankees led by Joe DiMaggio. Even in this giddy period of resurgence, the legacy of the unconventional still plagued the Dodgers. In Game Four, the Dodgers were poised to even the Series at two games apiece with two outs, no runners on base, and ace pitcher Hugh Casey on the mound. He got Tommy Heinrich to swing at a curveball for strike three, but, instead of ending the game, the ball kicked into the dirt and eluded catcher Mickey Owen. Before the next out was recorded, the Yankees had scored four runs and the Dodgers' hopes plummeted. Red Smith summarized the story in the *Herald-Tribune* the next day: "It could only happen in Brooklyn. Where else in this broad untidy universe . . . could a man win a World Series game by striking out?"

In 1943, Branch Rickey replaced MacPhail after a long and successful run as General Manager of the St Louis Cardinals. Rickey was intent on repeating his successful strategy that had produced six pennants (and four world championships) in St Louis between 1926 and 1942. He proceeded to build a strong scouting crew and expanded the number of Dodger minor league teams to produce a steady flow of new talent. Significantly, Rickey had been raised within a pious southern Ohio Methodist family that had

Figure 2.1 Managers Wilbert Robinson of the Brooklyn Robins and John J. McGraw of the New York Giants pensively examine a hatchet on opening day, which public relations officials said would "pry open" the new season of 1931. Both men were in the final stages of long and colorful careers in baseball. © Bettmann/CORBIS

been deeply involved in the anti-slavery movement, and he believed the time had arrived for baseball to move beyond the "gentleman's agreement" that had denied African-Americans opportunity to play at the highest level of the "national game" since the 1880s. In 1944 he quietly launched a quest to find the right person to break baseball's unwritten color ban.

Branch Rickey and Jackie Robinson

Rickey's social vision seamlessly melded with his intention of making the Dodgers a perennial National League contender. Thus, in October of 1945, he announced that the Dodgers had signed a 26-year-old shortstop away from the Kansas City Monarchs of the Negro Leagues. (One of the most vocal critics of this startling move was Larry MacPhail, now a senior executive with the Yankees.) After Jackie Robinson led the Montreal Royals to the 1946 Little World Series title and was named the International League's Most Valuable Player, Rickey promoted him to the parent club for the 1947 season.

When Commissioner Albert "Happy" Chandler shocked baseball by suspending Durocher for the entire 1947 season, Rickey selected a longtime associate, the 63-year-old baseball insider Burt Shotton, as Durocher's interim replacement. Durocher had incurred considerable criticism in New York newspapers for his proclivity for high-stakes gambling, his associations with alleged underworld figures, and his marriage to actress Laraine Day before her divorce had become official. The serene Shotton was a good choice to guide Jackie Robinson through his initial season. After a slow start, Robinson began to hit with authority in May and ended his rookie season batting .297. His dynamic base running and sharp fielding at first base helped lead the Dodgers to the pennant, just as Rickey had planned.

The much-anticipated World Series with the Yankees proved to be a classic. It featured Cookie Lavagetto's pinch-hit double in Game Four with two out in the ninth inning to break up Bill Bevens' no-hitter and gave the Dodgers a memorable, if improbable, 3–2 victory. In Game Six, the Dodgers managed to even the Series when substitute outfielder Al Gionfriddo ran at full tilt into the low fence in deep left-center field at Yankee Stadium to rob Joe DiMaggio of what seemed to be an almost certain home run, preserving a Dodger victory. Such heroics notwithstanding, the Yankees took Game Seven the next day in a 5–2 romp.

The stinging loss for Dodger fans, however, was mitigated by the fact that the Dodgers had become a National League power. Any reference to "Dem Bums" was now an historical footnote. During the next few years, Rickey continued building his team, signing several additional African-American players, including such standouts as pitchers Don Newcombe and Don Black and catcher Roy Campanella, while assembling a team that also included such stars as veteran shortstop Pee Wee Reese, center fielder Duke Snider, third baseman Bobby Cox, first baseman Gil Hodges, right fielder Carl Furillo, and pitchers Ralph Branca and Preacher Roe. In 1948 Jackie Robinson moved to his natural position of second base as he proceeded to build credentials for the Hall of Fame.

Figure 2.2 Jackie steals home! Jackie Robinson's electrifying base running was one of many reasons he was elected to the Hall of Fame. Here Robinson beats the tag of Phillies' catcher Andy Seminick during the heated 1950 pennant race. Philadelphia edged out the Dodgers for the National League title on the last day of the season. Hall of Fame first baseman Gil Hodges is the batter. © Bettmann/CORBIS

The always simmering but seldom bubbling rivalry between the Giants and Dodgers suddenly began to boil on July 16, 1948, when Rickey orchestrated one of the most famous personnel deals in baseball history. He coyly permitted Leo Durocher to opt out of his contract to accept the manager's position at the Polo Grounds. Durocher replaced the popular one-time Giant slugger Mel Ott, about whom Durocher had once indelicately said, "Nice guys finish last." This shocking midseason move to the Giants by the one individual Dodger fans had most closely identified with during their team's rise to the top of the National League produced true interborough nastiness. After 60 years of playing ball, an intense, embittered rivalry had finally emerged.

Sustained success on the field, however, did not translate into improved attendance. Although the Dodgers had become a perennial pennant contender, fans were not particularly appreciative. Attendance spiked to 1,800,000 in 1946, but even with the presence of Jackie Robinson and a pennant win in 1947, only 10,000 more fans paid their way into Ebbets Field. Although the Dodgers made another World Series appearance in 1949, attendance slipped to 1,635,000. And despite a close pennant race in 1950 in which they lost out to the Phillies on the last day of the season, attendance fell to below 1,200,000. The reasons were readily apparent: Brooklyn was an early victim of the impact of postwar affluence that stimulated a massive population shift of working- and middle-class white families to the suburbs. A modest three-bedroom house in a new tract housing suburb out on Long Island seemed an almost irresistible lure to a new generation of more affluent Brooklynites. As families departed Brooklyn for the crabgrass frontier, their apartments and small homes became havens for the less affluent. By the early 1950s, throughout the borough, a new underclass had begun to move into Brooklyn, and unemployment and crime rates began to rise; inevitably, storeowners and small manufacturers joined in the exodus. The general decline of Brooklyn was symbolized in May of 1955 when the legendary voice of the borough, the *Brooklyn Eagle*, ceased publication.

The Shot Heard "Round the World"

These trends were not lost on the new ownership of the Dodgers, headed by attorney Walter O'Malley. A tough-minded Machiavellian with an acute sensitivity to the bottom line, O'Malley had orchestrated Branch

Rickey's departure at the end of the 1950 season. The O'Malley family would control the Dodgers until 1998.

Walter O'Malley was a perceptive businessman and he understood that the aging Ebbets Field had become a serious liability. Its design flaws had been evident for years, and its location in a congested and rapidly deteriorating neighborhood intimidated many would-be ticket buyers. Consequently, despite a galaxy of baseball stars and a succession of spirited pennant races, attendance continued to fall. It was not unusual by the early 1950s for weekday crowds of less than 5,000 to be sprinkled lightly around the ballpark. O'Malley recognized that only a new ballpark could salvage the situation.

Unfortunately for Giants fans, similar conditions existed at the aging Polo Grounds. It also lacked adequate parking and was located on the edge of a transitional neighborhood. Much of the seating in the ball park was far removed from the field of play, and the park's elliptical configuration included several quirks, the most important being that the distance to the foul poles measured just 279 feet down the left field line and 258 to right field. The power gaps extended to a distant 450 feet while the center field wall and the green scoreboard stood a defiant 508 feet away from home plate. In 1923, an additional level of seating had been added above the 17-foot high fence in left field, and it curiously extended over the field of play by 21 feet. It was possible for a routine fly ball to become a cheap home run if properly placed. Adding further to the park's idiosyncrasies, the bullpens were actually located in the distant power alleys and well within the field of play. Thus, as the second half of the 20th century began to unfold, two of organized baseball's premier franchises were struggling to lure fans into aging and uninviting stadiums.

Thus the irony: during what has often been described as the "greatest baseball game ever played," nearly 20,000 seats in cavernous Polo Grounds remained empty. On Wednesday, October 3, 1951, a crowd of only 34,320 watched the third and final playoff game for the National League pennant between the cross-town rivals. Vast stretches of empty seats in the upper deck provided an apt metaphor for the general decline in attendance that concerned baseball executives. The Dodgers nicked Giant ace Sal Maglie for a run in the first inning when Jackie Robinson singled in Pee Wee Reese. By the bottom of the ninth inning, they had stretched that lead to a comfortable 4–1 margin.

Then one of baseball's enduring dramas unfolded. The Giants rallied to score a run and had the tying runs on second and third with two outs when Dodger manager Chuck Dressen decided to replace the exhausted Don Newcombe with veteran right-hander Ralph Branca, whose sharp curve and sneaky fastball had enabled him to win 13 games in his eighth season with the Dodgers. After looking at a called strike, third baseman Bobby Thomson connected with a Branca fastball that was well out of the strike zone. This famous pitch was high and inside, a waste pitch located precisely where Branca intended. The ball screamed off Thomson's bat on a line-drive trajectory down the left field line, smashing some 20 feet inside the foul pole into the lower deck seats. Left fielder Andy Pafko collapsed in disbelief at the base of the 17 foot fence as Thomson happily loped around the bases. After the initial shock set in, the crowd erupted in a roar. Giants broadcaster Russ Hodges famously screamed, "The Giants Win the Pennant! The Giants Win the Pennant! The Giants Win the Pennant! . . . I do not believe it!"

Thus did baseball's single most riveting moment occur on a gloomy Wednesday afternoon as autumn was descending upon Gotham. Unlike many seemingly great moments, this one never receded into the dim and hazy recollections of baseball history. It resonates yet today. In 1997, novelist Don DeLillo used Thomson's "shot heard 'round the world'" to set the stage for his prize-winning epic novel *Underground* that probed the dark contradictions of postmodern America. Thomson's home run instantly became one of the most memorable moments in baseball history, bringing a dramatic end to an exciting pennant race.

In mid-August, the Giants seemingly had fallen out of contention, trailing the Dodgers by 13½ half games. During the final weeks of the pennant race, the Dodgers compiled a lackluster 25–22 record, while the Giants went on a rampage, winning 37 games while losing just seven. In the final game of the regular season the Giants were extended to 14 innings before defeating Philadelphia to force a playoff.

In the years that followed, rumors began to circulate that Durocher had engaged in an unusual gambit that enabled the Giants to catch the Dodgers. Reports circulated in baseball circles that he had used a clandestine spying conspiracy that enabled the Giants to steal catchers' signals. Utility infielder Hank Schenz had brought a powerful Wollensak telescope home from the Navy in 1945. Durocher – always looking for an edge – perceived that the 35 mm telescope could easily distinguish the separated fingers as a catcher flashed signals, even from a considerable distance. By mid-July he had stationed pitching coach Herman Franks in his center field office, which had a small window that looked out on the field through the scoreboard. A former catcher, Franks was adept at reading catchers' signs. Peering through the Wollensak from more than 500 feet distant, Franks decoded the catcher's signals and buzzed an electronic signal to the Giants bullpen out in distant right field: One buzz meant a fastball, two buzzes a curve. On hearing the buzz, bullpen catcher Sal Yvars would cross or uncross his legs, alerting the hitter about the upcoming pitch. Conspiracy devotees point to the fact that the Giants won an unprecedented 85 percent of their home games in their epic drive to the pennant after Durocher perched Herman Franks behind the Wollensak. Although Dodger fans have found this a sinister explanation for their team's late season collapse in the signal-stealing caper, the arrival of 20-year-old center fielder Willie Mays two months into the season more than likely provides a better explanation for the Giants' surge.

In the years that followed Thomson's home run, rumors about the alleged caper began to circulate. Of course, stealing signs had long been a part of baseball, and no rule existed prohibiting what Durocher is alleged to have done. In this particular case, however, obvious ethical issues placed in jeopardy Thomson's transcendent moment of baseball fame. The story first surfaced publicly during spring training in 1962 when an Associated Press writer, without identifying his source, reported that Thomson had benefitted from pilfered signals. Durocher, Thomson, and other Giants naturally denied everything, but sports commentator Howard Cosell jumped on the story, giving it considerable credence. Over the years, the issue periodically reappeared. In 1980, Thomson categorically stated, "I had no help from any illegal sign-stealing on the homer," while Ralph Branca, whose life had been forever changed by one disastrous pitch that overshadowed an otherwise noteworthy pitching career, plaintively said, "The Giants cheated and stole the pennant in 1951, and that's the truth."

In 2006, journalist Joshua Prager told the story in great detail with considerable literary flair. Prager described a complex tale, replete with secrecy and intrigue, selective memories, massive egos, and massaged facts. Beneath it all lurked career baseball men naturally seeking an edge, however slight it might have been. The fact remains that, even if Thomson knew a 93 mph fastball was on the way, the signal from Franks via the bullpen could not have told him its location. Branca's fastball had plenty of movement and was located well out of the strike zone, but Thomson had somehow put bat solidly on ball. Of such mysteries – if not conspiracies – was the Dodger–Giants rivalry constructed.

Walter O'Malley and the "Great Betrayal"

Between 1951 and 1956, either the Giants or Dodgers won the National League pennant, with each pennant race intensifying the rivalry. In 1952 and 1953, the Dodgers won two tight pennants over Durocher's Giants, but in the World Series their futility continued when they lost twice in succession to the Yankees. Finally in 1955, they broke through, defeating the Yankees in Game Seven under the direction of second year manager Walter Alston. The Giants had lost to the Yankees in the anticlimactic 1951 World Series, but in 1954, listed by bookmakers as solid underdogs, they buried the Cleveland Indians in just four games. The opening game of the 1954 Series featured a spectacular over-the-shoulder, back-to-the-infield, running catch by Willie Mays in the vast expanses of the Polo Grounds center field off the bat of Vic Wertz, and a three-run pinch-hit homer by little-used outfielder Dusty Rhodes.

Although the Giants and the Dodgers enjoyed success on the field, their fans were not impressed. Attendance had fallen off by nearly 40 percent since 1948; fans were no longer willing to sit in poor seats in decrepit stadiums located in marginal neighborhoods where there was inadequate parking. Both teams had to confront the reality that they had to relocate to better venues, either in New York or elsewhere. For several years, Walter O'Malley had been quietly negotiating with New York's political establishment, seeking permission to build at his own expense (on land to be provided by the city) a 40,000-seat cantilevered stadium at a prime Brooklyn location at the corner of Atlantic and Flatbush Avenues. The land he coveted would provide adequate space for parking and was located near subway stations and the terminal of the commuter Long Island Railroad. But the most powerful man in New York City, master planner and political operative Robert Moses, wanted instead to use that space to build a large parking garage. The autocratic Moses adamantly insisted that O'Malley build outside of Brooklyn at Flushing Meadows (on the site where Shea Stadium would be opened in 1964 for the New York Mets). Frustrated by Moses' intransigence, O'Malley listened more carefully to overtures he had been receiving from city council members and Mayor Norris Poulson of Los Angeles, who promised him 307 acres of prime downtown Los Angeles land in Chavez Ravine on which to build his dream stadium.

O'Malley's decision to move west was – and still is – considered high treason by many New Yorkers. They accused him of abandoning Brooklyn's loyal fans because of cold-hearted greed, but in fact the fans had abandoned the Dodgers by their poor attendance, and city leaders never made a good faith effort to assist O'Malley in acquiring a suitable Brooklyn site. They apparently never could quite grasp that he would actually move his team out of their city.

On August 19, 1957, Giants owner Horace Stoneham announced that he had accepted an offer from the city of San Francisco that included a new 40,000-seat stadium with 12,000 parking spaces, all paid for from city coffers. Curiously, O'Malley did not make his intentions known until two months later, but he became the villain incarnate in the scenario. Angry New York writers refused to support the nomination of O'Malley for membership in the Hall of Fame, and only in 2007, on the 50th anniversary of his alleged "dastardly deed," did the Veterans Committee finally vote him in. Michael D'Antonio's biography of O'Malley (2009), based on extensive research into city planning records and the private papers of Moses and O'Malley, effectively demonstrates that O'Malley preferred to stay in Brooklyn but was virtually forced west by the intransigent and powerful bureaucrat Robert Moses.

Thus did the Dodger–Giants rivalry move to the Golden West.

New Cities, Still Rivals

The 1958 season opened on April 15 with the San Francisco Giants hosting the Los Angeles Dodgers at their temporary home field in aging Seals Stadium. In the first major league game played on the West Coast, the Giants defeated the Dodgers 8–0 behind Ruben Gomez's baffling screwball, but the next day the Dodgers bounced back with a 13–1 victory behind left-hander Johnny Podres. While just 25,000 spectators could squeeze into the Pacific Coast League ballpark in San Francisco, more than 78,000 fans greeted the two teams when they took the field on April 18 at the Los Angeles Coliseum.

The 100,000-seat Coliseum, home to professional football's Rams, was built in 1923 and in 1932 had hosted the track and field events of the Olympics. It had never been intended for baseball. Hastily drawn plans led to a convoluted baseball field that made a mockery of the game. Banjo hitters took aim at the left field seats located just 250 feet from home plate. Although guarded by a 140 foot long, 40 foot high screen, the result nonetheless was that pop flies often became four-baggers. Left-handed power hitters complained that they were unfairly penalized when the temporary six foot fence in right field was placed a distant 440 feet away.

Events on the quirky field, however, were overshadowed by the rising tide of political opposition to the city's contract with O'Malley that granted him control of Chavez Ravine on the edge of downtown. Many opponents were appalled that the city was turning over to a private entity such prime acreage, while others were swayed by heart-rending stories about the planned eviction of the few remaining low-income families. In June, voters turned out in large numbers to cast their ballots on a hotly contested referendum that would have killed the deal. Only a powerful campaign, led by the *Los Angeles Times* and supported by a flock of Hollywood celebrities, produced a narrow victory for the city government and the Dodgers; it passed by just 24,293 votes out of 666,577 votes cast. Following a series of lawsuits that upheld the land deal, bulldozers began resolutely leveling the ridges in Chavez Ravine and construction on Walter O'Malley's dream stadium commenced.

Sparkling Dodger Stadium opened on April 10, 1962, and was immediately proclaimed to be one of the world's best sports venues. Located near downtown Los Angeles, surrounded by palm trees and lush vegetation and with a dramatic view of the city's downtown skyline, it featured all of the amenities that had been lacking at Ebbets Field: 50,000 seats with unobstructed views, spacious aisles and walkways, readily accessible concession stands and restrooms, and even courteous ushers. Surrounding the park were 12,000 parking places with easy access to freeways.

Even before they moved into their new stadium, the Dodgers captured their first of five World Series titles in Los Angeles. It had taken them 72 years to win their only World Series in Brooklyn. After a disappointing seventh-place finish in 1958, a revamped Dodgers lineup defeated the Milwaukee Braves in two consecutive playoff games to win the 1959 pennant and then dispatched the Chicago White Sox in six games. The *Los Angeles Times*, one of the most ardent backers of the Chavez Ravine deal, was quick to point to the triumph as justification for providing the city's new team "with a decent playing yard." Across the sprawling, diverse metropolis of Southern California, a *Times* editorial writer explained, the Dodgers provided a unifying cultural force, "a sort of civic glue." O'Malley was thrilled that more than 2 million fans had paid their way into the Coliseum.

Although Bay Area sports fans embraced their new team, political factors conspired to impose upon the Giants the worst baseball stadium of modern times. The ballpark that opened at Candlestick Point in 1962 was the first of many circular stadiums built during the 1960s that were intended by cost-conscious politicians to accommodate both baseball and football. Consequently, sight lines for fans attending either sport were often poor. The decision to build the stadium 12 miles south of the city center on desolate and windswept Candlestick Point proved disastrous. Blustery cold winds, even during midsummer afternoons, made watching a game a matter of steely perseverance. Night games were routinely played in brutally cold weather, with fans bundled in parkas and stocking caps to ward off the damp cold and powerful gusts of wind.

In the 1961 All-Star Game, the image of an inhospitable Candlestick Park was forever etched in baseball lore when pitcher Stu Miller was caught by a blast off the Bay that apparently blew him off the pitching rubber; umpire Stan Landes called a balk, permitting a run to score. Some baseball buffs suggest that the story was greatly over-exaggerated, while others who witnessed the game swear that he was in fact thrown off balance by a vicious gust of wind. Whichever is true, the tale of Miller being "blown" off the mound persisted, and that moment came to symbolize for envious Giants fans the fact that they were stuck with an unappealing ballpark that lacked the many comforts of Dodger Stadium.

West Coast Mayhem

It did not take long for the rivalry that had existed in New York City to reignite on the West Coast. The Dodgers trailed the Giants in September of 1959, but swept a three game series from San Francisco to force the playoff with the Braves, knocking the Giants out of contention. In 1962, the two teams ended the season tied at 101–61 after the Dodgers lost ten of their last thirteen games. The Giants were led by the home run hitting of Willie Mays (49) and Orlando Cepeda (35), while the Dodgers featured the daunting pitching tandem of left-hander Sandy Koufax and right-hander Don Drysdale. Leadoff batter Maury Wills sparked the Dodger offense with his base running, ending the season with 104 stolen bases to break Ty Cobb's 1915 record of 96. The Dodgers led 4–2 at Dodger Stadium in the top of the ninth inning of the third and deciding playoff game, but the Giants rallied for four runs to take the pennant.

Angry Dodgers players punctuated their frustration by publicly denouncing a series of strategic moves (or blunders?) by manager Walter Alston, especially his refusal to use a rested Drysdale in relief to shut down the Giants' ninth inning rally.

However, all did not end well for the Giants, who lost the seventh game of the World Series at Candlestick 1–0 to the Yankees when Yankee second baseman Bobby Richardson made a leaping catch of Willie McCovey's screaming line drive with two men on base in the bottom of the ninth inning. This proved to be such a particularly agonizing moment for Giants fans that cartoonist Charles Schulz later immortalized it in his *Peanuts* comic strip. That crushing loss would hang heavy over the Giants for the next 27 years because they did not return to the World Series until 1989, while the Dodgers went on to win the pennant seven times during the same interval.

Despite many cries for Alston's firing, management stuck by their taciturn skipper, and he proceeded the following season to guide a weak hitting but strong pitching team to another World Championship, defeating the aging Yankees. In 1965, the power-challenged Dodgers managed to score only 608 runs, but the pitching staff turned in an incredible season, with an earned run average of just 2.81. The Dodgers compiled a 97–65 record, edging the frustrated Giants by two games in a season that scaled the heights of animosity between the two clubs. Sandy Koufax proved to be the difference-maker, compiling a 26–8 record on the strength of his near-unhittable fastball and a rich assortment of curves; he struck out a record 382 batters and had a remarkable 2.04 ERA. He also threw two no-hit games that season – one against the Giants in May, the other a perfect game against the Chicago Cubs in September in which he retired all 27 batters he faced. Koufax, however, pitched the entire season in constant pain – in spring training he had awakened one morning to see that his entire left arm had turned black and blue from serious hemorrhaging – and he would be forced to retire after the 1966 season.

With the 1965 pennant race between the two California clubs very close, and against the ugly backdrop of racial tensions that had produced a week-long riot in the Watts section of south-central Los Angeles, the Giants and Dodgers squared off at Candlestick Park on a bright Sunday afternoon on August 22 to close out a bitterly fought four game series. The tension of pennant race, combined with the backdrop of a 20-year history of high-stakes competition, meant that everyone was on edge. All season long, brush-back pitches had been frequent and uncomplimentary words had been uttered. On this seemingly pleasant afternoon, tensions ran uncomfortably high in both dugouts. The Dodgers had won two of the first three games, but a steady stream of sharp verbal exchanges had put tempers on edge. The Dodgers sent Koufax to the mound for the final game of the series, and the Giants responded with their ace right-hander, Juan Marichal. Early in the game, Marichal knocked down Maury Wills and Ron Fairly with high and tight fastballs that whistled by their chins. Koufax's teammates urged him to retaliate, but that was not his style. So, with Marichal at bat in the bottom of the second inning, catcher John Roseboro took it upon himself to respond: he fired two balls back to Koufax that ominously clipped Marichal's ear. After the second of these, the native of the Dominican Republic exploded in a fit of expletives, turned and belted Roseboro over the head with his bat, hitting him with two, possibly three, vicious blows. Blood spurted from a long gash on Roseboro's head, and 60 players and coaches were engaged in a major free-for-all. It took the umpires and a flying squad of policemen 14 minutes – with Willie Mays and Sandy Koufax attempting to play peacemaker – to quell the brawl. Roseboro, surprisingly, did not suffer a concussion, although 14 stitches were required to close his wound. "I thought it had knocked Roseboro's eye out," a shaken Dodger manager Walter Alston said afterwards. "There was nothing but blood where his left eye should have been." The Giants went on to win the game and the pennant race continued until late September before the Dodgers prevailed. Many a brawl had dotted the history of baseball, but old timers could not recall anyone taking a bat to an opponent's head.

Most baseball experts were appalled when National League president Warren Giles handed down what they considered a feeble punishment: an eight game suspension and a $1,750 fine for Marichal, plus he could not dress for the final two games of the season in Dodger Stadium. This incident, sometimes called the "ugliest moment in the history of baseball," highlighted the intensity that often was on display when the two teams met.

Dodger Blue Ascendant

As subsequent seasons unfolded, the Giants could never quite close the gap with the Dodgers. Not even the presence of such brilliant future Hall

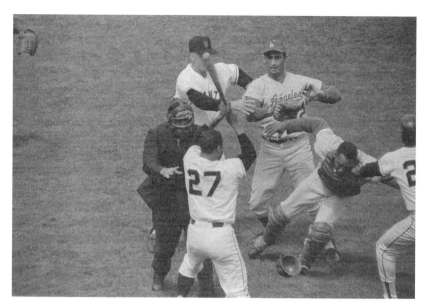

Figure 2.3   Giants pitcher Juan Marichal (27) prepares to take another swipe at the head of Dodger catcher John Roseboro on August 22, 1965, during a crucial game between rival teams caught up in a tight pennant race. Dodger pitcher Sandy Koufax plays peacekeeper while umpire Shag Crawford attempts to stop Marichal's next swing. National League President Warren Giles fined Marichal $1,750 and gave him an eight game suspension, a punishment that Dodger fans believed was not equal to the severity of the attack. © Bettmann/CORBIS

of Fame players as Mays, McCovey, Marichal, and pitcher Gaylord Perry could enable them to overtake the Dodgers. Between 1965 and 1969, the Giants finished in second place each year, but in the 1970s they tailed off badly. In 1972, the Giants shipped Willie Mays, now past his 40th birthday and nearing the end of his fabled career, to the New York Mets. His departure symbolized the franchise's decline. Attendance dropped to the point that owner Horace Stoneham came within a whisker of selling the team to the Labatt Brewing Company of Toronto in 1976. At the very last minute, local financier and civic leader Robert Lurie formed a consortium that purchased the team to keep it in San Francisco.

Things did not improve much under Lurie's ownership until general manager Al Rosen hired former Dodger pitcher Roger Craig as field manager and the Giants won their first National League pennant in 27 seasons in 1989. Craig managed shrewdly, sometimes using his instincts to go against conventional game strategy, maximizing the talent that featured the slugging of Will Clark and Kevin Mitchell and the all-round play of center fielder Brett Butler and second baseman Robby Thompson. But such was the Giants' luck that they ran into the multi-talented Oakland Athletics in the World Series. Even more powerful than the Athletics was the Loma Prieta earthquake, with a magnitude of 6.9, that hit the Bay Area during warm-ups an hour before Game Three. The stadium at Candlestick Point shook violently, and the upper deck undulated ominously. Fortunately, seismic reinforcement had been completed a few years earlier, and the stands were only half filled or the extra weight of spectators could have produced a disaster of incredible proportions.

When the Series resumed ten days later, the Athletics continued their own form of destruction, closing out the Giants in four straight games. To lose the World Series was difficult enough, but to do so in a blowout by the team from across the Bay was humbling indeed. The Giants once more descended into the doldrums. The nadir was reached in 1992. Voters turned down a referendum for an extensive remodeling of dreary Candlestick and, with attendance sagging, a frustrated Bob Lurie agreed to sell the team to buyers who intended to move them to St Petersburg, Florida, where a new domed stadium awaited. Only a last-minute intervention by league officials halted the sale, and the franchise was subsequently purchased by a group headed by the former CEO of the Safeway grocery company, Peter McGowan, who pledged to keep the team in San Francisco. Twice within 16 years, Giants fans had to deal with the very real possibility of losing their team.

While the Giants struggled to survive in the Bay Area, the Dodgers thrived in Los Angeles. In 1976, Dodger management nudged 64-year-old Walter Alston into retirement after 23 years of working under a succession of one-year contracts. During his long tenure, the quiet, unassuming Alston had won seven pennants and four World Championships. He ended his career with a glittering 2,040–1,613 won–lost record. After being named the National League's Manager of the Year six times, he was inducted into the Hall of Fame in 1983. But Alston's stolid demeanor did not work well in glitzy Los Angeles, and only the support he received from General Manager Buzzie Bavasi – who appreciated his steadfastness and loyalty – made the long tenure possible. He irritated locals when he made no secret that he preferred living in the crossroads

Ohio hamlet of Darrtown to living in Los Angeles. Alston's teams had lost their zest, reflecting the demeanor of their manager, and fans and Los Angeles sports writers began calling for Alston to be replaced by the flamboyant 49-year-old third base coach Tommy Lasorda. Bavasi finally agreed, and when Alston realized that there would not be a 24th contract, he announced his retirement on September 29, 1976. Lasorda was named manager two days later.

During Alston's final years, the Dodgers had become an unexciting team despite continuing their winning ways (including the 1974 league title). Fans still came in large numbers, but they did so without much enthusiasm, and the team played methodically if not mechanically. The Dodgers needed someone who could rekindle the team's fire. In Lasorda they found that person. The irrepressible enthusiasm of the former journeyman pitcher made for great media coverage. Lasorda became the team's number one cheerleader. He loved to point out that he had pitched for the Dodgers in Ebbets Field and had made a "great personal sacrifice" for the club in 1956 when he was traded to make room for rookie Sandy Koufax. A consummate pitchman, he raised the level of Dodger enthusiasm to the level it had enjoyed during the team's first years in town. He attributed wins to "the Big Dodger in the Sky," and loved to say that he bled "Dodger Blue." When Tommy Lasorda modestly proclaimed himself "Mr Dodger," few disputed that claim.

His personality and passion aside, Lasorda knew his baseball. He won over the blasé Los Angeles fans in his very first season in 1977, leading his team to 98 regular season wins and a tense playoff victory over the Philadelphia Phillies. He had plenty of talent to manage, getting strong play from such everyday standouts as Dusty Baker, Rick Monday, Reggie Smith, Ron Cey, Steve Garvey, and Davey Lopes, and he had a dependable pitching staff led by left-hander Tommy John and right-hander Don Sutton. The Dodgers lost the World Series to the Yankees in six games, but each game was close, the deciding factor being a home run barrage by "Mr October," Yankee outfielder Reggie Jackson.

By the end of his initial season as manager, Lasorda had become a leading celebrity in a city of celebrities, his smiling face routinely appearing on billboards and television screens endorsing a wide range of products. He was often seen dining with the likes of Frank Sinatra and Dean Martin – at posh Italian restaurants, naturally – and he became the personification of the ball club. Writers appreciated his accessibility, knowing he was usually good for a funny comment or a heads-up on a breaking story.

They also could get a large serving of one of Lasorda's favorite pasta dishes that he cooked up in the locker room. A second consecutive pennant in 1978 solidified his hold on the fans, although the Dodgers lost yet again to their nemesis – the Yankees, managed by Bob Lemon.

The season of 1981 was magical because the Dodgers were not considered contenders coming out of spring training. Their success revolved around the unexpected emergence of a charismatic, chubby left-handed pitcher, 25-year-old Fernando Valenzuela. An affable native of Mexico, he spoke little English but enthralled sports writers. He used an unorthodox delivery style during which he never looked toward home plate but instead peered toward the heavens as if asking for divine inspiration for his curveball. Despite this strange delivery, he baffled hitters with his large assortment of off-speed pitches and uncanny control. His "fastball" was not so fast, timed in just the mid-80s. In this, his rookie season, Valenzuela won his first eight starts, four by shutout, during which time he posted a 0.50 ERA. A 50 day strike in midseason seemed to reduce his effectiveness when play resumed in mid-August, but he finished the season with a 13–7 record and a league-leading 180 strikeouts. He was a runaway winner of the Rookie of the Year award. "El Toro" became a fan favorite across the United States, and "Fernandomania" brought new fans to the ballparks, including large numbers of Hispanics. Valenzuela pitched effectively in the playoffs against the Houston Astros and the Montreal Expos, and then beat the Yankees in a crucial World Series game when he threw 145 pitches, helping the Dodgers win in six nerve-racking games. Valenzuela continued to pitch creditably for the Dodgers for nine seasons before being released in 1991 when arm troubles occurred.

Lasorda's teams during much of the 1980s played to large crowds in Dodger Stadium, although their play after the 1981 triumph was often lackluster. Lasorda's cheerleading overshadowed the fact that the team had grown old. That situation began to change with the emergence of right-hander Orel Hershiser as a preeminent starting pitcher, and acquisition from Detroit of the former Michigan State tight end, right fielder Kirk Gibson. Throughout the 1988 season, the Dodgers never lost more than three games in succession, and, as the pennant race pushed into September, Hershiser began a streak that has to be considered one of the most impressive pitching feats in the history of baseball. He won five consecutive shutout games and then threw ten scoreless innings against San Diego to set a new major league record of 59 consecutive innings pitched without giving up a run (eclipsing the record set in 1968 by former Dodger Don Drysdale). During the playoffs, Hershiser extended his scoreless streak to 67 innings before giving up two runs to the San Diego Padres. He then shut out the heavily favored New York Mets in Game Seven of the league championship series and won two games (including yet another shutout) against the Oakland Athletics in the World Series.

Despite such heroics, Hershiser was not the biggest star of the 1988 World Series. That title fell to Gibson, who had provided timely clutch hitting all season long but, as Game One loomed, suffered from a severe hamstring pull. In the bottom of the ninth inning of Game One, with two outs and the Dodgers trailing by 4–3 and Mike Davis on first base, Gibson limped out of the dugout to pinch hit against the game's best relief pitcher, side-arming right-hander Dennis Eckersley. Thus unfolded one of baseball's most dramatic, made-for-Hollywood endings. Grimacing fiercely from pain, and with the count standing at 3–2, he connected on one of Eckersley's sliders and improbably lofted the ball over the right field fence. As he hobbled around the bases pumping his fist toward the evening sky, television announcer Jack Buck uttered his oft-repeated incredulous commentary: "I don't believe what I just saw!" The stirring come-from-behind victory capped by the wounded Dodger's home run propelled Los Angeles to a 4–1 World Series championship.

That memorable triumph, however, would be the last Dodgers appearance in the World Series, although they did make the playoffs in 1995, 1996, 2004, and 2008. Lasorda retired to a Dodgers vice-presidency in 1996, and his departure ended a period of stability that stretched back to 1954. He and Walter Alston had provided the only managerial leadership for more than four decades. In 1998, the O'Malley family sold the team to Australian media empire mogul Rupert Murdoch. The Dodgers had become a mere pawn in the portfolio of a multinational billionaire. In 2004, an indifferent Murdoch sold the team to Boston real estate mogul Frank McCourt.

The Long Shadow of Scandal

In the Bay Area, the Giants opted to emphasize the superstar potential of left fielder Barry Bonds as their ticket to success. Bonds was acquired as one of the highest paid free agents up to that time by new owner Peter McGowan before the 1992 season. The slender, lithe Bonds was a native of the Bay Area and his father Bobby was a former Giants star who signed on as first-base coach in 1993. In Barry Bonds' first season as a Giant, under new manager Dusty Baker, the club won 103 games and entered the final game of the season needing a victory to force a playoff with Atlanta. Heeding the distant echoes of a past rivalry now dimmed, the Dodgers ended the Giants' hopes with a 12–1 blowout that included a late-inning steal of second base by Dodger (and former Giant) center fielder Brett Butler, who broke one of baseball's unwritten rules of etiquette that one does not embarrass a vanquished foe in the late innings of a blowout. But this was just the Dodgers enjoying a little extra at the expense of their timeless rivals.

In 2000, the Giants moved into their privately financed new ballpark in downtown San Francisco at 24 Willie Mays Plaza. Pac Bell Park (later named SBC and finally AT&T Park as the corporate world of communications went through various financial permutations) was everything that Candlestick was not. The winds were relatively mild and the temperatures tolerable. The retro-designed stadium was a delight, even from the most distant seats, and fans in the upper deck enjoyed a stirring view of San Francisco Bay. That year Barry Bonds, long known for his speed and extra base hits, became a born-again home run slugger. As he entered his mid-30s, he began adding considerable muscle bulk, and regularly thrilled fans with a stunning increase in home run production; some of his mighty drives even sailed over the right field seats into McCovey Cove where a small flotilla of kayakers awaited the next splashdown.

The Giants appropriately won their division in their inaugural season in Pac Bell but lost out in the first round of the playoffs to the Mets. Team management opted to build their team around the often sullen and aloof Bonds, allocating about 25 percent of the payroll to his soaring salary that reached $22 million in 2004. Front office thinking revolved around his new-found home run stroke and its ability to attract capacity crowds. He responded by defying traditional baseball logic. At the age of 35, when baseball players usually have already begun the inevitable decline in productivity, Bonds entered into a seemingly inexplicable five year period in which he would hit 258 home runs. In 2001, playing in a home park with distant fences and incoming breezes off the Bay, Bonds hit a staggering 73 home runs. He reached the point where he approached the career home run mark of 755 set by Hank Aaron in 1973.

Whispers began to circulate that his power was derived from human growth hormones and/or steroid treatments. These whispers became pronounced when he was questioned before a federal grand jury in San Francisco looking into the dubious activities involving the Bay Area Laboratory Cooperative (BALCO). His denial of using illegal substances under oath, however, was leaked to the press. He continued his quest for Hank Aaron's record under a growing cloud of suspicion that his increased muscle mass was the result of more than, as he said, careful diet, use of approved supplements, and a tortuous exercise program. On the road, he was routinely booed and heckled, most fervently in Dodger Stadium. After publication in 2006 of a devastating book by two Bay Area reporters based upon leaks of Bonds' grand jury testimony, he became the center of a raging national controversy. Most San Francisco fans gave him a pass and robustly cheered his every home run, but elsewhere his achievement was viewed with contempt. When his 756th career home run landed in the bleachers on the evening of August 7, 2007, Baseball Commissioner Bud Selig pensively watched from a luxury box, displaying no emotion, and pointedly did not participate in the on-the-field celebration. Even before the season ended, Giants management announced that Bonds would not be re-signed for the 2008 season. With 762 home runs credited to his name in the record book, he was then hit with a federal indictment for perjury in his testimony before the grand jury back in 2003. Baseball fans noticed that the Giants finished in last place in the Western Division the year Bonds surpassed Aaron.

In 2002, the Giants, under manager Dusty Baker, had used Bonds' 46 home runs to reach the World Series as a wild card team, beating Atlanta and St Louis in the playoffs. As Game Six of the World Series unfolded, it seemed that the Giants would finally win the franchise's first World Series since 1954. Leading three games to two and sporting a 5–0 lead in the bottom of the seventh inning against the Los Angeles Angels, Baker opted to replace starter Russ Ortiz and curiously presented him with the "game ball" symbolizing the Giants' impending World Series title. Baker's gesture was a bit premature, as Scott Spiezio hit a three run homer and the Angels rallied to defeat the Giants 6–5 and then proceeded to win Game Seven over a dispirited San Francisco club.

As the new millennium began to unfold, the fire seemed to go out of the rivalry. Perhaps it was because of corporate-style management, or maybe a consequence of diminished fan identification with teams owing to the steady shuffle of rosters that resulted from free agency. One factor was the lack of head-to-head divisional pennant races. Attendance remained strong in both cities, but the fans lapsed into a stifling torpor. Even the traditional chant of "Beat LA! Beat LA!" that had long resonated across the Bay lacked enthusiasm when the colorless Dodgers came to town. And, at Dodger Stadium, where the fans seemed to come out to the game as if by habit and not drawn by anything remarkable, the once ardent catcalls that were hurled at Barry Bonds somehow seemed perfunctory and stale. Maybe a good old-fashioned brawl was in order. A crucial ingredient in maintaining an incandescent rivalry is certainly the existence of a fierce battle for supremacy between two exciting, competitive teams in an all out drive for the top honors.

Battle Along Tobacco Road

Duke and North Carolina Basketball

There's absolutely no doubt in my mind, baby, Duke–Carolina is the best rivalry in college basketball, and probably in all of athletics. Even a one-eyed broadcaster can see that! (Dick Vitale)

Less than ten miles separates the campuses of two of the most successful major college basketball teams in history. To be precise, the distance is just 8.5 miles as the crow flies, but the cultural and political distance between the two institutions is great. Founded in 1789, the University of North Carolina in Chapel Hill is the nation's oldest public university and has long enjoyed a lofty rating as one of the nation's great public universities. Duke University, located in Durham, enjoys a place in the top echelon of elite private institutions. Both schools pride themselves on their world-class faculties, wide range of graduate and professional programs, high admissions standards, and impressive research. It is significant that both institutions have managed to mount prominent athletic programs on campuses where high academic standards are *de rigueur* and athletes graduate at very high rates. These factors have all contributed to the very special basketball rivalry that exists along Tobacco Road.

North Carolina and Duke began playing each other in basketball in 1920 (Tar Heels 36, Blue Devils 25) but basketball at the time was not in the spotlight because, in the decades between the wars, both schools attempted to field nationally ranked football teams. During the 1930s, Duke enjoyed considerable success under coach Wallace Wade, and UNC moved into a short-lived national prominence between 1947 and 1949 behind running back Charlie "Choo Choo" Justice. During the 1950s, however, fans discovered the magic of basketball and, in effect, football took a back seat on both campuses.

Ironically, the embracing of basketball along Tobacco Road occurred because of a heavy influx of Yankees. When the Tar Heels under basketball coach Tom Scott lost 43–40 to one of Hank Iba's efficient Oklahoma A & M teams in the NCAA championship game in 1946, no one paid much attention. This cavalier attitude toward basketball changed when coach Frank McGuire arrived for the 1952–3 basketball season. A native New Yorker, the slick-talking Irishman had been the successful head coach at St Johns. In his fifth season in Chapel Hill, McGuire pushed and prodded the Tar Heels to the national championship, upsetting a Wilt Chamberlain-led Kansas. McGuire's top-ranked Tar Heels capped off an undefeated season by defeating Phog Allen's Jayhawks in three overtime periods, 54–53.

McGuire's starting five had all arrived in Chapel Hill via the "Reverse Underground Railroad" that McGuire operated to bring in top talent to Dixie from his native New York. The 1957 national championship team was fondly known throughout heavily Baptist North Carolina as "Four Catholics and a Jew." All five – Pete Brennan, Tommy Kearns, Bobby Cunningham, Joe Quigg, and Len Rosenbluth – hailed from the New York City area and they made basketball something special in North Carolina. They managed to squeak by in several close games during the season – including five overtime games – to end their season 32–0. Most notable among their regular season games was a hard fought 75–73 victory over Duke, which was the first game in the rivalry to be televised across the state.

In that special season, basketball moved into a position of centrality in the world of North Carolina sports, and there it remains. UNC would return to the Final Four of the NCAA tournament 16 more times thereafter, winning four additional championships, while garnering 21 Atlantic Coast Conference championships. Not willing to allow its neighbor to dominate things, Duke, under athletic director and former basketball coach Eddie Cameron, upped its commitment to its basketball program, making its first appearance in the Final Four in 1963. The Blue Devils would ultimately take 14 trips to the Final Four and capture three national championships. Along the way, they won 18 ACC crowns.

Ever since the two schools committed themselves to basketball excellence, they have battled for local (and national) bragging rights, squaring off twice during the regular season and often meeting in the ACC postseason tournament. More often than not, national ranking, a high tournament seeding, and the distinct possibility of a Final Four appearance rested on the outcome of their battles. Ever since the two teams became nationally prominent, only a handful of programs can claim comparable long-term success – Indiana, Kansas, Kentucky, and UCLA – but none of these has been fueled by the existence of a powerful rival located almost within shouting distance. Without question, year in and year out, Duke and North Carolina basketball has provided college basketball's most enduring – and exciting – rivalry.

Two Universities, Distinct Missions

The two institutions have markedly different missions. The University of North Carolina enjoys the distinction of being the first publicly funded state university in the nation. Created by the North Carolina General Assembly in the same year that George Washington was inaugurated as President, it was located near the middle of the state to encourage public access. UNC always enjoyed a special place in the hearts and minds of North Carolinians, and it emerged in the 20th century as a leading public university. Today, with 30,000 students, it is recognized as one of the premier public research universities in the United States. Coaches and administrators at Duke have long complained that their institution does not receive the same local support as their rival, but that is because Duke draws most of its students from outside the state; consequently, the fiercely loyal UNC alumni living in the state outnumber Dookies by a factor of about ten to one.

In 1892, a small Methodist college was relocated from Randolph County to Durham after receiving a substantial gift from tobacco magnate Washington Duke. Trinity College was renamed Duke University in 1924 after becoming a primary beneficiary of the James B. Duke endowment that enabled it to grow rapidly in size and academic prestige after the Second World War. Today, considered one of the nation's leading universities, its enrollment is capped at 13,000, divided equally between undergraduate and graduate students.

Frank McGuire and Vic Bubas:
The Rivalry Takes Shape

Although most fans trace the rivalry to the hiring of Frank McGuire in 1952, followed in 1959 by the appointment of Duke's first prominent coach, Vic Bubas, in many ways it resulted from the appointment of legendary Indiana high school coach Everett Case, who was hired to take over a lackluster program at North Carolina State in 1946. Case had won four state championships in basketball-crazed Indiana before the Second World War, and at the age of 46 set out to energize the Wolfpack program. He recruited relentlessly, teaching an up-tempo style of play that thrilled spectators accustomed to the traditional set pattern style. His teams dominated the old Southern Conference, winning its last six championships. With the establishment of the Atlantic Coast Conference in 1951, he proceeded to capture its first three titles. Case popularized basketball in North Carolina by hosting the much-loved Christmas-time Dixie Classic in the (then) enormous 12,500-seat arena on the Raleigh campus. He also convinced the ACC to top off its regular season with a tournament that would determine the conference's lone-entry in the NCAA tournament. That tournament – the first of its kind – put enormous pressure on coaches and players and provided a suspenseful climax to the basketball season. Case won his first 15 games against UNC and did almost as well against Duke. In response to Case's dominance, Duke and UNC modernized their basketball facilities, increased budgets, and hired high-profile coaches to fend off the Aggie school in Raleigh.

UNC's flamboyant McGuire established his credibility when he won his first game against eighth-ranked North Carolina State in January of 1953. Duke's soft-spoken coach Harold Bradley produced the national player of the year in 1952 in guard Dick Groat and managed to win two ACC regular season titles (but not the all-important ACC tournament) in his nine years at the helm. Things got interesting in the fall of 1959 when Duke hired Vic Bubas to replace Bradley. A former star player and assistant coach with Case for six years at NC State, Bubas was hired primarily for his recruiting abilities. At the press conference where he was introduced, Duke's legendary Athletic Director Eddie Cameron closed the session by pointedly asking his new coach, "Don't you think it is now time to go recruiting?" The stakes had been raised.

The arrival of Bubas on the Durham campus greatly stimulated fan interest. The charismatic coach attracted a steady procession of top talent to campus. When he landed a top prospect from McGuire's home turf of New York, the tension between the two schools accelerated. Art Heyman was one of the most heavily recruited players in the nation in 1959, and knowledgeable observers expected him to end up at Chapel Hill. McGuire had frequently bragged that when it came to recruiting, he "owned" New York City. And so it seemed. The previous year McGuire landed guard Larry Brown out of a Long Island high school and the following year signed the sensational 6'5" power forward Heyman to a scholarship letter, apparently beating out Kentucky and Indiana. Brown and Heyman had competed for rival high schools and now they seemed destined to play together as McGuire went in quest of another NCAA title. But that letter was not binding until July, and Bubas worked relentlessly to convince Heyman that he should play in a darker shade of blue. At the last moment, Heyman opted for Duke, infuriating McGuire and Tar Heel fans. By luring the heralded – if temperamental and unpredictable – Heyman away from his signed commitment to Carolina, the new kid on the block had seriously upped the ante along Tobacco Road.

During Bubas' first season, his inexperienced and outmanned team lost twice to North Carolina by large margins and entered the ACC tournament only slightly above a .500 average. But the Blue Devils caught fire late in the season and surprised the Tar Heels in the tournament semi-finals with a pesky 1–3–1 zone, holding off a last minute rally to win 71–69. The next day Duke defeated Wake Forest 63–59 and went on to win two games in the NCAA tournament, falling one game short of making the Final Four. In just one season, Bubas had established himself as a coach to be reckoned with, and the Blue Devils enjoyed the emotional rush of a high national ranking.

It seemed that an exciting time loomed: the veteran McGuire versus the upstart Bubas. But such was not to be, for McGuire had run afoul of the NCAA on a series of recruiting infractions. In midseason 1961, Carolina was hit by a year's probation, and, despite a number five national ranking, was prohibited from playing in the upcoming NCAA tournament. His scatological denunciations of the NCAA committee (reported by the press in a sanitized form) and the embarrassment of NCAA sanctions did not sit well with North Carolina's chancellor William Aycock.

McGuire knew that his time at UNC was near its end, but he went out in style in one of the most memorable games in Duke–Carolina history. The major narrative was not that the Tar Heels dropped a tense 81–77 game before an impassioned overflow crowd; it was the ten minute free-for-all that occurred in the final seconds of the game that resonated for years thereafter. Emotions had run high all night at Duke's Indoor Stadium, with sophomore Heyman the brunt of many anti-Semitic taunts from Carolina fans (who overlooked the fact that their sophomore star Larry Brown was also Jewish). On the floor, trash talking was constant,

Figure 3.1 Point guard Larry Brown drives into the key against North Carolina during a game at Duke's Indoor Stadium in 1961. Shortly after this picture was taken, Brown became in involved in scuffle with Duke's Art Heyman that set off a major brawl. At 5′9″, Brown played professionally in the short-lived American Basketball Association before launching a 40-year coaching career. He won the NCAA championship at Kansas in 1988 and the 2004 NBA title with the Detroit Pistons. Reproduced by permission of UNC Athletic Communications, University of North Carolina Athletic Department Archives

as were the tossing of sharp elbows and the setting of hard screens. Late in the game, Heyman roughly fouled Brown from behind as he went up for an easy layup. Fists flew and benches emptied as fans poured out of the stands to join in the fun. A flying squadron of policemen was required to restore order. The game ended with Bubas and McGuire exchanging unpleasantries at midcourt, and the fight – as well as which team was responsible for its instigation – remained a major point of contention for years to come. The rivalry had become red hot.

These nasty events occurred within the larger national shadow of a new gambling scandal. Four North Carolina State players were implicated in 1960, and rumors that Duke's upset of North Carolina the previous year might have been tainted by the national gambling scandal swirled around McGuire's head. No charges that his players had shaved points or thrown the game were ever leveled, but these tense times provided the opportunity for Chancellor Aycock to bluntly warn McGuire to clean up his act. Thus it was no great surprise that the embattled coach resigned that summer to take the head coaching position of the Philadelphia Warriors in the NBA. Perhaps he was motivated by having the opportunity to coach Wilt Chamberlain, but he undoubtedly knew it was time to move on.

The Dean Smith Era

Chancellor Aycock wasted little time in promoting 31-year-old assistant coach Dean Smith to replace McGuire. Aycock found the earnest young Kansan's quiet demeanor a refreshing contrast to McGuire. He told Smith to "Make us proud of our student-athletes. Make sure your players graduate, no problems with gambling, and no recruiting violations." Smith would follow those instructions closely over the next 36 seasons in which he established himself as one of the all-time great coaches in the history of college basketball. When he retired in 1997, he had won the largest number of games of any college coach – 879 – a record that stood until surpassed in 2006 by Bob Knight.

Smith had played for the famed Phog Allen at Kansas, where he was a substitute guard on the national championship team in 1952, and served as a graduate assistant during the 1952–3 season. A native of Emporia, Smith had grown up in the Midwestern town where he regularly attended the Baptist Church, starred on teams coached by his father, and earned an academic scholarship to attend Kansas. He came to Chapel Hill after a brief coaching stint at the Air Force Academy.

Smith's first season was not auspicious. Thanks to McGuire's indiscretions, his team was on probation and concerns about the gambling scandals had led to the suspension of the midwinter Dixie Classic and a shortening of the Tar Heel schedule. Despite the talented presence of senior Larry Brown, the Tar Heels were short-handed. They struggled to an 8–9 record, including two losses to Vic Bubas' high-flying Blue Devils. It would be the only losing season that Dean Smith endured in his lengthy career. During his second season his team improved to 15–6 and made the semi-finals of the ACC tournament, but to demanding Tar Heel fans the new coach was coming up short against Bubas, whose team was ranked in the top ten and dominating the ACC.

Meanwhile, Bubas was extending his recruiting net into the Midwest, luring such top prospects as Lexington native Jeff Mullins away from Adolph Rupp and the University of Kentucky. To make matters worse for Smith, the Blue Devils played in the Final Four in 1963, and the following season went to the national championship game before losing to the high-flying UCLA Bruins in 1964 as coach John Wooden captured the first of his ten NCAA titles. In 1966, Duke once more made an appearance in the Final Four, while North Carolina remained home.

Despite high expectations and increasing fan criticism, Dean Smith knew what he was about. He persevered in the face of adversity and the occasional call for his firing. He established himself as a firm disciplinarian, instituting close scrutiny of off-court behavior and academic progress of his players, establishing a year-round conditioning program, and bringing to an end the casual practices run by McGuire. His carefully structured practices were clinical exercises in teaching of fundamentals. Even at tournament time, he insisted on repetitive drills on first principles. By 1965, with Duke the center of national attention, Carolina fans expressed increasing irritation with the Tar Heel's inability to catch up with Duke. One February morning, an effigy of Smith was found swinging in the morning breeze. This tasteless ploy only served to rally the team behind their young coach; shortly thereafter, led by senior forward Billy Cunningham, the Tar Heels gave Smith his first win over Duke by a narrow 65–62 score. By 1966, he had his own recruits in place, and his teams would never again finish lower than third in the ACC.

Smith was fascinated by the intricacies and subtleties of arcane basketball rules and strategy. Early on, referees discovered in the heat of a close game that he knew the rules book as well as, if not better than, they did. He was forever testing new theories and experimenting with new tactics that might provide a slight advantage. Smith fervently believed that basketball was a team game, and he always emphasized team over individual. Even the most talented of All-Americans had to buy into his system. His teams became known for an offense that was based on constant player movement incorporating precise screens, sharp cuts to the basket, and crisp passing; his tenacious defenses were designed to create turnovers that led to easy scores off a controlled fast break. To appreciate Tar Heel basketball was to appreciate basketball grounded in proper technique. At the same time, Smith was flexible, always tweaking his system to accommodate the special qualities of his players.

That said, Smith will probably be best remembered as the coach whose slowdown "four corners" offense prompted the NCAA to implement a 45 second shot clock in 1985. Some basketball purists insist that another Kansas basketball alumnus, John McClendon, actually originated the offense, but Smith apparently developed his own version as a by-product of his penchant for innovative game strategies. Four corners had its origins in his second season when his underdog team visited Kentucky to play Adolph Rupp's top-ranked Wildcats. For several weeks, he had his team practice a stall offense and decided to give it a try at Lexington. With Larry Brown holding the ball at midcourt and the other four Heels stationed near the four corners of the frontcourt, the stall forced Rupp to pull his team out of its tight defense, allowing the quick Larry Brown to slip through the Wildcats, making sleight-of-hand passes to teammates cutting toward the basket. The result was a stunning 68–66 upset. Convinced that he had found a useful tactic, Smith continued to tinker with the spread offense and, much to the frustration and anger of opponents, used it to control the tempo and draw fouls late in games while protecting a narrow lead.

Fans in North Carolina got a full dose of the new offense when an overmatched UNC team played Final Four-bound Duke in the semi-finals of the ACC tournament in 1966. Knowing that his team could not run with the more talented Blue Devils, Smith began the game in four corners and stayed with it throughout the first half, later expressing surprise that Bubas did not instruct his team to apply pressure. Smith was roundly booed and irate fans showered him with debris and obscenities as he left the court at half-time, but the Tar Heels led the heavily favored Blue Devils 7–5. He stayed with his strategy in the second half. However, after controlling the entire game, his team lost its composure in the last few minutes, made a few bad passes, and permitted Duke to tie the game at 20–20. With just four seconds remaining, Duke's all-conference guard Mike Lewis sank a free throw to give his team a 21–20 victory. The Blue Devils went on to defeat NC State in the finals and eventually lose to Kentucky in the Final Four. Much to the consternation of UNC opponents, the four corners had become an integral part of Carolina basketball.

Because rival coaches, players, and fans detested the four corners, UNC fans naturally embraced it, even beginning to collectively hold up four fingers late in games when it seemed appropriate. That its employment led to far more victories than defeats over closely matched opponents best explains fan enthusiasm. One of the favorite watering holes in Chapel Hill was even named the "Four Corners." During a nationally televised game in 1982, Carolina ran the scheme for more than 12 minutes in the ACC tournament championship against Virginia without taking a shot, and viewer disgust made it inevitable that the NCAA would adopt a shot clock, something it had resisted for three decades after the NBA installed a 24 second clock in 1954.

To Dean Smith, however, the four corners was merely one weapon in his diversified arsenal. His coaching style and philosophy did not change much, but he was always open to innovations and willing to challenge conventional wisdom. Such was the case in 1966 when he made the decision that the time had come for Carolina to recruit black athletes. He undoubtedly recalled that his father, a young coach at Emporia High School, was ordered by his principal to drop a black player from his team due to pressure from the head of the Eastern Kansas Conference. Alfred Smith responded that he would quit his position before bowing to racist pressure; his principal relented and Smith kept his job.

By 1966, the issue of southern teams stubbornly sticking to their lily-white policy had come to a head. The Voting Rights Act of 1965 had just been signed into law, and it was only a few years earlier that the first black students had been enrolled in southern public universities despite widespread resistance. In 1963, Mississippi State University administrators had publicly defied an order from Governor Ross Barnett and permitted the Bulldogs to play Loyola of Chicago in the NCAA basketball tournament even though the Ramblers had four blacks in its starting lineup. College sports officials everywhere were quietly contemplating the significance of the March 1966 NCAA championship game in which Kentucky was decisively beaten by a little-known team from Texas Western College in El Paso that featured an all-black starting lineup supplemented by two top black substitutes. Although Smith, well known in Chapel Hill for his liberal political views, received considerable recognition for recruiting a black athlete, he undoubtedly realized that the time had arrived.

Smith's decision to sign Charles Scott out of Laurinburg Institute in North Carolina came only after he had learned that Lefty Driesell, the aggressive young coach at Davidson, had received a verbal commitment from the blue-chipper. Smith invited the 18-year-old for a weekend visit, where he introduced him to black Chapel Hill citizens and faculty and took him to a concert featuring Smokey Robinson and the Miracles and the Temptations. When Scott informed Driesell that he had decided to attend UNC, the spurned coach responded angrily, but to no avail. Driesell believed (with good reason) that Scott was his key to winning a national championship at Davidson, which he envisioned as his response to the decision by his alma mater in 1959 to hire Vic Bubas rather than himself.

The athletic 6'5" Scott lived up to Smith's expectations, leading the Tar Heels to ACC league and postseason tournament championships in 1968 and 1969. However, Smith more than once was prompted to respond to racist comments hurled at his star player during away games. At South Carolina, his assistant coaches had to restrain him from going into the stands to confront a particularly obnoxious heckler, and he publicly criticized the white sports writers who left Scott off their top five selections for conference Most Valuable Player in 1969, an obvious racist slight given Scott's stunning level of play.

Due to the rule that freshmen could not play at the varsity level, Scott starred for the freshman team in 1966–7 while fans awaited his debut the next season. Smith's persistent recruiting had resulted in his most promising team since taking over from McGuire. In 1964, he had out-dueled Bubas to land guard Bob Lewis out of Washington, DC, and he signed the highly recruited 6'4" forward Larry Miller the following year from the mill town of Catasauqua in western Pennsylvania, an area previously considered to be a Duke recruiting preserve. In the fall of 1966, they were joined by three of Smith's best recruits who stirred hopes among Tar Heel fans: 6'11" center Rusty Clark, 6'8" forward Bill Bunting, and point guard Dick Grubar. This sophomore-dominated team beat Duke twice during the regular season as it compiled a 21–4 record, but Smith's first ACC regular season championship did not provide automatic entrance into the NCAA tournament. They still had to win the ACC tournament, now played at Greensboro Coliseum. Inevitably, Duke and Carolina won close semi-final games, setting up their third meeting of the season. The ACC tournament – which determined the conference's sole entry into the 16-team NCAA tournament – placed enormous pressure upon coaches and players. "People today don't understand what kind of pressure that was," Larry Miller later recalled. "I couldn't eat, couldn't sleep. My stomach was in knots." Most of the 9,000 fans crammed into the Coliseum were more concerned about who would enjoy bragging rights in North Carolina than earning entry into the NCAA tournament.

This pressure-packed game gave Smith his full acceptance by Carolina fans. Duke had dominated the rivalry ever since Bubas had arrived, winning four regular season and four ACC tournament championships and having appeared in three Final Fours. Many pundits believed that the Blue Devils would win over the talented but sophomore-dominated Tar Heel contingent because of their experience. Duke broke out to an early nine point lead, but a Miller-led charge turned the tables and Carolina went ahead by six points. With seven minutes left, a hot shooting streak put Duke up by five, at which point Miller initiated a late game rally and the Tar Heels celebrated an 82–73 victory. Smith was carried off the floor by his jubilant team. But Smith's young team was not quite finished for the season, as they defeated Princeton and Boston College in the first two rounds of the NCAA tournament to enter the Final Four in Louisville. There they ran into a red-hot Dayton team led by All-American forward Donnie May and went down to a 15 point defeat. They then lost by 22 points in the consolation game to Elvin Hayes and a powerful Houston team, but Carolina fans were ecstatic nonetheless, cheering excitedly as their vanquished team left the floor, "We're Number Four! We're Number Four!" Those cheers were stinging reminders to the Duke fans back home that Carolina basketball was back.

The Tar Heels continued their upward swing and made the Final Four in the next two seasons after capturing the regular season and ACC tournaments again. In 1968, they defeated Ohio State in the semi-finals but were blown out by arguably one of the best college teams of all time, the UCLA Bruins led by Lew Alcindor and Lucius Allen. Even an effort in the first half to slow down the Bruins with the four corners failed. Forced to play straight-up basketball after trailing by ten at half-time, an overmatched and undermanned Carolina team got waxed 78–55. The following year, the Charles Scott-led Tar Heels once again dominated the ACC, while Duke slipped to a 12–12 record and a dispirited and burned-out Vic Bubas announced his retirement from coaching.

Yet, there was time for one more dramatic confrontation that added more fuel to the rivalry. Bubas' team managed to slip by the early rounds of the ACC tournament, only to face the heavily favored Tar Heels in the finals. With point guard Grubar out with a knee injury, Carolina fell behind the determined Blue Devils by 11 points early in the second half. At that juncture, Dean Smith's decision to recruit Scott was rewarded as the senior went on a scoring spree, hitting on ten long bombs, driving for acrobatic lay-ins, and nailing midrange jumpers. In one of the most impressive single-game performances of any player in UNC history, Scott ended up scoring 40 points (it would have been 50 if the three point line rule had been in effect). This memorable achievement, however, was not sufficient to persuade five sports writers to include him on their all-conference ballot – an egregious demonstration of bigotry. In the NCAA tournament, Scott proceeded to lead his team past Duquesne. Following that, he netted a last second jumper to pull out an 87–85 victory over Davidson and Lefty Driesell. In the first round of the Final Four, however, Purdue rode guard Rick Mount's 36 point output to an easy win over Carolina. Within a few years, Dean Smith had elevated UNC basketball to national prominence; now, it was his inability to win a national title that irritated exacting Carolina fans.

Charles Scott changed the face of ACC basketball. In self-defense, all teams in the Atlantic Coast Conference began to recruit African-Americans. It was at this critical juncture that Bubas moved to an administrative position at Duke, stating that he had no energy left for coaching at such a high level of pressurized basketball. There were too many close games, too many recruiting battles, too many second guesses by petulant "boosters." Some perceptive observers, however, wondered if he feared that it would not be possible to recruit top black athletes to what had become an elite, private (and overwhelmingly white) university. Whichever the case, Bubas left having helped establish one of basketball's greatest rivalries and elevate ACC basketball to national prominence. He had made the 9,300-seat Indoor Stadium the place to be on game night. As the 1970s dawned, Vic Bubas and Dean Smith, both natives of the Midwest, excellent recruiters, master teachers, and top bench coaches, had put basketball's special rivalry firmly on track.

North Carolina Takes Control

During the 1970s, the pendulum swung in favor of North Carolina as Smith's Tar Heels won 23 of the 31 games played between the two schools. Bubas' replacement, former West Virginia head coach Bucky Waters, lasted only four seasons before resigning; his slowdown offense and penchant for picky team rules proved unattractive to recruits. When Duke suffered their first losing season in 23 years – the third in school history – the unpopular Waters demanded but was denied a contract extension. He thereupon resigned in September of 1973 and was replaced on an interim basis for the season by assistant Neil McGeachy. His hopes of landing the job on a permanent basis were undone by one of the most stunning comebacks Dean Smith ever orchestrated. Trailing 86–78 with just 17 seconds left at UNC's Carmichael Court, Smith called time out to plot an improbable counterattack. After a series of mishandled passes and a missed free throw by Duke, freshman Walter Davis sank a 28 foot off-balance heave to tie the game. The Tar Heels won in overtime. McGeachy was not retained and the 43-year-old Bill Foster, who had enjoyed considerable success at Utah, was named the new Duke coach.

Carolina continued to win while Foster struggled to rebuild the sagging Duke program. Throughout the 1970s, Smith's teams won 20 or more games each season, capturing five regular season and four tournament ACC championships and making two more trips to the Final Four, only to lose in the semi-finals to Florida State in 1972 and to Marquette in the championship game in 1977.

Fans had come to expect Smith to recruit well, and they watched a long procession of talent go through the program during the late 1970s. Among them were forwards Walter Davis and Mike O'Koren, centers Mitch Kupchak and Tom LaGarde, and guards John Kuester and Phil Ford. Smith routinely produced 20-plus victory seasons, but a national championship continued to elude him. That problem seemed to be nearing resolution when his 1977 team struggled through a season of injuries to win the ACC regular season championship and then slipped by Virginia in a rugged tournament game without the injured Davis and after Ford fouled out. Hard-fought victories over Purdue, Notre Dame, and Kentucky put them into the Final Four against an upstart Runnin' Rebels team from UNLV coached by Jerry Tarkanian. Freshman Mike O'Koren rattled home 31 points in an upset victory and Smith seemed on the verge of his first national championship, but the Heels faced the sentimental favorite Marquette, led by Al McGuire who was coaching his final college game. Midway through the second half, Carolina had a two point lead, but Davis and Ford were struggling with their injuries and LaGarde was on crutches. It was the obvious time to go to the four corners, but for some unknown reason Smith ran it with O'Koren sitting for more than four minutes at the scorer's table. Smith decided that he did not want to burn a timeout in that situation, but the player who could best flash to the basket for a pass from Phil Ford off this unique offense remained on the sidelines. Marquette had prepared for the four corners and stopped it cold, and, with O'Koren on the bench, Carolina's momentum fizzled. Late in

Figure 3.2 Walt Davis fires one of the most memorable shots in UNC history. He banked in this 28-foot heave in February of 1974 against Duke to send the game into overtime. The Tar Heels improbably closed an eight point deficit in the final 17 seconds and prevailed in overtime. Reproduced by permission of UNC Athletic Communications, University of North Carolina Athletic Department Archives

the second half, the Warriors took the lead for good, giving the teary-eyed McGuire a 69–57 retirement present.

Meanwhile, Foster had replenished the barren Duke roster he had inherited in 1974, bringing in such future stars as Jim Spanarkel, Mike Gminski, Tate Armstrong, Kenny Dennard and Gene Banks. By 1977–8, Foster had Duke back in the national rankings while enjoying a 27–7 season, winning the ACC tournament, and powering their way to the NCAA finals where they lost to Kentucky after upsetting heavily favored Notre Dame in the semi-final game, 90–86. During the next season, Duke's national championship hopes were dashed by a series of debilitating injuries to key players. Meanwhile, the relationship between Smith and Foster grew testy, especially after the Senior Night game at Duke in February of 1979. Duke opened in a tight zone defense, and Smith ordered his team to hold the ball, which they did for 12 minutes. The slowdown continued, and at half-time Duke led by the zany score of 7–0. Both teams played the game straight in the second half, each scoring 40 points. Foster, who loved a high-paced game, was infuriated with Smith and unleashed one of his many zingers in the postgame press conference, sarcastically questioning Smith's strategy and echoing a standard Duke sensibility that Carolina "owned" the local sports pages.

Foster's frustration from playing second fiddle to Smith and UNC undoubtedly contributed to his decision to depart for South Carolina. Foster left Duke after a so-so 1979–80 season but he had rehabilitated the program. He compiled a 113–64 record that included several impressive wins over UNC, two ACC championships, and three deep runs into the NCAA tournament. A blowout loss to Carolina at season's end, however, convinced Foster that the time had come to move on. His sparkling performance has been slighted in Duke basketball lore, due in part to his relatively short tenure and to the fact that his time as coach was sandwiched between two Duke legends, Vic Bubas and Mike Krzyzewski.

As Foster departed Duke, Smith was riding high. Following the departure of O'Koren, Ford, and Davis in 1979, he rebuilt by bringing in a bevy of talent: guard Jimmy Black, 7′0″ center Brad Daugherty, and forwards Sam Perkins and James Worthy. Properly reloaded, the Tar Heels once more won the ACC regular season (although losing to Virginia, and 7′4″ Ralph Sampson, in the ACC tournament), and powered themselves to the NCAA championship game by defeating Virginia in the semi-finals of the Final Four, a team they had lost to twice during the season. However, this time they lost to Indiana as the Hoosiers won a second national championship under Bob Knight, 63–50. Carolina kept the game close until Worthy got into serious foul trouble early in the second half. For the third time, Dean Smith felt the sting of coming ever so close but not sealing the deal.

That changed with the arrival of Michael Jordan the next season. A late bloomer as a high school player, Jordan began to attract the attention of recruiters during his senior year. By that time, Smith and assistants Bill Guthridge and Roy Williams had convinced Jordan to attend UNC. Breaking with a long tradition of limiting freshmen to back-up roles, Smith inserted Jordan into the starting lineup at the beginning of the season.

He quickly became an integral part of a special team. As a freshman, Jordan shot 53 percent from the field and scored in double figures in 29 of 34 games. His work ethic became legendary, and he bought into Smith's team-first philosophy. (After he became a star in the NBA, Carolina fans loved to ask the question: "What one person was able to consistently prevent Michael Jordan from scoring?" Answer: Dean Smith.) By midseason, the game plan called for freshman Jordan as the next option if the defense had denied All-Americans James Worthy or Sam Perkins the ball.

In the ACC final against the Sampson-led Cavaliers of Virginia in 1982, Smith used the four corners throughout much of the second half, infuriating television announcers and fans across the nation. Virginia coach Terry Holland refused to order his team out of a tight zone defense. Jordan responded to the pressure by hitting four crucial jump shots from around the key. The Tar Heels went on to win 47–45, but the game was clearly a catalyst for introducing a shot clock for college ball. After slipping past an upset-minded James Madison by two points in the opening game of the tournament, Carolina breezed into the Final Four, where they were pushed to the limit by a Clyde Drexler-led Houston team before prevailing. In the finals against sophomore super-center Patrick Ewing and the Georgetown Hoyas, Worthy and Perkins battled Ewing to a draw. With Georgetown having regained the lead by one point with 32 seconds left, a calm Dean Smith called a timeout. Reasoning that rival coach John R. Thompson would have his defense set for Perkins and Worthy, he diagrammed a play for his special freshman. His players never would forget Smith's words as they broke the huddle: "Knock it down, Michael."

And of course he did, with 14 seconds left on the clock. When the Hoyas threw the ball away desperately attempting to set up a final play, the monkey had finally been lifted from Dean Smith's back.

Coach K

The surprise appointment of the unknown 32-year-old Mike Krzyzewski to replace Foster in 1980 did not sit well with many Duke fans. They had expected a big-name coach and instead they got an unknown guy whose West Point team had just come off a less-than-stirring 9–17 season. It also seemed to Duke loyalists that, despite the strong recommendation provided by his former coach at Army, Bobby Knight – "He has all of my best qualities and none of my bad ones," Knight told Athletic Director

Tom Butters – he was unprepared to be a head coach in the ACC. His north side Chicago working-class Polish Catholic background did not resonate well in Durham, and he was possessed of a name that dedicated Duke fans initially could neither pronounce nor spell. He not only had limited head coaching experience, but it was at a school that played basketball at a level well beneath the ACC. All in all, his background seemed to indicate that he was not a good fit for an elite private southern university.

Krzyzewski's first three years were rocky (17–13, 10–17, 11–17) but Butters remained firmly behind his embattled coach who was struggling to rebuild a program. In 1983–4, fortified by a contract extension given by the heavily criticized Butters, he led his stylish 1982 recruiting class to a breakout 24–10 season and an appearance in the NCAA tournament. His sophomore-laden team included Johnny Dawkins, Mark Alarie, Jay Bilas, and David Henderson. The young coach had returned the program to a nationally competitive level and the rivalry with Carolina was about to enter its most exciting era.

Figure 3.3   Mike Who? Duke fans were not overjoyed when the unknown Mike Krzyzewski was introduced at this press conference in 1980 as the new Blue Devil coach. Thirty years after this picture was taken, Krzyzewski had risen to the top of the coaching profession and his critics had long since been silenced. *The Chronicle*/Duke University Archives

From the beginning, the relationship between the young but swaggering Krzyzewski and the middle-aged, reserved Smith can be described as strained cordiality. During their first game coaching against each other on December 5, 1980, Krzyzewski's overmatched team squared off at Greensboro against the tenth-ranked Tar Heels led by Sam Perkins, and James Worthy – both destined to be first round NBA draft choices – but hung tight only to lose 78–76. Asked by a reporter in the post-game press conference what it was like to be coaching against a man of such stature as Smith, Krzyzewski bluntly responded: "I didn't feel anything tonight I haven't felt before. There are a lot of good coaches around, and I have confidence in my ability." And, he added, "I'm a good basketball coach too."

Everything about the two men seemed to invoke sharp contrasts. Although both hailed from the Midwest, Smith grew up in a conservative community in Kansas and became a liberal Democrat, while Krzyzewski was raised in an ethnic, working-class neighborhood of Chicago, but became a Republican. Smith was a long-time cigarette smoker, and Krzyzewski abhorred the habit. Smith was a scratch golfer, but it was a game Krzyzewski disliked. Krzyzewski was a competent weekend tennis player; Smith never had learned the game. Smith took pride in never (well, rarely) uttering a swear word; Krzyzewski became famous, if not infamous, for his use of salty barracks language in practice, on the sidelines during games (loudly and repeatedly), and even in press conferences. His defenders explained away his frequent resort to profanity as a product of his working-class origins and his years spent at West Point being groomed by Bob Knight. Nonetheless, his detractors made many caustic references to his intemperate and sometimes questionable behavior, often contrasted with Smith's adherence to the social niceties of intercollegiate competition. The angry expletive-filled screeds that became Krzyzewski's wont along the sidelines seemed to be most unbecoming of a Duke man.

Their style of play was, not surprisingly, distinctly different. Smith's offense was always under control, following a familiar, disciplined, almost scripted pattern, while Krzyzewski's teams were encouraged to play a more free-flowing game, instinctively reading and reacting to what was occurring on the court. Fans expected to watch the Carolina point guard dribble up the court while looking to Smith to signal a play; Krzyzewski's teams were expected to attack swiftly without the controlling influence of their coach.

One episode is instructive. In a close game between the two rivals in 1984, Smith surprisingly lost control of his emotions when he failed to get the attention of the referees to discuss a technical rules matter. He rushed to the scorer's table, hammered it with his fist, striking by accident the scoreboard control buttons that put 20 additional points for his own team up on the scoreboard. After losing by five points, an angry Krzyzewski told the press that the failure of the officials to assess Smith with a technical foul in that uncharacteristic instance was a classic example of the "double standard" that pervaded the ACC – one for the exalted Smith, another one for everyone else. On another occasion, he sarcastically referred to his rival as "God." Other ACC coaches privately concurred, quietly pleased with his outbursts. However, ten years later his rivals would be saying the same thing about Krzyzewski and his alleged influence on officials.

The competitive fervor intensified as Duke narrowed the gap, and by the latter half of the 1980s Duke had seemingly surpassed the Tar Heels. In 1986, Krzyzewski's program kicked into high gear, when his first great recruiting class reached its senior year: the daunting quartet of Dawkins, Alarie, Bilas, and Henderson, supplemented by standout junior guard Tommy Amaker and freshman forward Danny Ferry. Duke entered the NCAA tournament with only two losses – one to North Carolina – and after barely escaping a first round upset to 16th seed Mississippi Valley State, easily moved into the Final Four and dispatched Kansas 71–67 to meet Louisville in the finals. After leading at half-time, Duke went cold and missed several wide open shots, closing to within one point in the final seconds, only to lose 72–69.

The intense rivalry rekindled in the mid-1980s would remain white-hot until the present day. Each year, preseason publications would elevate fan expectations, and, as the season unfolded, high national rankings and frequent Final Four appearances became commonplace for both teams. And, each school captured two national championships. Extensive regional and national television coverage, intensified by the pressures of cable sports network scrutiny and the proliferation of talk radio, meant that enormous amounts of money were now at stake. All of this tended to intensify the pressure – and constant focus – upon the head coaches.

The Dean Dome and Krzyzewskiville

The rivalry naturally involved the fans. Cramped 10,000-seat Carmichael Hall had long been a rowdy venue in Chapel Hill, with students located near the floor. That changed when the 21,700-seat Dean Smith Center opened in 1986. As part of the fundraising effort that financed the $33 million facility, big donors and prominent boosters were given priority seating on the lower level, with students largely relegated to the nose-bleed sections. The older, more reserved fans did not generate the enthusiasm that had characterized Carmichael, prompting a derisive comment that game time at the "Dean Dome" resembled a faculty "wine and cheese" gathering.

Although that characterization did not give proper credit to the enthusiasm of Tar Heel fans, the fact was that the raucous atmosphere in venerable 9,300-seat Cameron Indoor Stadium was much more compelling. In 1986, with student tickets in great demand, Duke students created "Krzyzewskiville," pitching hundreds of tents outside the ticket office days in advance of a game to establish their ticket priority. As the tent city grew with winning seasons, the Duke student government published a 5,000-word set of rules that governed the overnight ticket vigils and uniformed monitors were in place to preserve order and enforce the rules. Over the years, the university installed wireless Internet service, electric outlets, cable television, and portable sanitary facilities to make the campout tolerable. By tradition, Coach K would make an appearance at the encampment before the UNC game to rally the troops and encourage high-spirited cheering.

Many of the residents of Krzyzewskiville were hard-core members of the "Cameron Crazies," who painted their faces blue and white, shouted clever – if not off-color – chants at opponents, engaged in bizarre body gyrations to distract opposing team free-throw shooters, and generally raised hell. Sometimes their attempt at humor and satire went over the line. In 1989, the Crazies held up signs directed at Carolina's All-American forward J. R. Reid that proclaimed, "J. R. Can't Reid." After the game Dean Smith ignored his team's 20 point victory and instead focused on what he charged was a racist slur. If Reid were white, he snapped, the sign would not have been hoisted by a group of elite white students. A week later, he added additional fuel to the fire when he noted that his two black starters, Reid and Scott Williams, had a combined SAT score higher than Duke's two white stars, Christian Laettner and Danny Ferry. He also pointedly observed that he had recruited all four players and had copies of their academic records in his files. Kzryzewski responded the next day, suggesting that Smith had violated federal confidentiality regulations and that his comments "really piss me off."

Off the court, the competition raged year-round as both programs recruited nationally. Nearly every year, a few heavily recruited blue-chip players came down to making the tough decision of whether to don the dark blue of Duke or the light blue of Carolina. Recruiting became another way for fans to keep score. Inevitably, both schools won some and lost some in this never-ending saga. Krzyzewski edged Smith for the services of such blue-chippers as Danny Ferry, Christian Laettner, Bobby Hurley, Grant Hill, Steve Wojciechowski, Quinn Snyder, Shane Battier, Mike Dunleavy, and J. J. Reddick, but Smith countered by signing J. R. Reid, Cliff Rozier, Eric Montross, Rasheed Wallace, Donald Williams, Jerry Stackhouse, Vince Carter and Antawn Jamison.

In 1988, forward Danny Ferry and guard Quinn Snyder provided Krzyzewski the nucleus for a rejuvenated team. The Blue Devils began the season ranked number one in the country, won 27 games, but lost in the NCAA Final Four to Seton Hall. The following season freshman Christian Laettner made his debut after a highly publicized recruiting struggle with North Carolina. In 1989–90, Bobby Hurley, a high school star from New Jersey who most observers initially thought was headed for North Carolina, worked his magic at point guard and the Blue Devils powered their way over the favored Arkansas Razorbacks to meet the high-flying Runnin' Rebels of UNLV in the NCAA Championship Game. The media had a good time framing the game as between an elite private school and a public university with less stringent admissions policy coached by reputed renegade Jerry Tarkanian. With Hurley fighting intestinal flu, Duke came out flat and were then flattened by the fired-up Rebels led by future NBA stars Stacy Augmon, Greg Anthony, Anderson Hunt, and Larry Johnson. When the carnage in Denver was over, the score read 103–73, the most lopsided championship game in history.

Payback came the following season and featured the leadership of another Duke high-profile recruit, Grant Hill, son of the former Yale and Dallas Cowboys star running back Calvin Hill. The Blue Devils entered the Final Four on a roll, having won 30 games, but in the semi-finals ran smack into the same UNLV outfit that had humiliated them the previous year. This time, however, Krzyzewski had a healthy and more experienced Hurley running the offense, and the surprisingly disorganized Rebels could not mount a last-minute miracle as Duke moved into the finals against Kansas 79–77. The title game against Kansas resulted in a 72–65 Duke victory. With senior Laettner and freshman Hill doing the heavy lifting, Krzyzewski had his first national championship. He and Smith now owned one title apiece.

Figure 3.4 Dean Smith, at the top of his game, is pictured here in 1993 as he directs his team. Smith coached the Tar Heels to two national championships and amassed an 879–254 career won–lost record between 1961 and 1997. The Tar Heels now play in the 22,000-seat Dean Smith Activity Center. Reproduced by permission of UNC Athletic Communications, University of North Carolina Athletic Department Archives

That tie lasted only one year, because Duke made it two straight, capping the 1992–3 season with a 34–2 record, defeating Michigan and its freshman-laden "Fab Five" team in the final game by a decisive 20 points. The Blue Devils won what many observers believed was the true national championship game in the semi-finals when they narrowly edged Indiana and Krzyzewski's mentor Bob Knight after erasing a 12 point half-time deficit. However, the big story of that dream season was *THE PLAY* against Kentucky in the regional finals. Trailing by one point with just 1.8 seconds left, Krzyzewski diagrammed a play that had Hill tossing a perfect 70 foot football-style pass down court to Laettner, who flashed from the baseline to the foul line and in one motion caught the pass, wheeled to his left and drilled an 18-footer as the buzzer sounded. It remains one of the most stunning plays in college basketball history; Laettner scored 31 points in the game, making ten for ten from the field and another ten free throws without a miss.

The next season, a foot injury to Grant Hill assured that Duke would not make a sixth consecutive trip to the Final Four, but such an eventuality also was unlikely given the determination of the Tar Heels to catch up with their neighbors. Led by senior forward George Lynch and 7′0″ center Eric Montross, Carolina defeated Kansas in the semi-finals and upset the favored Chris Webber-led Michigan team. Late in the game, a suffocating double-team prompted Webber to call a timeout, but the Wolverines had previously used up their five timeouts. The resulting technical foul enabled the Tar Heels to win 77–71. Many observers said that Webber's goof had cost his team the game. Angered by comments that his second national championship was "lucky," Smith noted that the double-team defensive play was one that his team routinely practiced, and added for good measure, "Call us lucky if you want. But also call us champions."

The intensity of the rivalry dropped off in the mid-1990s when Krzyzewski was forced to take a leave for the second half of the 1993–4 season due to exhaustion, which stemmed from the slow and painful recovery he was making from hip replacement surgery and his unwillingness to follow doctor's orders and stay away from his office in order to recuperate. His young team was 9–3 when he stepped aside and assistant coach Pete Gaudet took over, but the Blue Devils went into a tailspin and lost 12 of the remaining 16 games. Krzyzewski returned the following season and a rebuilding process ensued.

Although rumors were swirling that Smith was contemplating retirement, his Tar Heels continued to dominate the series with Duke and reached the Final Four in 1995 and 1997. Smith was determined to retire on his own terms and to assure that his successor would be his loyal, long-time assistant of 30 years, Bill Guthridge. Smith did not announce his retirement until October of 1997, just weeks before the new season was to begin, and athletic director Dick Baddour had little choice but to accept Smith's recommendation. Smith's career record was 897–254, and his many honors included four national Coach of the Year awards, eight ACC Coach of the Year recognitions, and induction into the Basketball Hall of Fame. He had won two national championships, taking his teams to 27 NCAA tournaments, and made eight Final Four appearances. He also had dominated Duke 59–35, even winning 18 of 36 games in the hostile confines of Cameron Indoor Stadium. Head to head with Krzyzewski, Smith won 24 of 38 match-ups.

The Beat Goes On

After Smith departed, Krzyzewski gained a clear upper hand over Carolina. In the ensuing decade, he emerged as a special person on the Duke campus, earning an estimated $2 million salary, holding a professorship in the university's Fuqua School of Management, and being inducted into the Basketball Hall of Fame. He toured the country giving motivational speeches at corporate meetings, became a familiar face on national commercials, and was named the coach of the 2008 United States Olympic team, where he coached a team of NBA superstars that captured the gold medal without a single loss. Between 1997 and 2003, Krzyzewski won five ACC regular season and tournament championships. His 2001 team, led by Shane Battier, captured the national championship after losing narrowly in the finals in 1999 to Connecticut; the Blue Devils also lost to eventual champions Connecticut in the Final Four semi-finals in 2004.

At one point during this amazing era, the Blue Devils had reached nine consecutive Sweet Sixteens. In the process, Kzryzewski's team had become a constant on national television, prompting the emergence of a loyal national following not unlike that of the Notre Dame football "subway alumni." Duke's success and prominence, not to mention the seemingly fawning treatment given by national sportscasters, inevitably produced a growing legion of Duke detractors. Each year controversies erupted over whether or not television commentators gave Krzyzewski and Duke deferential treatment, and every time an official's call in a close game went Duke's way, thousands screamed foul.

The Carolina program initially did not to miss a beat under Bill Guthridge. His first team won 34 games and lost in the Final Four, but his second year saw an uncharacteristic ten-loss season that was capped, much to the glee of Duke fans, by a stunning first-round loss to Weber State in the NCAA. His third and final season saw further slippage to an un-Smith-like 18–13, although the Tar Heels surprised with a late run but ultimately lost to Florida in the Final Four. Guthridge retired the following summer, and everyone close to the Carolina program assumed that former Tar Heel assistant Roy Williams would leave Kansas to return to his alma mater. While Smith had displayed his fealty to loyal assistant Guthridge, everyone knew that he considered Williams his ultimate long-term successor. In fact, it appeared that Guthridge timed his retirement announcement based on the presumption that Williams would return home.

A 1972 graduate of UNC, Roy Williams had played junior varsity basketball but his talents lay in coaching. He became an attentive student volunteer in the program, and in 1978 returned to Carolina as an assistant coach where he proved to be a skilled recruiter and an astute teacher of the game. In 1988, Williams moved to Kansas to replace another former Tar Heel, Larry Brown. Williams became wildly popular at KU, winning more than 80 percent of his games, earning a berth in the NCAA every year of his tenure (except the first, when KU was on probation), and bringing to Allen Fieldhouse an endless procession of superb talent. Jayhawks fans admired his down-home personality and his up-tempo style of play. At one point, KU won 62 consecutive home games. Had the offer to return to his alma mater come earlier, Williams undoubtedly would have left, but in 2000 he had in place a group of players with whom he had developed a close relationship and whom he believed could win a national championship. When he opted to remain at Kansas, he shocked many North Carolina faithful. His Kansas teams went 90–19 the next three years, reaching the Final Four in 2002 but losing to Syracuse by three points in the championship game in 2003.

Stunned by William's decision, and caught without a back-up plan, UNC athletic director Dick Baddour hired first-year Notre Dame coach Matt Doherty, a fiery forward who had played for Smith on his 1982 championship team and had worked under Williams for several years as an assistant at Kansas. Despite being a former UNC player, Doherty did not seem to appreciate the close family-like culture that Smith had instilled in the program. Doherty brought in his own staff from Notre Dame, and did not retain any of the long-time Smith/Guthridge assistants. Even the popular Phil Ford was let go, and Smith quietly fumed. Doherty's antics on the sideline – in marked contrast to Smith and Guthridge – was amusing to some; when he got a technical foul in his first home game, Carolina fans actually cheered. But Doherty's act did not wear well, and most Carolina fans began to complain about what they considered Doherty's sophomoric sideline coaching style.

As his teams encountered difficulties, Doherty's erratic behavior alienated department staff and turned off his players. It did not help in his first season that Duke had a 35–4 record, beat his team twice, enjoyed a season-long number one ranking, and defeated Arizona to win the national championship. In Doherty's second season, with the number of lopsided losses mounting, Duke clobbered Carolina by 30 points at the Dean Smith Center, and Carolina fans heckled their own coach. Carolina went an abysmal 8–20, but rebounded the next year to win 19 games. This was not a performance equal to the Dean Smith standard; for the second straight year, the Tar Heels were not invited to the NCAA. The fact that they won the NIT – the equivalent of college basketball's bronze medal – could not save Doherty. Rumors of anticipated player transfers and the obvious lack of support from Dean Smith prompted his resignation.

Given another opportunity in 2003, Williams decided that he would return to his alma mater. In his second season back in Chapel Hill, Williams utilized the talents of some of Doherty's top recruits – Sean May, Rashad McCants and Raymond Felton – and captured the ACC title en route to a National Championship victory over Illinois. With the addition of Williams' own blue-chip recruits – Tyler Hansbrough, Ty Lawson, Brandon Wright, and Wayne Ellington – in the 2007 and 2008 seasons, Carolina won 67 games, enjoyed high national rankings, and moved into the 2008 Final Four with only two losses, only to be blown out by 20 points by, of all teams, the Kansas Jayhawks. KU proceeded to win the championship over Memphis in overtime. In 2009, however, a determined senior-dominated Tar Heel gave Williams his second NCAA title, handily defeating Michigan State in the finals 89–72.

The UNC resurgence under Williams restored balance to the rivalry. Between 1998 and 2004, Duke had won 16 of the 21 games between the two schools, including two horrendous blowouts by scores of 87–58 and 93–68 during Doherty's dismal 2001–2 season. By 2006–7, however, Williams had recharged the rivalry, as Carolina swept the two games played that year and had his team ranked number one for most of the season while Duke, now playing on the "Coach K Court" at timeless Cameron Indoor, fielded a squad dominated by freshmen and sophomores. Nonetheless, what was billed as a "rebuilding" season produced a 28–6 record and a second-place finish in the ACC behind Carolina.

The future of college basketball's greatest rivalry seems assured. Both programs appear destined to continue their winning ways. Fans of both teams can anticipate that excellent talent will continue to migrate to Durham and Chapel Hill to play for great coaches and national honors. Along Tobacco Road, the basketball beat goes on.

4 Mayhem on the Midway

The Bears and the Packers

The game was murder. They were ready to kill each other right from the gun. One personal foul after another – shoving, kicking, late hitting. The tension was unbelievable. We knew it was going to be one of those tough, miserable games with a lot of fouls . . . (Referee Jerry Markbreit, describing a 1986 Bears–Packers game)

It all began inauspiciously enough. On November 27, 1921, the Staley Starch Makers defeated the Acme Meat Packers 20–0 in a rugged game of football played on a cold and blustery Chicago Sunday afternoon. As but a sign of things to come, clouds of deceit and foul play soon hung over the relationship when the Starch Makers reported to league officials that the Meat Packers had illegally played some hotshot collegians under assumed names. With ill will already evident, the teams did not meet in 1922 but resumed their competition in 1923. By this time the Chicago team had taken the name of Bears. Once more the Chicagoans emerged victorious, 3–0, before an estimated 4,000 fans in a game played in a Green Bay city park.

The two teams have played each other every autumn thereafter, making this Midwestern match-up the longest running in the history of professional football. Over the years, the teams have had many ups and downs, but whether or not a championship was on the line, they always found plenty of incentives to give a special effort when they played each other. Proximity and familiarity played important roles in fostering this rivalry, as did loyal fans who provided core support for both teams. Both teams became early members of the National Football League, and their respective founding head coaches provided crucial leadership and stability for the NFL during the lean times of the 1920s and 1930s when professional football was struggling to survive.

George Stanley Halas resolutely guided the Bears as club president from their inception until his death at age 88 in 1983. During that time he served as head coach on four separate occasions, compiling a 321–148–31 record. Halas also provided leadership that was instrumental in guiding a league of thinly capitalized teams through many a financial dilemma and laying the foundation for the financial behemoth it would become. Earl "Curly" Lambeau of the Packers had less to do with league politics than Halas but he was responsible for the creation and ultimate success of one of the NFL's most venerable teams, located improbably in a small Wisconsin mill town. Lambeau served as the general manager and head coach of the Packers from their establishment in 1919 until he was forced to step aside in 1950. To understand the Packers–Bears rivalry is to appreciate the leadership that these two founding fathers of the NFL provided.

Throughout the time that these two men competed they had to deal with recurring economic crises that threatened to shut down both teams, even the league itself. They persevered when most football fans preferred the college game and generally viewed the professionals with indifference, if not disdain. The Packers and Bears, however, became a reliable constant for the struggling league. For much of the first 20 years of the rivalry, attendance hovered between 5,000 and 10,000, occasionally reaching 15,000. By the late 1930s, crowds of 40,000 or more became commonplace in Chicago, with about half that in Green Bay. Between 1921 and 1941 the teams each won five league championships. Overall, the two teams have won 21 of the 87 NFL championships, and 48 of their players have been inducted into the Pro Football Hall of Fame. The Packers have won three Super Bowls (1967, 1968, 1996) and the Bears one (1986), and each team has lost once in the ultimate professional game. As the 2009 season was about to begin, the Bears held an edge of 91–80 over the Packers, with six games ending in a tie.

Halas and Lambeau

The two founding fathers of the NFL came from similar backgrounds. They were raised in the Midwest by hard-working immigrant families. George Halas was born in 1895 in a working-class Czech neighborhood in Chicago. He enrolled at the University of Illinois in 1914 where he lettered in football, basketball, and baseball and earned a degree in civil engineering. At 180 pounds, he played both ways at end, but his football career at Illinois was hampered by injuries. Upon graduation, he joined the Navy and was assigned to the Great Lakes Naval Station, where he became a player-coach of the base football team. The ruggedly handsome "Curly" Lambeau was the son of Belgian immigrants. Born in 1898, he grew up in a working-class family in Green Bay, where he was a multi-sport standout at East High School. As a schoolboy he came to love football, demonstrating his fascination with the technical aspects of the game, especially with the recent innovation of the forward pass. In 1919 he played alongside the famed George Gipp in the backfield at Notre Dame.

Lambeau returned home in 1920 to accept an offer from the Indian Packing Company to organize a football team that would publicize the company's name. At age 21, Lambeau became the head coach, quarterback, and general manager of a typical slapdash semi-professional team during an era when businesses often sponsored sports teams as a means of advertising themselves. Lambeau made the forward pass an integral part of his team's offense and the Meat Packers won ten games against regional foes in their initial season. Home games were played in Hagemeister Park where spectators stood along the sidelines to watch the action. At a time before free substitution, squads were comprised of 16 to 20 players, and each was paid a salary somewhere between $10 and $25 per game. Thus was a modest foundation established for what would become one of the most storied of professional sports franchises.

A few hundred miles to the south, a similar story was unfolding. In Decatur, Illinois, businessman A. E. Staley decided that a football team carrying the name of his starch manufacturing company would be a good way to promote his products. After sitting on the bench of the New York Yankees as a seldom-used utility outfielder in 1919, George Halas moved back to Chicago to work as a bridge engineer for the Chicago, Burlington, and Quincy Railroad. One of Staley's associates had watched Halas coach at the Naval Station, and so an offer was made: Halas would use his engineering skills to make the starch machines hum by day and coach the football team after work. A schedule with similar company-sponsored teams was arranged and the Staleys finished the season 10–1–2.

On September 17, 1920, Halas met with like-minded men in Ralph Hay's Hupmobile dealership in Canton, Ohio, where they agreed to establish the American Professional Football Association (APFA). It was a shaky, poorly capitalized enterprise. Of the 11 founding teams, only four remained for the second season. Members scheduled their own games,

sometimes with non-Association teams, and the championship was determined by a vote of the surviving teams at season's end, not by a playoff
or even on the basis of won–lost records. Before the start of the 1922
season, at Halas' suggestion, the Association changed its name to the
National Football League.

In the spring of 1921, due to financial problems, Staley permitted Halas
to move the team to Chicago and assume ownership. Because the 1921
the team played their games at Cubs Park (renamed Wrigley Field in 1926),
Halas considered renaming his team the Cubs, but he surmised that
football players tended to be larger and less docile than their baseball
counterparts; hence, he selected the obvious name of Bears. The Bears
drew several home crowds of 5,000 that first season – enough to pay the
bills – and went 9–1–1, claiming their first league title.

Green Bay joined the league in the summer of 1921 and local businessmen donated money to install 1,000 seats in Hagemeister Park. The
Meat Packers finished 3–2–1 in league competition, including the initial
loss to the Bears. The 1922 season in Green Bay proved to be disastrous.
Bad weather hurt attendance and Lambeau was unable to pay the $2,000
guarantees he had promised to lure competitors to town. With the team
on the verge of folding, the publisher of the *Green Bay Press-Gazette*, George
Howard, contributed $5,000 to help establish a non-profit community
corporation that would own and operate the team; individual stock
shares were sold for $5 a share. The Green Bay City Council built a wooden
stadium to accommodate 6,000 spectators. Over the years, the capacity
of City Stadium increased incrementally to 20,000, but it remained a
primitive place with wooden planks for seating. Lambeau continued in
his role as general manager/coach/quarterback and recruited players from
across the Upper Midwest. The team responded by ripping off six consecutive winning seasons, going 43–20–8 during that period. Community
support grew, with attendance averaging above 5,000 for home games.

The nickname "Titletown USA" was adopted during the heyday of
Vince Lombardi in the early 1960s, but it could have been applied when
the Packers captured the NFL championship for three consecutive years
between 1929 and 1931. The community turned out to welcome the
team home with a victory parade after the Packers defeated the Bears 14–0
to clinch their first championship and cap-off an undefeated season.
Lambeau played sparingly in 1929 and then retired to the sidelines as
the full-time coach. Despite its winning ways, the franchise was always
teetering on the edge of financial disaster. Nonetheless, the Packers had

become an integral part of the community. By the early 1930s, this modest working-class city of 37,500, home to paper processing plants and a polyglot immigrant population, had carved out a niche for itself in the modest world of professional football.

The Packers found their natural rival in the big-city team 200 miles to the south. The rivalry was encouraged strongly by both coaches, who appreciated that it was good for ticket sales. Chicago's Halas liked to say that it was the "happiest series of games" he ever participated in. As Jeff Davis writes in his biography of Halas, "When they began the annual home-and-home series in 1925, with each team winning at home, the series was under way in earnest. It became the NFL's most storied rivalry, a colorful, rollicking, hard-fought, insult-filled, ego-driven battle between two teams and between their hard-drinking, boisterous fans and proud cities. Nothing could have been more wonderful."

When he arrived in Chicago, Halas asked former Illinois teammate Ed "Dutch" Sternaman to join him as partner to operate the Bears. The corporation was capitalized in 1922 at $15,000. Thus was born the franchise that remains yet today in the Halas family and is worth an estimated $980 million. For the first 20 years, however, Halas had to take out many a bank loan to get through budget crunches. Attendance was barely sufficient to keep the team operating, and Halas recognized that he had to do something dramatic to stimulate fan interest. His attention was inexorably drawn downstate to his alma mater, the University of Illinois, where coach Bob Zuppke had assembled a winning team led by the first superstar of college football, halfback Harold "Red" Grange. Halas had found his meal ticket.

The Red Grange Era

During his junior season in the fall of 1924, Grange had led Illinois to an undefeated season, highlighted by an incredible performance against a powerful Michigan team when he scored four touchdowns in the first quarter – a 95 yard return of the opening kickoff and runs from scrimmage of 67, 55, and 44 yards. Grange scored a fifth touchdown in the second half and passed for yet another. The hyperbolic sportswriter Grantland Rice looked on in amazement at this stunning performance and dubbed Grange the "Galloping Ghost." Blending speed, agility, and athleticism, Grange was capable of scoring anytime he touched the ball.

Halas recognized that the talented halfback could make professional football much more popular; he was someone who could lure large numbers of fans to Cubs Park on Sunday afternoons.

When Grange took to the field at Ohio Stadium in Columbus on November 21, 1925, everyone believed that this would be the last time he carried a football because his eligibility was at an end. Only a few insiders knew that astute public relations man C. C. Pyle had quietly cut a deal with Halas to get Grange a big payday. In the locker room after the Fighting Illini had defeated Ohio State 14–9 before 85,000 fans, Grange stunned reporters when he announced he was turning pro – immediately. Much to the consternation of purists, who at the time tended to denigrate professional athletes and exalt amateurs, Grange announced he would sign with the Bears for an exhibition swing around the United States. He would pocket one-half of the ticket sales.

Critics denounced C. C. Pyle as "Cash and Carry," but the ensuing barnstorming tour turned out enormous crowds to watch the Galloping Ghost, beginning with a sell-out crowd of 36,000 at Cubs Field on Thanksgiving Day. The Bears played ten more games in the next three weeks in major cities on the East Coast, highlighted by a crowd of 73,000 in the Polo Grounds for a match-up with the New York Giants. Large crowds turned out also in Miami and then Los Angeles. The tour ended in Seattle in January with Grange running at will against a band of so-called Washington All-Stars. He pocketed an estimated $250,000.

Grange's salary demands for the upcoming regular season were rebuffed by the penny-pinching Halas, and so Grange played for the short-lived New York Yankees. Ironically, Grange's attraction as a ball carrying whirling dervish ended in the fourth game of the 1927 season *against* the Bears at Wrigley Field. Grange suffered a serious knee injury when George "The Brute" Trafton slammed into him as he attempted to catch a pass. He sat out the 1928 season making motion pictures of dubious quality (*The Galloping Ghost, One Minute to Play, The Racing Romeo*), and in 1929 rejoined the Bears and played effectively but not spectacularly. He no longer could make the quick cuts that had made him so elusive, and he became a straight-ahead runner, an effective blocker, and one of the NFL's better defensive backs.

Grange joined the team at the time that Halas decided to end his dual career as player-coach to concentrate on running the business side of his club's operation. In 1932, Halas borrowed money to buy out partner Ed Sternaman and took complete control of the team. He would remain the sole owner until the team was passed to his oldest daughter, Virginia McCaskey, at the time of his death in 1983. As head coach, Halas had won only the 1921 championship, but throughout the 1920s the Bears had the best overall record in the league, 75–29–17. New coach Howard Jones was an innovative football man who installed an experimental offensive formation in which the quarterback received a direct snap from the center with three running backs lined up three yards behind him.

The Bears entered the final game of the 1932 regular season under Jones against a determined Green Bay team that had compiled a 10–2–1 record and was seeking a fourth consecutive league title. The Bears stood at an improbable 5–1–6, but because ties were not computed, the Bears could ease past the Packers with a victory at Cubs Park. With six inches of snow on the ground and the temperatures in the teens, less than 5,000 fans turned out to watch. They saw the Bears triumph on a 20 yard run off tackle by Bronko Nagurski. This narrow victory put the Bears into the NFL's first postseason playoff game to determine the league championship. Their opponents sported a similar record of 6–1–4 and came from the small river town of Portsmouth, Ohio.

This set up one of the most unusual games in which the Bears ever participated. It was scheduled for December 18 in Chicago, and the weather had only become more brutal following the snowy victory over Green Bay. Predictions for game day included near-zero temperatures with snow and ice covering the frozen turf. Fearing that only a handful of fans would turn out, Halas got permission from Commissioner Joe Carr to move the game indoors to the Chicago Stadium. The hastily designed playing field was only 80 yards long with elliptical end zones, and a wooden fence stood within a few feet of the sidelines. A circus had just departed the Stadium and so a six inch layer of dirt conveniently covered the concrete floor. Substantial residue deposited by elephants and horses also remained, to give the game a unique redolence. With 11,000 spectators looking on late in the fourth quarter, the score was knotted at 0–0. The Bears drove down to the two yard line and, on fourth down, fullback Bronko Nagurski took a handoff and headed into the line; but he stopped, stepped backwards, and threw a short jump pass to Grange, who caught the ball in the end zone while lying flat on his back. Portsmouth Spartans coach Potsy Clark angrily claimed that Nagurski was not five yards behind the line of scrimmage when he released the ball, as required by rule, but the officials signaled a touchdown. The Bears went on to win their first championship since 1921 by a 9–0 score. The Spartans lasted one more year in Portsmouth, and the franchise was sold to Detroit radio station owner George Richards for $15,000, who renamed them the Lions.

Following that championship season, Halas sensed that the NFL was about to fold due to the extreme economic conditions of the Great Depression. The league had been reduced to just eight franchises, and several of those were in serious trouble. Halas also recognized that the product on the field had become less and less exciting. Team strategies were built primarily around single wing offenses that produced few long gains. Many games amounted to little more than bone-jarring plays run into the center of the line. In 1932, an average of only 16 points was scored per game, and half the teams averaged less than seven points a game. Halas led an effort to change the rules to encourage a more exciting style of play. The ball itself was made slimmer to permit more precise passing, and rules liberalizing substitution were passed, although free substitution would not occur until the 1950s. With the Nagurski-to-Grange disputed forward pass in mind, a forward pass could now be thrown from anywhere on the field behind the line of scrimmage. It was also decided that when a play ended near the sideline or out of bounds the ball would be put back in play ten yards from the sideline. Goal posts were moved from the end line to the goal line to encourage more field goal attempts. These changes had their desired effect as offenses perked up, and ticket sales began to steadily increase despite the economic hard times. By 1939, games averaged 20,000 spectators.

Halas returned as head coach in 1933. Whether he did so to save money remains unclear, but it was evident that he missed coaching. Halas' second stint as head coach produced 88 wins and three NFL titles in the next ten years, unquestionably establishing him as one of the league's all-time top coaches. His 1933 team defeated the Packers in three hard-fought games that served to solidify the rivalry. The rivals entered the season with each team having won 11 games in the series (along with three ties). The Bears won the first game 14–7 when star end Bill Hewitt blocked Arnie Herber's punt in the last minute of the game, picked up the bounding ball, and lumbered into the end zone. That victory put the Bears ahead of the Packers in the series rivalry, and they have maintained an advantage ever since. Their third victory over the Packers came in early December and put the Bears in the postseason playoff championship game against the New York Giants. Trailing 21–16 before 26,000 fans in Wrigley Field with less than a minute to play, Bronko Nagurski connected on a pass to Hewitt on the Giant 19 yard line. About to be tackled, Hewitt flipped a lateral pass to rookie Bill Karr, who ran in for the winning touchdown. Halas had crafted this trick play, calling it the "Stinky Special."

Don Hutson: Pioneer of the Passing Game

In 1935, the last year before the NFL instituted a player draft, Lambeau signed All-American end Don Hutson out of the University of Alabama. At a slender 6′2″ and 170 pounds, most "experts" considered him too frail for professional ball. Hutson, however, possessed sub-ten second times in the 100 yard dash and was blessed with superb instincts, including an uncanny nose for the football. On his first offensive play as a rookie, he took a short pass from quarterback Arnie Herber and eluded tacklers for an 87 yard touchdown. He would catch 98 more touchdown passes in a career that lasted 11 seasons. Hutson essentially created the position of modern pass receiver as he ran crisp routes that included fakes and sharp cuts. He and his quarterbacks utilized precise timing patterns in which the ball would be in the air before Hutson made his cut. In 1941, Hutson became the first NFL player in history to catch 50 passes in one season and the following year became the first to amass over 1,000 yards receiving in a season. In an era of limited substitution, Lambeau played him at safety on defense where he flourished, intercepting 30 passes during his final six seasons. For good measure, Hutson kicked seven field goals and 172 extra points, altogether scoring 823 points in his Hall of Fame career.

The Packers thus became famous for their passing attack, winning championships in 1936, 1939, and 1944. In 1936, they defeated the Boston (soon to become Washington) Redskins in the championship game 21–6, highlighted by a 48 yard touchdown pass from Herber to Hutson in the opening minutes. The following year, the Bears edged out the Packers on the strength of Bronko Nagurski's power smashes and the outside running of halfback Ray Nolting. They beat the Packers twice en route to a 9–1–1 season that ended with a 28–21 loss to Washington in the championship game. Former TCU All-American "Slingin' Sammy" Baugh ignored 15 degree temperatures in Chicago when he connected on three touchdown passes. The Packers went 8–3 in 1938 but, before 48,000 spectators, lost in the championship game in the Polo Grounds to the Giants, 23–17. The following season they regrouped behind new quarterback Cecil Isbell to edge out the Bears for the Western title and shut out the New York Giants 27–0 in the championship game played in Milwaukee before a crowd of 33,000. The Packers had begun playing two or three "home" games at the old State Fair Grounds in Milwaukee and later played games in the baseball County Stadium to attract larger crowds, a practice that they continued until 1994.

Papa Bear

Halas watched with interest as such passers as Baugh and Isbell worked their aerial magic. Not only were their teams winning games, but also spectators clearly liked the exciting action. So Halas went hunting for a passer and found him on the campus of Columbia University. He worked out a deal with Art Rooney of the Pittsburgh Pirates (renamed the Steelers in 1940) to acquire All-American Sid Luckman in the 1939 draft. Luckman quickly became a star performer, his passes adding a potent new dimension to the Bear offense. Luckman became a transformative figure in football as the sparkling offense he led during a dominating 1940 season convinced coaches everywhere to abandon the single wing for the pass-friendly T-formation.

By this time Halas had become a leading, if controversial and contentious, figure in Chicago, with a reputation as a fiery, profane, demanding, penny-pinching sports executive. As a coach, Halas' reputation revolved around his sideline antics. He patrolled up and down the edge of the gridiron like a general commanding his troops in battle, and his frequent emotional outbursts and obscenity-filled tirades at game officials became a part of his public persona. His recurrent confrontations with players during contract negotiations also enhanced his gruff image. Many a player carried resentments from their salary battles with him long after their playing days had ended.

Halas' relationship with the men who covered the team for Chicago's newspapers was often combative – he, of course, wanted cheerleaders, not hard-nosed reporters. Thus his rough-hewn image as "Papa Bear" was not that of a cuddly teddy bear, but rather that of a "surly, snarly, sinister, and smart" businessman who always looked to gain an edge in financial dealings and on the field. Biographer Jeff Davis aptly concludes that he was "a hard man, a true godfather who saw fit to run his team, his league, and his family in his own image." Demanding, intense, confrontational, and not always fair or consistent in personnel decisions, Halas was both

Figure 4.1   George Halas intently watches his Chicago Bears during a
35–14 victory over the New York Giants in Yankee Stadium in November of
1955. Halas was not only the owner and chief operating officer of the Bears
from 1921 until his death in 1983, but he spent four decades on the sidelines
as head coach. © Bettmann/CORBIS

admired and reviled. He knew football as well as any coach, but he was
never viewed as an innovator in the mold of a Paul Brown or Bill Walsh.
Rather, he was the man who worked hard, but with little imagination,
and produced tough-minded, physical teams that took pride in their
fearsome reputation. Sixteen foot high statues of two of his coaching
rivals – Vince Lombardi and Curly Lambeau – are proudly displayed today

outside of the home field of the Packers and the Super Bowl trophy is named the Lombardi Trophy. No such public tributes exist for Halas, and, indeed, there is little left today to remind us of his role as the man who helped found and nurture the NFL through decades of good and not-so-good times and who created the Chicago Bears in his own testy image.

Monsters of the Midway

On the eve of the Second World War, Halas was at the height of his career and his team enjoyed its greatest period of dominance. In 1940, Luckman quarterbacked the Bears to a magical season in which they acquired the nickname "Monsters of the Midway." They defeated the Packers decisively in both meetings as they rolled to another divisional title, setting up a championship showdown with George Preston Marshall's Washington Redskins in Griffith Stadium on December 8.

Halas secretly prepared to hit the Redskins with some new offensive wrinkles out of the Bears' T-formation. In the week before the game, he huddled with former University of Chicago head coach, Clark Shaughnessy, then head coach at Stanford, who had installed his own innovative version of the T-formation. Shaughnessy had introduced the man-in-motion as a means of confusing the defense, and adjusted offensive line sets to gain blocking advantages. For the game with the Redskins, Shaughnessy suggested a new wrinkle that he had been toying with – the counter-play that used misdirection to confuse defenses. As the blockers moved toward one sideline, the ball carrier would cut back against the grain to take a handoff from the quarterback. Shaughnessy also designed new passing routes off the man-in-motion designed to exploit weaknesses he and Halas had detected watching Redskins film.

The result was stunning. Arthur Daley's oft-quoted lead paragraph in the Monday *New York Times* told it all: "The weather was perfect," he wrote, "and so were the Bears." Indeed. On the second play from scrimmage, Bill Osmanski broke a 68 yard touchdown run on a perfectly executed counter-play. The Redskins attempted to come back, but a perfectly thrown ball by Baugh to the wide-open Charlie Malone on the five yard line was inexplicably dropped. At that moment, the wind went out of the Redskins sails and the rout was on. When he was not handing the ball off to his hard running backs, Luckman riddled the Redskins secondary with pinpoint passes. For good measure, the Bears defense returned three interceptions of Baugh passes for touchdowns. Final score: 73–0.

That lopsided game signaled the emergence of professional football as an accepted part of the American sports scene. For two decades the NFL had struggled to survive, its legitimacy often questioned. But now it was gaining widespread interest. Millions of Americans listened to Red Barber describe the game live on the Mutual Broadcasting System; 37,000 fans were in attendance; and a record-setting 150 sportswriters were issued credentials. This was not only the most one-sided score in NFL history, but was also the last game in which one player did not wear a helmet. That dubious distinction belongs to Bears end Dick Plasman.

The dismantling of the Redskins proved to be a transformative moment for all of football. Coaches everywhere wanted to know more about the T-formation, which meant that Halas and Shaughnessy were much in demand for clinics and lectures, and their book *The Modern T-Formation with Man in Motion* was eagerly purchased by high school and college coaches. Several NFL teams adopted the new offense during the war years, and in 1947 Curly Lambeau also joined the "T-Party." By 1950, all NFL teams except the Pittsburgh Steelers had made the switch. Notre Dame, under new head coach Frank Leahy, became the first major college team to jump aboard, and by 1950 most high schools and college teams also had adopted the system. When Tennessee and UCLA finally scuttled the single wing in the late 1950s, the triumph of the Chicago Bears' innovative offense was compete.

In 1941, the Bears proved that their demolition of the Redskins had not been a fluke. Halas had drafted well for several years and assembled one of the most dominant teams in professional football history. The Bears and Packers met in Green Bay in September to open the season. A full house of 25,000 crowded into the obsolete wooden City Stadium to harass the Bears, who came onto the field in their newly designed uniforms that have not been substantively changed to this day: navy blue helmets, white visitors' jerseys with three orange stripes on the sleeves and blue numerals (navy blue jerseys were worn at home), and white pants with blue and orange stripes. The Packers wore their traditional blue jerseys with yellow leather helmets and matching yellow pants. It was not until the 1950 season that the Packers switched to forest green home jerseys. The Bears scored late to win 25–17 and went undefeated until the Packers, determined to even the score, came to Wrigley Field the Sunday after Thanksgiving. They held a 16–0 lead going into the fourth quarter and barely hung on to win 16–14. The next week the Bears defeated the cross-town Cardinals on a fourth quarter comeback that featured the passing of Luckman and the catching and running of halfback George McAfee. Late in the first half, however, the enthusiasm of the 41,000 spectators was dampened when they were informed by the announcer that the Japanese had bombed Pearl Harbor.

That victory set up a playoff with the Packers for the Western Division crown, and this time the Bears were ready. The offensive line chopped large holes in the Packers' defense for McAfee and fullback Norm Standlee, and the game that many considered to be for the NFL championship resulted in a relatively easy 34–14 Bears triumph. The title game against the New York Giants proved anticlimactic as the team and its fans had their minds focused on the war. McAfee and Standlee ran at will and the Bears dominated 39–7, but only 13,000 turned out at Wrigley Field on a surprisingly warm December day. Pearl Harbor had changed everything.

Halas, whose rusty engineering skills were still in demand, was off to the Navy and the South Pacific in early 1942, but the team he had assembled continued its strong play. Under co-coaches Hunk Anderson and Luke Johnson, the Bears lost by a touchdown to the Redskins for the NFL championship in 1942, after once again edging out the Packers for the Western title. In 1943, the Packers finished second to the Bears, who gained revenge on Washington 42–21 in the championship game. But everyone knew it was not the same. Between the 1942 and 1944 seasons, 20 of the 28 men on the Bears roster had departed for the military, and interim coaches were signing men in their 40s to fill the roster. In 1944, however, the Packers won it all with their own slapdash collection of 4-F draft rejects and aging veterans, defeating the Giants 14–7 in the title game.

Halas returned from the South Pacific for the 1946 season and his team, made up largely of military veterans, won the Western Division. A victory over the Giants at the Polo Grounds in the championship game, however, was clouded by allegations that two members of the Giants backfield, quarterback Frank Filchock and fullback Merle Hapes, had been offered $2,500 each to make certain the favored Bears covered the ten point spread. Commissioner Bert Bell suspended Hapes but permitted Filchock, who denied everything, to play. Filchock played bravely after Bear end Ed Sprinkle broke Filchock's nose, obviously attempting to demonstrate that he was not on any gambler's payroll. Late in the game, Luckman drove the Bears to the 19 yard line and then faked a handoff to McAfee and bootlegged the ball around end for the winning score. A late field goal by Frank Maznicki put the game at 24–14. The Bears had won, but the Giants had kept them from covering the spread.

Doldrums

Curly Lambeau was forced to resign after a disastrous 2–10 record in 1949, at a time when the team once more faced financial collapse. Another stock issue – $25 a share – prevented the team from folding. To compound matters, the inadequacies of City Stadium prompted the league to threaten to move the franchise to Milwaukee, but Green Bay voters responded by overwhelmingly approving a bond issue to finance a modern 32,500-seat stadium. Recognizing the importance of a viable Packers franchise for his own team's wellbeing, George Halas spent time in Green Bay urging voters to pass the ballot measure. A new City Stadium opened in September of 1957, the first stadium in the NFL specifically designed for football. In 1965, it was expanded to 60,000 seats and renamed Lambeau Field. In 2003, a major renovation added an additional 12,000 seats along with an immense retro-style atrium that houses year-round consumer attractions. It is now widely considered one of the best venues for watching a game in the NFL.

The Bears also fell on hard times. Halas had always displayed an obsessive concern for money, but these tendencies became more pronounced as he aged. Consequently many players left in disgust, including high-profile quarterbacks Johnny Lujack and George Blanda. For some reason – some thought sheer stubbornness – Halas repeatedly refused to play the multi-talented Blanda, a future Hall of Fame inductee, essentially relegating him to field goal kicker. Blanda's independent streak apparently threatened Halas' need for absolute control. Unwilling to bend to Halas' will, Blanda retired in 1958, but in 1960 signed with the Houston Oilers of the American Football League. He later played for the Oakland Raiders as a superb back-up quarterback and place kicker and did not retire until he was 48 years of age. Asked about Halas after he had retired, a still-bitter Blanda snarled, "He was too cheap even to buy me a kicking shoe."

In 1956, following several mediocre seasons, Halas retired from coaching once more, turning the team over to assistant Paddy Driscoll. After two lackluster seasons, Halas returned once more as head coach. He soon discovered that he had met his match in the latest new Green Bay head coach. After Curly Lambeau departed, three coaches were hired and then sent packing as the losses mounted. The third of those, Scooter McLean, posted a 1–10–1 record in 1958 and was fired after one season. The gloom that hung over the small city was palpable. Packers president Dominic Olejniczak searched carefully for the right man, interviewing a large number of candidates, apparently assuming that it was make-or-break time for the franchise. His search turned up several promising candidates, but the one that resonated was Vince Lombardi, the offensive coordinator of the New York Giants. "I shouldn't tell you this," Halas told Olejniczak, "but he'll be a good one. I shouldn't tell you because you're liable to kick the crap out of us!" At the time, however, the media looked with considerable skepticism upon the appointment, noting that Lombardi had been rejected several times by other NFL teams in his quest for a head coaching opportunity.

Titletown USA

The appointment of Vince Lombardi as head coach and general manager produced the greatest era in Packer football. He took control quickly, releasing several players and trading for and drafting those who fit his template – hard-working, mature, team-oriented professionals. He installed an offensive system based on precise timing and execution rather than raw power. His system revolved around what he called "option blocking," a technique epitomized by the famed "Green Bay Sweep." Blockers were taught to move their man in the way that seemed most advantageous while the ball carrier made his cuts up field by reading the block – what Lombardi called "running to daylight." Lombardi emphasized precise execution rather than providing his team with a lengthy playbook, and practices were consumed by endless repetitions to get things fine-tuned. Early in his first season the Packers defeated the Bears 9–6 as a full house screamed enthusiastically in City Stadium, and they went on to compile a 7–5 record, breaking that miserable 11 year losing spell. Lombardi was voted Coach of the Year. The following year he placed the distinctive oval G on the yellow helmets, and with Bart Starr installed as quarterback, the Packers won their first Western Division title in 16 years. They lost 17–13 in the championship game at Philadelphia when fullback Jim Taylor was tackled short of a first down at the Eagles eight yard line in the final minute of play.

Figure 4.2 Coach Vince Lombardi confers with quarterback Bart Starr during the first Super Bowl. The Packers won convincingly over the Kansas City Chiefs 35–10 on January 15, 1967. All-Pro fullback Jim Taylor is on the left, and in the background without a helmet is Hall of Fame halfback Paul Hornung. © Bettmann/CORBIS

In 1961, Green Bay went 11–3 and manhandled the New York Giants 37–0 in the championship game. This Packers team included ten future Hall of Fame members. The coolly efficient quarterback Bart Starr ran the offense, bolstered by running backs Jim Taylor and Paul Hornung, popularly knows as "Mr Inside and Mr Outside." They worked their ball carrying magic behind an offensive line that included Forrest Gregg, Fuzzy Thurston, Jerry Kramer, and Ron Kramer. Lombardi delegated the details of the defense to coordinator Phil Bengston, who deployed such standouts as linebacker Ray Nitschke, end Willie Davis, tackle Henry Jordan, and defensive backs Herb Adderley and Willie Wood.

The following year, the Packers dominated the league, finishing a memorable 13–1 while outscoring their opponents 415 to 148. Once more they defeated the Giants in the NFL Championship Game played on a bitterly cold day at Yankee Stadium; Jerry Kramer's three field goals sealed the victory as the Packers won 16–7. In just four seasons, Lombardi had transformed the franchise from perennial loser to champions. Green Bay fans happily took to calling their small city "Titletown USA."

Just a few months after the Packers' classic victory, Lombardi was stunned when NFL Commissioner Pete Rozelle informed him that he had solid evidence linking All-Pro Paul Hornung to betting on NFL games (but not Packers games). Lombardi agreed that Rozelle was correct to suspend his star halfback for the 1963 season. His dream of winning three straight NFL championships was derailed by a combination of Hornung's ethical lapse and a series of injuries to key players.

The Bears Come Out of Hibernation

Opening day 1963 found George Halas and a group of determined Bears visiting City Field. The Packers had won the previous five games between the rivals, but now Hornung was absent. Halas was so determined to turn the tables that he even signed linebacker Tom Bettis, who had been released after a run-in with Lombardi, solely because he could obtain information about the Packers' defensive schemes. After a hard-hitting battle, the Bears left town with a 10–3 victory. The Packers responded with an eight game winning streak, but lost Starr midseason to a broken wrist. In late November, the Bears ended any hope that the Packers might have had for a third consecutive championship when they pelted the Packers 26–7 at Wrigley Field in a game that brimmed over with hostility between the two teams. The Bears had slain their rivals twice, and they struggled through several close games, winning largely on supreme efforts by the defense coached by the ebullient George Allen. Led by defensive end Ed O'Bradovich and tight end Mike Ditka, the Bears defeated the Y. A. Tittle-quarterbacked Giants in Yankee Stadium 14–10 to claim the 1963 NFL Championship.

After the game, many Bears players effusively praised the coaching of "George," but it was the popular Allen, not the crusty 68-year-old Halas to whom they referred. Halas had become an aging, remote figure to most of the players and, with another championship in hand, the time seemed propitious for him to go out on top. Instead, he coached another five seasons, each one marked by dissension and a steady erosion of talent and victories. Before the 1968 season, facing two hip replacement surgeries, Halas turned the team over to assistant Jim Dooley. At age 73, Halas left coaching for the last time, with 324 career victories, a league record. It was not until 1992 that Don Shula of the Miami Dolphins surpassed that mark.

Halas said that he decided to leave coaching because his painful hips no longer permitted him to run down the sidelines to curse at officials, but the reality was that he had lost touch with the game and, especially, his players. His reputation in Chicago as a tight-fisted owner who would trade top players rather than submit to their salary demands had become more pronounced. Halas, however, ran the club for the next 15 years in much the same fashion as in days of yore. Despite the presence of sterling running back Gale Sayers and middle linebacker Dick Butkus, things did not improve under Dooley; he was terminated after four losing seasons, and three other coaches followed in short order. After the 1982 season, an aging Halas, suffering from multiple health problems, hired former player Mike Ditka as his new coach, hoping that the tempestuous Iron Mike could return the Bears to their winning ways. Halas would

Figure 4.3   One of the greatest middle linebackers in NFL history, Dick Butkus of the Bears, is about to smack Green Bay quarterback Don Horn just as he released the ball at Wrigley Field in December of 1968. © Bettmann/CORBIS

not live to see that day, however, because midway through Ditka's first season, the Papa Bear died (October 31, 1983) at the age of 88.

Many of Halas' most significant accomplishments occurred beyond public purview. Throughout his career he provided strong and progressive leadership among league owners. One of Halas' enduring legacies was his role in developing an enlightened television policy. During the initial years of commercial television in the late 1940s, Halas watched incredulously as the new medium wreaked devastation among many minor league baseball teams, even entire leagues. Etched deeply into his mind was the last Bears home game in December of 1949 against the cross-town Cardinals; it was a sellout, and fans without tickets demanded the game be televised. Halas was persuaded (for a good fee) to permit a local station to televise the game live. Game day brought a cold rain, and less than 15,000 ticket holders showed up for the kickoff. Halas and other league officials recognized that television could stimulate new fan interest, but if not handled properly, could produce financial ruin by cutting into ticket sales. Halas convinced his fellow club owners to support his plan to ban the telecasting of home games on local networks. A protracted legal battle ensued, but in 1952 a federal judge ruled that the local blackout was permissible if away games were shown locally and no ban on radio broadcasts was imposed.

This policy went a long way toward growing the NFL and it became the foundation for Pete Rozelle's inspired plan implemented ten years later in which all teams shared equally in the television revenues generated from a single league-wide contract with a major network. Little did they know just how large that one bundle of money would become after Rozelle received congressional immunity from antitrust liabilities. When the first open bidding for the entire league was held for the seasons of 1964 and 1965, CBS won the contract with a bid of $28,200,000, a quantum jump in television revenue. Halas believed revenue sharing would enable all teams in the league to compete on a more-or-less equal basis by providing financial equality; he also knew that it would enable the Packers, located in a city of less than 100,000 residents, to remain competitive.

"Winning Is the Only Thing"

As Halas struggled through his final years on the sidelines, Lombardi drove his team back to the top of professional football. Two seasons, in 1963 and 1964, without a championship turned him into an even more demanding coach. He plastered the Packers locker and weight training rooms with posters and motivational messages, including the one that would be interpreted as a "win-at-all-costs" philosophy that journalists attributed to Lombardi. Actually, the controversial slogan, "Winning isn't everything, it's the only thing," was most likely first uttered in a 1953 motion picture in which John Wayne played a college football coach. Biographer David Maraniss emphasizes that Lombardi's primary coaching objective was to achieve proper execution and full effort on all plays, *not* winning at any cost. If a full effort were expended, and proper execution achieved, winning would take care of itself. Maraniss quotes wide receiver Carroll Dale that, even in victory, Lombardi would not tolerate mistakes: "He would not overlook them. He would correct them, immediately. Winning wasn't everything for him, he wanted excellence. There's a difference."

In the last championship game played before the introduction of the Super Bowl, the Packers defeated the Cleveland Browns 23–12 in the snow and mud of Lambeau Field; the key play was a perfectly executed 13 yard touchdown run on a Green Bay Power Sweep by Paul Hornung that was led by the blocking of linemen Jerry Kramer and Bob Skoronski. Hornung made a classic cut "to daylight" as he went untouched into the end zone. This run was captured perfectly by ground-level cameras and became a staple in the popular NFL Film series. In the ensuing 1966 season, the Packers continued their dominating ways, winning the NFL championship game 34–27 over Tom Landry's Cowboys in Dallas on the strength of four Bart Starr touchdown passes.

In 1966, an important new wrinkle had been added to professional football. The recent merger with the American Football League had led Commissioner Pete Rozelle to propose what later came to be called the Super Bowl. Despite having won the NFL crown again, the Packers' work was not complete. Lombardi became a man possessed in Santa Barbara, where he prepared his team to defend the honor of the older NFL in the cavernous Los Angeles Memorial Stadium against Hank Stram's Kansas City Chiefs. Losing to the upstart AFL would have been an enormous humiliation. Interestingly, 40,000 tickets priced at just $12 went unsold, but the yawning expanse of empty seats did not bother the Packers who won handily, 35–10.

Lombardi's last season in Green Bay produced one of the most memorable games in football history, the famous "Ice Bowl" played in Green Bay. At stake in late December was the NFL championship and a return trip to the Super Bowl. The press talked effusively about Landry's so-called Doomsday Defense, anchored by Hall of Fame tackle Bob Lilly, and the innovative multiple set offensive operated by quarterback Don Meredith throwing to a fleet of speedy receivers.

The temperature registered a brisk minus 13 degrees at kickoff time and a surreal haze produced by the condensation of the breaths of 60,000 fans hovered over Lambeau Field. After the Packers jumped on top 14–0, the Cowboys clawed back to within four points at half-time. Midway through the fourth quarter the Cowboys took the lead 17–14 on a 50 yard pass from halfback Dan Reeves to Lance Rentzel. With four minutes remaining in the game, the Cowboys held that slim lead when Packer Willie Wood returned a punt to his 32 yard line. The Packers were 68 yards from the distant, frozen goal line, but Starr moved his team methodically downfield on short passes intermixed with straight power runs. With just 16 seconds left on the clock, the Packers were on the Cowboy one yard line, and, with Lombardi having decided against attempting a tying field goal, Starr surprised everyone by diving into the end zone behind an effective Kramer block on tackle Jethro Pugh. The entire drive was a testimony to Lombardi's coaching philosophy of eliminating mistakes. There were no penalties, no fumbles, no dropped passes, no missed assignments; it was an efficient, disciplined effort by a superbly coached team playing under extreme pressure in extreme weather conditions. Packer announcer Ray Scott later said, "That final drive was the greatest triumph of will over adversity I'd ever seen. It was a thing of beauty."

Iron Mike and "Da Bears"

After Lombardi departed for the Washington Redskins in 1968, the Packers soon fell from atop the league. Four coaches came and went without returning the Packers to the glory days of the Lombardi era. The Bears suffered through a similar fate into the mid-1980s, but came out of hibernation briefly when Halas named former Bears star Mike Ditka as head coach in 1982. Halas wanted to return the Bears to their Monsters of the Midway image, and found his man in Iron Mike. In what has to be one of the shortest head coaching job interviews in history, Ditka responded bluntly to an initial question about his "coaching philosophy." "Coach, what do you want me to do, bullshit ya? Your coaching philosophy is the same as mine: I want to win. I know how to win." Interview over. No other candidate was seen.

Ditka took over the team with full knowledge that he would have to deal with the inept Michael McCaskey sometime in the near future. He was the eldest son of Halas's oldest daughter Virginia who assumed ownership of the franchise when Halas died during Ditka's second season as head coach. From the beginning, Michael seemed out of touch with the team and professional football and displayed an instinctive ability to make the wrong decision at the worst possible time. George Halas's last words on his deathbed to his daughter were reportedly that he had established a competent management team by appointing attorney Jerry Vainisi to run the front office operation with Ditka as coach. "I already have my men in place to run the team," he whispered plaintively. "Anybody but Michael."

But Michael it was, named by his mother as the club's new president. Meanwhile, Ditka put his stamp on the team, molding it in the form of the great Bears teams of the past. Middle linebacker Mike Singletary provided the spark for a rejuvenated defense, Walter Payton became one of the greatest ball carriers in league history, and quarterback Jim McMahon, of limited physical skills but possessing enormous leadership qualities, guided the team with authority. After a turnaround 10–6 season in 1984, the Bears dominated the NFL in 1985 and overwhelmed the Giants and Los Angeles Rams in the playoffs before embarrassing the New England Patriots 46–10 in the Super Bowl. The defense, led by Singletary, Richard Dent, Dan Hampton, and Wilber Marshall, held the Patriots to a stunning minus 19 yards total offense in the first half. Late in the game, Ditka used a ploy that delighted Chicago fans but which many football insiders believed to be inappropriate because it seemed intended to embarrass the opponent: he inserted 320 pound defensive tackle William "The Refrigerator" Perry into the backfield to score a touchdown on a one yard plunge into the line. Because of his enormous size and jovial personality, Perry had become a fan favorite. He made for good copy, described by one journalist thusly: "He possesses rolls of fat and empty spaces where his front teeth should be."

The Bears of 1985 are widely considered to be one of the most powerful teams in history, rivaling the 1940–41 Bears and the undefeated 1972 Miami Dolphins. But there would be no dynasty. In addition to fighting with Michael McCaskey over matters big and small, Ditka nursed a personal grievance because his team had not only carried him off the

Super Dome field in January, but also defensive coordinator Buddy Ryan. Throughout the season, the fiery Ditka and the headstrong Ryan clashed repeatedly, their massive egos producing a major rift. Ditka had turned much of the defense over to Ryan, who received enormous praise in the media for his attacking defensive plays. Ditka could not abide Ryan, and by midseason the two men barely spoke. At one point they nearly came to blows on the sideline during a game.

There would be no repeat in 1986. Ryan departed for the head coaching position in Philadelphia, and while Ditka publicly rejoiced ("I'm elated he's gone"), the Bears defense never returned to its 1985 level. Several players reported to summer camp out of shape, including the massive Perry who had obviously raided his own refrigerator far too often and had ballooned to nearly 400 pounds. McMahon's passing was severely hampered by an early season shoulder injury, and when Ditka and Vainisi acquired quarterback Doug Flutie at a high salary and inserted him into the starting lineup to replace the charismatic McMahon, the team was riddled by dissension. A late November game against the Packers at Soldier Field, the Bears' home ground since 1971, effectively ended their hopes for a return to the Super Bowl. It also ended McMahon's season – several seconds after he had thrown an interception, Packers defensive end Charles Martin picked up the quarterback from behind and brutally slammed him, right shoulder first, into the hard artificial turf. Referee Jerry Markbreit immediately ejected Martin, but McMahon ended up undergoing surgery on his passing arm and never returned to his Super Bowl form. The Bears limped into the playoffs under Flutie and were eliminated in the first round, playing uninspired football as they lost badly to the Washington Redskins. The following day Michael McCaskey, seeking a scapegoat, fired general manager Vainisi, and Ditka exploded in a rage. Things went rapidly downhill from there.

Packers Resurgence, Bears in Retreat

By 1992, the Bears had returned to their dismal 1970s level, and Ditka was fired. The franchise continued to flounder into the next millennium. Up in Green Bay, however, after 20 years of wandering in the post-Lombardi wilderness, the Packers began to remind fans of those glory days. In 1991, the Board of Directors decided the time had come to start anew and brought in the experienced personnel guru Ron Wolf from the Oakland Raiders as general manager. Wolf appointed the offensive coordinator of the highly successful San Francisco 49ers, Mike Holmgren, as the new head coach. Holmgren's resume included ten years working under one of the game's most innovative coaches, Bill Walsh. Wolf also acquired from the Atlanta Falcons a young quarterback out of Southern Mississippi, Brett Favre, who Falcon coach Jerry Glanville publicly stated lacked NFL-level ability. Wolf also signed free agent defensive end Reggie White to provide team leadership and anchor the defense.

Holmgren inserted Favre into the starting lineup midway through the 1992 season and a six game winning streak ensued, the longest the club had enjoyed since 1965. Beginning in 1993, the Packers made the playoffs in six consecutive seasons. Under Holmgren's tutelage, Favre evolved into a perennial All-Pro quarterback. He played the game with such enthusiasm that he became one of the most popular players in Packers history. Favre led the Packers to the Super Bowl during the 1996 season where they easily defeated the New England Patriots under head coach Bill Parcells. The exuberant quarterback threw for 246 yards, including touchdown passes to Andre Rison and Antonio Freeman, and ran for another in the 35–21 romp. The following season the Packers lost 31–24 to the Denver Broncos and quarterback John Elway in Super Bowl XXXII.

Holmgren left to assume the combined duties of executive vice president and head coach of the Seattle Seahawks in 1999. He had compiled an overall record of 75–37 and had set a new team record by leading the Packers to six consecutive playoff berths. Wolf named former Philadelphia head coach Ray Rhodes to replace Holmgren, but after an initial dissension-riddled 8–8 season, Wolf replaced him with the offensive-minded Mike Sherman, former Holmgren assistant. Despite the turnover in coaches, Favre continued to flourish. His public admission that he had overcome an addiction to painkillers, his wife's courageous battle with breast cancer, and his down-home qualities of a good ol' boy from rural Mississippi – not to mention his winning ways – endeared him to Packers fans. In December of 2003, Favre's standing rose even higher when he elected to play in an important Monday Night game with playoff implications just one day after learning his father had died of a heart attack. Sublimating his grief, Favre threw four touchdown passes in the first half against the Raiders.

As Favre passed his 35th birthday, rumors began building as to when he might retire. He did so after the 2007 season, which almost ended in a storybook fashion. He led the team to a 13–3 season and defeated

Holmgren's Seahawks in the second round of the playoffs. Against the New York Giants in the NFC Championship game in Green Bay, the game went into overtime, but instead of leading his team to a dramatic victory as a motion picture script might have been written, he instead threw an untimely interception that enabled the Giants to win on a 47 yard field goal. The Giants went on to upset the New England Patriots in Super Bowl XLII. A Super Bowl appearance would have provided the perfect ending to Favre's record-setting 17 year reign in Green Bay. Following that devastating defeat, Favre announced that he was retiring. But, as the 2008 training camp prepared to open, the idea of his possible interest in returning for another season began to ripple through the media. By this time, the Packers had announced the elevation of their 2005 first-round draft choice Aaron Rodgers to the starting quarterback position. For several months rumors flew about Favre's possible return, which was overwhelmingly encouraged by Packers fans. Packers general manager Ted Thompson and coach McCarthy, however, were not enthused, and Favre eventually approved a trade to the New York Jets, where he tailed off in effectiveness late in the 2008 season after an initial promising start. Obviously furious with Green Bay management for a perceived personal slight, in the summer of 2009 Favre signed with the neighboring Minnesota Vikings of the same division. This move alienated many of his devoted fans who believed he was acting out of spite to gain revenge on the Packers management. For a time, at least, the most primary rival of Packers fans had become the Vikings, and it promised to remain so as the long as Brett Favre was wearing a Vikings uniform.

While the Packers were enjoying a renaissance, the Bears were languishing as criticism of team president Michael McCaskey continued to mount. Despite various gaffes, his mother resolutely stood by her eldest son. McCaskey's selection of Dave Wannstadt (1993–8) and Dick Jauron (1999–2003) as head coaches produced only two brief appearances in the playoffs, and the crescendo of fan disappointment continued to grow amidst lackluster team performances. In February of 2001, Virginia McCaskey finally ran out of patience with her son and announced she was replacing him with Ted Phillips. A long-standing family business associate, Phillips became the first non-member of the Halas family in history to serve as president of the organization.

Phillips began the difficult task of rebuilding the relationship with city leaders, especially mayor Richard Daley, that Michael McCaskey had shattered. This included resumption of derailed negotiations for the remodeling of Soldier Field. In 2003, a revamped home for the Bears opened. Before the 2004 season, the Bears named defensive specialist Lovie Smith as their new head coach. Smith's revamped defense, keyed by linebacker Brian Urlacher, made up for the deficiencies of a sputtering offense and the Bears reached the playoffs after the 2005 season. The following season they captured the NFC crown despite a glaring deficiency at quarterback, but lost to the New England Patriots in the Super Bowl. The team fell to 7–9 the following year as continuing quarterback woes made for an anemic offense. Bears faithful had to wonder: would "da Bears" fall into another long funk as after the spectacular 1985 season?

Despite the many ups and downs during 90 years of football, both the Chicago Bears and the Green Bay Packers have persevered. Both teams enjoy the support of legions of faithful fans and are considered among the most valuable NFL franchises. In Green Bay, nearly 5 million non-negotiable shares of stock are dispersed among more than 110,000 shareholders. The team, which has sold-out every game since the early Lombardi years, has a reputed backlog of 74,000 names on a waiting list for season tickets. In 2007, a national financial magazine estimated the value of the Bears at $984 million, while the dollar value of the community-owned Green Bay Packers is, in truth, impossible to assess. With a rivalry that dates back to the 1920s, devoted fans of both teams can look forward to exciting football when these two storied franchises meet twice each autumn in what has rightfully been called "The Black and Blue Division" of the National Football League.

We just wanted to beat each other's brains out. But we had no interest in bad blood. (Jack Nicklaus, 2006)

The face of American golf in the 1950s was that of the austere Ben Hogan. Although he made a gallant comeback after suffering near-fatal injuries in 1949 when his Cadillac collided head-on with a bus on a foggy west Texas highway, he never enjoyed widespread popularity. Hogan approached the game with an intense analytical focus and, over years of exhaustive practice, had developed a picture-perfect swing and a sure putting stroke. His mastery of the game earned him respect and admiration, but did not garner him public affection. He was all business on the course, his grim visage of concentration giving no indication of emotion or joy in the game he played so well. Off the course, he was withdrawn and reclusive.

With his image as a cold and calculating technician who had uncanny control of his shots, Hogan was never embraced by the average golf fan. Even his several instructional books aimed at the weekend golfer were laden with detailed technical language that left most readers more baffled than enlightened. For this intense man, golf was a business, never a game. At the peak of his game in the early 1950s, he remained an aloof figure, admired but not loved. Toward the end of his reign, golf began shedding its elitist image. Millions of new players were taking up the game – beneficiaries of the postwar economic boom – but it was the emergence of two compelling newcomers that created a new era for American golf.

Arnie: The Blue-Collar Golfer

The first to make his appearance was a charismatic Pennsylvanian whose enthusiasm for the game was infectious. At a muscular 5'10" and 175 pounds, Arnold Palmer exuded both confidence and excitement when he played the game. He loved to compete, and he captured the affection of spectators with his exuberant approach to the game. Palmer tended to see opportunities when his opponents saw only potential dangers. His fans came to expect him to get into trouble, often falling well off the lead, but make a miraculous shot to spark another come-from-behind "charge" on the last day of big tournaments. It was an exciting time, and Arnold Palmer helped transform golf into a popular mainstream sport. As Palmer once noted, "It was a time when the American people were beginning to feel that anything might be accomplished if only we were bold enough to try." That was how he approached his golf: not afraid to try, almost too willing to go for broke.

Part of Palmer's appeal was that he exemplified the American Dream. He was the son of working-class parents who instilled in him a strong work ethic and determination to succeed. Arnold Palmer was the anti-Hogan, a magnetic figure whose unmistakable joy in playing the game he loved attracted millions of middle- and working-class fans. That his approach to the game was reflective of his blue-collar origins was part of his appeal. Unlike most golfers, whose strokes had been perfected by years of coaching, Palmer's lunging swing was enough to make any golf instructor cringe; some said that it resembled a hockey player attempting a slap shot. However, he followed his father's advice and never let anyone change a swing that produced low, slightly hooking shots. His tee shots routinely carried 275 yards or more, and seldom did they rise higher than 30 feet off the ground. As he says, "the running joke" on the tour was that "you could tell when Arnold Palmer had been on the [practice] tee – the grass in front of it was scorched." Palmer's putting form was equally unorthodox – "I hunched over the ball, knock-kneed and leaning, and gave the ball a firm wristy rap" – and was the subject of much second-guessing. His putting can be only described as "uniquely aggressive."

Confident in his abilities and enjoying the competition and attention, he would often interact with the gallery, sharing a laugh and sometimes stopping to sign an autograph. Palmer became a top touring professional at the beginning of network television's early efforts to broadcast the final holes of major tournaments. It was little wonder, then, that Palmer's impact was to democratize the game, to make it attractive to millions who had never before given much thought to golf. Everything about Arnold Palmer's personality and playing style resonated with the loud and boisterous legions that tramped around the course with him.

Palmer was the son of a greens keeper and teaching professional at a nine hole private golf club located in the small mill town of Latrobe, Pennsylvania. From an early age he worked on the course assisting his father, learning to drive a tractor mower, manicure the greens, and groom the sand traps. In the 1930s, golf professionals were viewed by club members as mere hired hands and typically not accorded much respect. Such was the case with Deacon Palmer, who was expected to use the side door and not to make himself comfortable in the bar or restaurant. Arnold learned at an early age that he was only permitted to play the course early in the morning before the members arrived for their rounds, or after the last member had departed. But play he did, essentially teaching himself the game, with an occasional suggestion from his father.

By the time he entered high school, he had decided to bypass football and baseball to concentrate on golf. He became a promising juniors player, winning the Pennsylvania High School Championship twice. His talent secured a golf scholarship at Wake Forest, where he won two Southern Conference titles as well as two National Intercollegiate Medalist titles. But the death of a close friend in an automobile accident during his junior year greatly affected him and he departed college for a three year stint in the Coast Guard.

The pivotal moment in Palmer's career occurred when he entered the 1954 US Amateur Championship in Detroit. He won his first six match-play rounds and in the semi-finals sank a difficult five foot side-hill putt on the 36th hole to force a playoff against a veteran tournament player. He eventually won on the third extra hole. Palmer then came from two holes behind against 43-year-old Robert Sweeney, an experienced amateur player of considerable reputation, to win the tournament. Herbert Warren Wind watched the 25-year-old Palmer in the finals against Sweeney: "The contrast in their backgrounds was obvious, and quite frankly, nearly everybody wanted Arnold to win. . . . He was so engaging: there was a wonderful brightness and niceness about him. At that point he wasn't a finished golfer but, even then, there was an aura about him."

Palmer's victory in Detroit gave him the confidence to compete at the highest levels of the game, but he had been hesitant to turn professional. He was aware that most professional golfers at that time had to hold club professional positions to make ends meet, and he was recently married to Winnie Walzer, whom he had met at a tournament in her hometown of Coopersburg, Pennsylvania. However, basking in the glow of his marriage and with an offer of a $5,000 endorsement contract from

Wilson Sporting Goods in hand, on November 15, 1954, Palmer turned professional. He struggled in his first events as he and Winnie drove from tournament to tournament pulling a small house trailer. The bleak financial realities that he confronted on the tour, coupled with his vivid childhood memories of growing up during the Great Depression in a house without indoor plumbing and only a fireplace for heat, would mold his entire future. Even after he began to win major tournaments and was flooded with endorsement offers, Palmer never changed his apprehensive view of his financial prospects.

Arnie's Army on Maneuvers

Palmer got a major boost in August of 1955 when he won the Canadian Open. He shot a record-shattering 64 on the opening day and followed with a 67, 64, and 70 to win the tournament in a record low score of 265. In 1956, Palmer won two tournaments, earning $16,145, and the following year his tour experience helped him win four tournaments and a place in the top ten 17 times. He took home all of $27,800.

Based on his growing success, Palmer had become well known to serious golfing fans, but in 1958 he captured the imaginations of sports fans everywhere when he won his first major, out-dueling Ken Venturi and Doug Ford on the final day at the Augusta National Golf Club to capture the Masters. On that day, he nailed a spectacular eagle on the par 5 13th hole to take the lead, thrilling the record crowd of over 30,000. Palmer's victory had, in fact, been partially fueled by a caustic comment made by Ben Hogan on the eve of the tournament. Having witnessed for the first time Palmer's unconventional swing during a Wednesday practice round, golf's precision ball striker was not diplomatic. In the locker room afterward, with Palmer well within hearing range, Hogan pointedly asked Jackie Burke, "How in the hell did Palmer get an invitation to the Masters?" An irritated Palmer later commented, "Hogan was just another one of the goddam guys on the tour as far as I was concerned. All I wanted to do was beat him, and I did." Palmer won the tournament in dramatic fashion, by one stroke. He was clearly the favorite of the large galleries, which included off-duty soldiers from nearby Fort Gordon who took to calling themselves "Arnie's Army," cheering loudly as he played aggressively in the face of enormous pressure. Convinced that he had a future in the game, Palmer and Winnie signed a contract to build a modest three bedroom house on a three acre plot overlooking the Latrobe Country Club. The ever-prudent Arnie insisted on paying cash.

With a major title on his resume, Palmer was well on his way to stardom. In 1960, he zoomed to the top of the annual money-winners list. He had become the most popular golfer in the United States. In that year, Palmer won eight tournaments, including his second Masters, and captured his first US Open in a memorable final round at Cherry Hills in Denver. Early in the season, he had won his third consecutive tournament at Pensacola with what became his trademark late "charge," coming from behind in the final round to defeat Doug Sanders by one stroke when he holed out a 32 foot putt on the 18th green. That dramatic winning putt had been made possible by racking-up six birdies in the last ten holes, an improbable feat that prompted Al Geiberger to gasp, "I was awestruck! You can't do that in golf."

In 1959, Palmer had lost the Masters with careless play on the final two holes to permit Art Wall to win. The following year, he approached the same 400 yard 17th on the final day, trailing Ken Venturi by one stroke. He slugged his tee shot long down the middle and then smacked a crisp 8-iron that stopped 27 feet short of the hole. As he scurried onto the green, he gave the line a quick read, took one practice jab with the putter, and rammed the ball into the hole. Arnie's Army thundered its approval. On the 18th, Palmer drove 260 yards into the wind and then knocked a 6-iron to within five feet, with Venturi looking on helplessly from the clubhouse. With only a moment's hesitation, he snapped his putter and the ball hit the back of the hole and settled home. Television announcer Jim McKay exclaimed, "Arnold Palmer is the Masters champion of 1960!" It was, he breathlessly intoned, "one of the greatest displays of courageous golf that anybody has ever seen!" Palmer's spectacular play that day sealed his standing as a living golf legend. The next day, President Dwight Eisenhower arrived at Augusta, feeling privileged to have the opportunity to play a round with the most famous golfer in America. *Sports Illustrated* labeled Palmer "the brightest star of a new generation of professionals," concluding that, "From a wild climax, Arnold Palmer emerged as an authentic and unforgettable hero."

If anyone thought that *Sports Illustrated* had engaged in unnecessary hyperbole, they changed their minds two months later after Palmer had performed the equivalent of a golfing miracle to win the US Open. After two rounds at Cherry Hills in Denver, he stood in 15th place, far off the pace. The Open would conclude according to a tradition begun in 1898 with 36 holes on Saturday. This was enough pressure-packed golf to test even the most seasoned veteran's endurance and concentration. After his morning round, Palmer trailed the leaders by seven strokes. Ominously, a burly 20-year-old amateur from Columbus, Jack Nicklaus, had inched near the top of the leader board. Palmer began his afternoon round by driving the ball to within 25 feet of the hole on the 365 yard downhill fairway. He tapped his second putt in for a birdie, and then proceeded to birdie five of the next six holes to pull into contention.

Approaching the 17th hole, a weary Ben Hogan stood on the brink of what would have been a crowning championship to cap his storied career. As it turned out, the 47-year-old Hogan was making his last stand. He knew that his tired and aching body would not enable him to prevail in an 18 hole playoff the next day, and so he determined the time had come to take a risk to win the match outright. Instead of pitching up near the elevated green to avoid a large water hazard, Hogan attempted to go for birdie to seal the tournament. His shot to the green landed a few inches short of perfect; for a moment it lingered, but then the heavy backspin Hogan had imparted with his wedge took hold and the ball spun backward down the embankment and into the water. After taking a bogie, an exhausted Hogan hooked his tee shot on the 18th into the water, taking a triple bogie. Palmer, for a change, played it safe and coasted home with two pars. He had shot a record-setting 65 in his final round to win the championship.

Jack the Giant Killer

Palmer's stunning finish in the Open proved to be one of the most pivotal moments in the history of professional golf – it marked the end of the Hogan era. After missing a short putt for a devastating seven, Bantam Ben grimly tipped his hat to the crowd, walked off the 18th green, and dropped out of competitive play. A new chapter had been opened with dramatic flair by the charismatic man from Latrobe. But on the same day that Palmer took center stage and Hogan bid farewell, there emerged a newcomer who would soon engage Palmer in the greatest rivalry in the history of golf. In that final round at Cherry Hills, 20-year-old Jack Nicklaus was paired with Hogan. A student at Ohio State, Nicklaus was playing as an amateur. As they teed off on that fateful 18th, Nicklaus and Hogan were tied, just one stroke behind Palmer. Thinking that he was several strokes off the lead, and apparently shaken from having just witnessed an uncharacteristic meltdown by golf's reputed most accurate shot maker, Nicklaus played the final hole lackadaisically, taking a bogie. Only afterwards did he realize his big mistake. He had finished at 282, just two strokes off Palmer's winning score. He had been in a position to birdie the hole, which would have placed him in a playoff with Palmer. Nicklaus vowed that he would never again make that mistake. Supremely confident in his abilities, on that day Nicklaus set his sights on Palmer.

Other than their love of the game of golf and their fierce competitive drive, the two men destined to dominate golf for years to come shared little in common. Nicklaus had been raised in an upper-middle-class suburb on the northwest edge of Columbus. His father operated four pharmacies, which made it possible for him to invest substantial sums in Jack's golfing education. Jack's father was a member of the exclusive Scioto Country Club, and it was there that the husky youth received extensive instruction from acclaimed golf instructor Jack Grout. Encouraged by his parents, Nicklaus soon became the talk of Columbus – and well beyond. He won the Ohio State Junior Match Play Tournament at the age of 13, defeating boys several years his senior. As his game improved, he spent more and more time with Grout. By the time he enrolled at Ohio State, Nicklaus had won 14 amateur tournaments, including the United States Amateur. Following his record-setting second-place finish as an amateur at Cherry Hills, he won the US Amateur for the second time in 1961, a victory that gave him the confidence to turn professional.

The Palmer–Nicklaus rivalry took root at the 1962 Open played at Oakmont Country Club near Pittsburgh. Legendary for its narrow fairways and 210 bunkers, including the famed "Church Pews," Oakmont was just 40 miles from Latrobe and Palmer had played the course many times. The previous August, he had won the British Open and in April had turned back his good friend Dow Finsterwald and the up-and-coming South African Gary Player in an 18 hole playoff to win his second Masters. Going into the tournament, Oakmont had the feel of an impending coronation for the guy from nearby Latrobe.

In his initial foray onto the tour, Nicklaus had yet to live up to the lofty predictions that had accompanied his announcement the previous November that he was turning professional. He had been well off the lead in all 16 tournaments that year while Palmer came to Oakmont with considerable momentum. Ten years Nicklaus' senior, Palmer had seven years of professional experience, during which time he had won 30 tournaments, including five majors. At the peak of his game at age 33, he was on a big-time roll. Beginning with the Palm Springs Classic in January, he had won six tournaments, including a dramatic come-from-behind victory in the Masters over Gary Player that prompted Augusta sports editor Johnny Hendrix to call Palmer "the greatest comeback player golf has ever seen." But everyone, including a wary Palmer, knew that "the fat kid" with the high, long fade off the tee was ready for a breakthrough, and the tournament directors understood as much, placing them in the same threesome for the opening round on Thursday. Palmer had first encountered Nicklaus, still in high school, in 1958 when they played an exhibition at Ohio University in Athens. Palmer recalled being amazed by the strong kid "with a butch haircut and a high fade," who demonstrated stunning distance during a driving contest with Palmer. "I made [then] a mental note on the spot to always keep an eye on this upstart kid, because with his skills and eerie composure under fire it was probably only a matter of time before he was giving us all a run for the prize money."

A record crowd of over 17,000 showed up at Oakmont for opening day, and it seemed as if nearly all of them were enlistees in Arnie's Army. After two rounds, Palmer was tied for the lead with Bob Rosburg and held a three stroke advantage over Nicklaus. However, the biggest story of the tournament was the behavior of Palmer's fanatic supporters. Perhaps the fans thought they were at a Steelers football game as they trampled all over the niceties of golfing etiquette. They boisterously cheered Palmer's every shot, and yelled even louder when one of Nicklaus' putts slipped by the hole. It was their raucous attempt to intimidate or distract Nicklaus that was so shocking. As Nicklaus calmly went about his game, he tried to ignore the many taunts about his weight. Nicklaus had permitted considerable bulk to accumulate around his waist. His thick thighs and broad shoulders gave a heightened impression of his size. He had suffered the indignity of a headline in *Sports Illustrated* labeling him "One Whale of a Golfer." Thus as the 22-year-old first year professional made his way around the course, he heard himself crudely called out as "Ohio Fats" and "Fat Gut."

On the second day, with the two adversaries once more playing in the same group, additional marshals were summoned to help preserve a reasonable level of spectator decorum. A reporter for the *New York Herald Tribune* said that he felt as if he were "covering a lynching." Palmer would apologize to Jack for his supporters' behavior, and Nicklaus would say that he had blocked out the taunts. But Nicklaus had read a comment in the Pittsburgh newspapers from Palmer on the eve of the tournament: "Everybody says there's only one favorite, and that's me. But you'd better watch out for the fat boy."

The deplorable crowd behavior, however, only made Nicklaus more determined. He ignored the hostile gallery and focused on his game. In the end, it was Palmer who felt the pressure, trying extra hard to please his army of fans and anxiously attempting to fend off his youthful challenger. As the 36 hole marathon on Saturday began to unfold, Palmer seemed confident and in control. With just 11 holes to play, he had edged out to a five stroke lead, but then the momentum of the match turned. After slugging a long 3-wood to the right side of the ninth hole, Palmer inexplicably dubbed a chip out of the tall grass, and instead of scoring a possible eagle, ended up with a mere par after missing a ten foot putt. Meanwhile, Nicklaus was getting hot, ripping off a string of birdies. By the 14th hole, they were tied for the lead and Arnie's Army, which had mellowed with their man far out in front, resumed their nasty verbal assault upon the upstart who dared challenge their local hero. On the 18th, Nicklaus narrowly missed a 15 foot birdie putt and ended the tournament at 283. Palmer had left his approach shot 10 feet short, and suddenly the enormous crowd of 24,000, which had shaken the course all day with its riotous cheering, became deathly silent as Palmer went into his familiar knock-knee putting stance, looking for a birdie to seal the win. His putt slid by the hole and his Army let out an anguished groan.

The 18 hole playoff on Sunday established the rivalry. Palmer pulled his opening drive on number one into the rough on the right and Nicklaus made a statement about the upcoming playoff when he blasted a 300 yard drive down the right side of the fairway. The enormous gallery was at least 95 percent for Palmer, but Nicklaus quieted his antagonists by parring the hole in workmanlike fashion while Palmer took a discouraging bogie; Jack extended his lead to two strokes on number four with a birdie putt. Some members of Arnie's Army had even taken to stomping their feet while Nicklaus putted, but to no avail. By the 10th hole, Jack, playing methodically, had a four-stroke lead. Palmer closed to within one stroke on the 15th, but he lost his emotional edge as he watched Nicklaus continue to play errorless golf. On the final hole, Palmer gambled by attempting to knock in a downhill chip, but it rolled past the hole, resulting in a double bogie. Nicklaus calmly putted out for a three-stroke victory.

"I just wanted to win so badly," Palmer lamented. "I can't play any better than I played here, and I still couldn't win. And that Nicklaus

Figure 5.1 Arnold Palmer gives rival Jack Nicklaus a friendly tap on the jaw after Nicklaus defeated him in an 18-hole playoff for the 1962 US Open title at Oakmont. © Bettmann/CORBIS

. . . he played super." Palmer later conceded that his young rival was "a different animal altogether . . . he didn't seem the slightest bit bothered by the electricity of my charge and the cries by my supporters. If anything, they seemed to drive him further into that hard cocoon of concentration. I had never seen anyone who could stay focused the way he did – and I've never seen anyone with the same ability since." As the two golfers accepted their prize money and made their final comments to the press, Palmer prophetically said, "Now that the big guy is out of the cage, everybody better run for cover." On that Sunday afternoon in June of 1962, the chubby 22-year-old with the buzz haircut had won his first tournament, the first of 18 majors he would accumulate. Jack Nicklaus had metamorphosed from "the fat guy" into "the big guy."

Golf's Greatest Rivalry

And thus did the two giants settle into a decade of stirring duels. Palmer recovered from his disappointment at Oakmont by winning his second consecutive British Open, playing the daunting Troon course with his usual flair, while Nicklaus stumbled badly, taking a horrendous ten on the 11th hole the first day and staggering to finish a humiliating 29 strokes behind Palmer. That proved to be a mere blip on golf's radar screen, however, as Nicklaus won the 1963 Masters despite a bursitis attack in his hip. During the final round, he saw defending champion Palmer disappear under a flurry of bogies. On the back nine, veteran Sammy Snead finally wilted, and Nicklaus edged Tony Lema by one stroke. "Just think," Palmer mused as he slid the size 44 Green Jacket over Nicklaus's imposing 215 pound frame, "he has ten years more to go before he's as old as I am today." For Palmer, his spot atop the world of golf had become precarious. He recognized that in Nicklaus he had a rival who had elevated golf to a new level.

Palmer entered the 1964 Masters determined to reclaim the Green Jacket from his adversary. He was now 34 years of age, and even some of the most ardent soldiers in his Army feared that he might have passed his prime since he had not won a major the previous year; winning majors had become the demanding criteria that many journalists and fans used, however unfairly, to measure the status of an elite golfer. All the while, the more-or-less "friendly" rivalry between Palmer and Nicklaus continued to grow. At the 1963 World Series of Golf tournament in Akron, a made-for-TV event that paired the four major tournament winners in a 36 hole competition, Palmer, who had not won a major the previous year, was invited to participate after winning a special "qualifying play-off." He joined with British Open champion Bob Charles, US Open winner Julius Boros, and Nicklaus, who had won both the Masters and PGA. At a pre-tournament media confab, Nicklaus, with a smirk on his face, kicked Palmer's chair for effect as he said, "If this is a contest for champions, then Arnold doesn't belong here. Arnie's strictly an also-ran in the major events. Isn't that right, Arnie?" The next day, sports pages across the country reported the incident with the term "also-ran" heavily emphasized. After Nicklaus captured his second consecutive World Series, Palmer and his millions of fans were even more determined to reverse the onrushing tide.

Opening day of the 1964 Masters witnessed Palmer resolutely taking a two stroke lead over Jack with a 69. Nicklaus was once more subjected to constant barbs tossed out of the gallery by Palmer supporters. When Palmer teed off on Sunday for the final round, he held a compelling nine stroke lead over Nicklaus, and, with a three-round total of just 206, stood on the brink of erasing Ben Hogan's 1953 tournament record of 274.

But Nicklaus was not about to go away, and by the 14th hole, he had shaved five strokes off of Palmer's seemingly insurmountable lead, making a Palmeresque charge. On the 16th hole, however, Nicklaus narrowly missed a 30 foot putt that would have had Arnie squirming and Palmer then cruised to a comfortable six-stroke victory over Nicklaus and Dave Marr.

A New Way to Keep Score

By the time that Nicklaus slid the Green Jacket over Palmer's shoulders that April evening, the two men had moved their competition on to another level – which man could turn his golfing fame into more money. In 1960, Palmer secured the services of Mark McCormack, head of the innovative sports marketing firm International Management Group (IMG), to help create Arnold Palmer Enterprises. Palmer had recognized that his golfing success could lead to many financial opportunities, but his gut instinct told him that he could also be played for a fool by a fast-talking sharper, and so he wisely turned to McCormack.

After Palmer won his second Masters in 1960, McCormack moved quickly to capitalize. The endorsements flooded in with a rush to Arnold Palmer Enterprises. When McCormack could not persuade Wilson Sporting Goods to agree to amend its contract with Palmer to permit him to actually design the clubs that were marketed under his name to his own specifications, he stunned the Wilson hierarchy by permitting the contract to expire at the end of 1963 and then contracted with a Chattanooga company to make and market clubs actually designed by Palmer. Within a year, Wilson executives undoubtedly wished they had been amenable to Palmer's wishes, for the new company sold over 100,000 sets of clubs in its first year of operation.

McCormack shrewdly exploited Palmer's golfing fame as well as his attractive physical appearance and engaging personality. Palmer now commanded a $5,000 fee to play exhibitions, an amount that would escalate over the years. He drank Coca-Cola on the course while playing in tournaments, and so he naturally became a spokesman for the soft drink company. By 1965, Palmer's smiling face appeared in magazine advertisements, on television, and on billboards, proclaiming the virtues of a wide array of goods including shaving lotions, deodorants, automobiles, petroleum products, shoes, power tools, and golfing equipment and attire. You could learn to play the game by reading his instructional books, carry your Arnold Palmer signature golf clubs in an Arnold Palmer bag, and play a round wearing Arnold Palmer golfing clothing and shoes. And afterward, you could even have those clothes cleaned at one of 110 Arnold Palmer franchised dry cleaning establishments. In 1967, Palmer ended up a close second on the tournament earnings list with $184,000, but his ancillary projects more than tripled his winnings. McCormack told the *Wall Street Journal* that his client had become so popular that, "He has reached the point where his on-course successes aren't terribly important to his enterprises anymore."

A Changing of the Guard

Mark McCormack may have satisfied Palmer's desire for financial security, but Palmer had to live with the fact that on the golf course he was falling further behind Nicklaus. At the 1967 US Open at Baltusrol Golf Club in New Jersey, he thought he had a good chance to reclaim the top spot. He had played very well in 12 tournaments that year, winning the Los Angeles and Tucson Opens, and finishing among the top four finishers seven other times. His hopes were further encouraged by the fact that Nicklaus had fallen into an uncharacteristic slump. They teed off on Sunday tied for second, one stroke behind Marty Fleckman. Palmer proceeded to shoot a blistering 69, finishing the tournament at 279, which would normally produce a championship. But Nicklaus returned to top form on the final day, recording a remarkable 65; his tournament score of 275 broke Ben Hogan's US Open record. Nicklaus later said, matter of factly, that as that final round ended he came to the realization that he would not lose another major to Palmer. "I just felt like I was the better player," he recalled. "Arnold was the best player in the world for about seven years, but then he ceased being so."

Nicklaus was correct: Baltusrol had indeed signaled that Palmer's stay at the top of the world of golf was coming to an end. In 1968, Palmer shot a 79 on the second day and missed the cut at the Masters, and in June he finished 59th at the US Open. After finishing an encouraging tenth at the British Open, he made his final charge at a major in San Antonio at the PGA, the only major he had never won. But he missed an eight foot putt on the 72nd hole to finish one stroke behind Julius Boros. The following year, he suffered the indignity of having to qualify for the US Open because he had failed to meet any of the standard criteria for automatic entry (i.e., having won a major in the previous five years, having finished in the top 15 at the previous Open, or being among the top 15 PGA money winners). He managed to win the Danny Thomas and the Heritage tournaments in 1969, but time was rapidly taking its toll on his game.

When Palmer turned 40 in September of 1969, *Sports Illustrated* featured him on the cover, somberly announcing a "Farewell to an Era." In 1958, as he was surging to the top of his profession, Palmer had prophetically said, "The trouble with golf is that as you learn more, you get older and you start to lose out physically and in concentration. If there was a way you could stay young for 30 years and keep learning all that time, you might have a perfect golfer." Two years later he reluctantly admitted that his eyesight had deteriorated; for a time he wore eyeglasses, but they bothered his concentration. He soon opted for contacts, but found that his eyes became dry and itchy on windy days. "I'm 42," he explained. "I'm not going to try to birdie the world anymore." He won his last tour victory in 1973, capturing the Bob Hope Desert Classic for the fifth time, slipping in a birdie putt on the final hole to edge his playing partner, Jack Nicklaus, by a stroke.

His last hurrah came at the US Open at his old haunt at Oakmont. The media played up the rivalry: Nicklaus was in his prime; Palmer was barely hanging on, but he rallied and stayed in contention throughout the tournament. On the back nine on the final day, however, his short game deserted him. Significantly, at tournament's end, he and Nicklaus ended up tied, just as they had at the remarkable 1962 Open played on the same course. But this time there would be no playoff, because Johnny Miller had gone on an incredible final day birdie binge (eight) and won the tournament going away when he shot a record 63. Ironically, relatively few people saw many of Miller's amazing shots that day for most spectators had signed on for one of the last marches of Arnie's Army.

Precarious Enterprises

Palmer's descent from the top tier of competitive golf was disappointing to his fans, but he moved into the twilight of his career playing with the same verve and determination as ever. The fact that he absolutely loved the game of golf gave him the motivation to continue to play despite the disappointing results. His decline was paralleled by Jack Nicklaus' ascent to the unquestioned top of his profession. Palmer had won seven majors during his prime, and Nicklaus, at age 30, surpassed that in 1970 when he captured the British Open. At this juncture, Nicklaus had undergone a major transformation. He rid himself of the "fat guy" reputation by entering a Weight Watcher's program, shedding 25 pounds to bring his weight down to a svelte 185 pounds. He also responded to his wife's prodding and recast his sometimes bland, sometimes garish golfing wardrobe to jump-start the launching of his own golf clothing line. He also let his buzz cut grow into a mod foppish look that made him, for the first time, a truly photogenic target on the golf course.

Appreciative fans dubbed him The Golden Bear, and with Palmer fading, he found a much more appreciative audience as he practiced his craft. No longer did he hear caustic comments about his weight as he walked down fairways, and the applause was much more spontaneous and generous, although he never reached the level of adoration heaped upon Palmer. Significantly, no one emerged to replace Palmer as a major adversary. There were major competitors, of course, and Nicklaus had many a lively battle with Lee Trevino, Johnny Miller, Tom Watson, and Gary Player. Nicklaus appreciated the fact that fans now began to display real affection toward him. "Yea, absolutely, I liked that," he recalled. "Here you are a little fat boy and all of a sudden you've got a different image. Sure, of course you like that. Why wouldn't you?"

Although he had surpassed Palmer on the golf course, Nicklaus recognized that he was woefully behind in the money game. Mark McCormack and IMG had made Palmer a very wealthy man, and, in 1963, Palmer generously agreed to relax his exclusivity agreement so that McCormack could also work his financial magic for Nicklaus. Despite their rivalry, the adversaries had become friends off the golf course, each appreciating the talents of the other, but in competition they were still driven to beat the brains out of each other every time they met. Palmer flew Nicklaus to tournaments aboard his twin-engine Commander Jet, but that one-upmanship could not last; of course, Nicklaus had to have his own private airplane, which he learned to pilot. Nicklaus says that he became convinced that a private aircraft was a good investment in part because of the travails of flying commercial – especially when his golf clubs got lost – but also because, like Palmer, he found a personal aircraft was a major time-saver. With his private jet, named Air Bear, Nicklaus said, "I can make almost as many stops around the United States in a day as I could in a week flying commercially, and still often eat breakfast or dinner in my own home." He came to look upon his airplane as "my most essential and efficient business tool."

Palmer was the clear winner in the subtle competition for off-course revenue that the two men found themselves engaged in by the mid-1960s. McCormack could not work the same financial magic for Nicklaus as he did for Palmer. The reason was simple: "Arnold was King and Jack was the Prince who was more like the ugly duckling," recalled a CBS producer for golf telecasts. "Jack was the baby blimp with big, fat pleated trousers that made him look even bigger. He was no matinee idol." It all began with their playing style: Palmer was the irrepressible, exciting, go-for-broke gambler; Nicklaus, remained the ever-so-careful golfer who studied each shot and was often excruciatingly slow to putt, whose play was as methodical as the tick-tock of a clock. Palmer simply had that indefinable something that Nicklaus lacked: charisma. And, as their two autobiographies indicate, Palmer clearly enjoyed devoting much more time to his business enterprises on a sustained basis than did Nicklaus.

Mark McCormack undoubtedly owed his first allegiance to Palmer. However, try as he might, he found Nicklaus's public persona hard to sell. Jack did not see it that way: "They [IMG] represented me for nine years and I made no money. That's why I left. Arnold was most important to them. . . . and so I said, 'Well, the only way I'm going to do this is to do it myself.'" Thus, in 1970, Nicklaus decided to go his own way.

Having severed relations with McCormack and IMG, Nicklaus joined forces with a long-time friend and successful owner of a heavy construction company who had the imposing name of Putnam Sandals Pierman. Nicklaus was entering a field in which he lacked experience. Up to this point in 1970, he had concentrated nearly all of his attention on golf and his family and, unlike Palmer, he never exhibited the almost-obsessive concern with the details of his business interests. Nicklaus and Pierman called their new venture Golden Bear, Inc. and brought in a team of six executives to head up the various divisions. For a time, Nicklaus did immerse himself in the decisions involved in getting his company up and running but he soon opted to delegate day-to-day operations of Golden Bear to Pierman. In 1975, however, Pierman departed for new adventures and Nicklaus found himself making decisions that had multimillion dollar implications. He later confessed that he was overwhelmed by "the mass of daily decisions involving detail as well as policy" to the point where he could not devote enough time to his primary goal in life, "winning golf tournaments."

Nicklaus thereupon hired Charles "Chuck" Perry to take on the day-to-day operation of Golden Bear. His new executive had significant experience in running a publishing company as well as serving as the founding president of Florida International University. Their relationship seemed to work well for nearly a decade but, with Nicklaus focused on golf, Perry operated aggressively, investing in ventures that were far removed from anything even remotely connected to golf. As long as profits were realized, that was fine with Nicklaus, but in 1985 he was shocked to learn that Golden Bear had taken on a staggering debt load. There were large investments of dubious quality and Nicklaus faced an ocean of red ink: "I basically had the obligation of over a hundred million dollars, which I had no way in the world of ever repaying." Some estimated his liabilities to be as high as $150 million. He confronted "imminent financial disaster," with bankruptcy a distinct possibility.

Nicklaus and a new set of advisors managed to renegotiate many of the obligations, and obtain sufficient refinancing and important contract extensions and modifications to satisfy his creditors, but the experience was traumatic. It took more than five years to erase the problems. Nicklaus ultimately was able to satisfy his obligations "to the tune of a lot of millions of dollars." As Ian O'Connor observes in his book, Nicklaus, the baby-boomer raised in a country club setting by relatively affluent parents, was a conservative golfer who got himself into deep financial trouble by being "a reckless businessman." That situation contrasted sharply with the conservative business philosophy consistently followed by Arnold Palmer, the oft-reckless golfer, as he built his massive financial empire.

Golf's New Architects

By the early 1990s, Nicklaus had righted his severely listing financial ship, and he did so by channeling much of his business activity into his golf course design company. It was something he enjoyed and understood, and he demonstrated a unique flair that brought in many lucrative contracts. He had begun dabbling in course design early in his career, and in 1969 he and Pete Dye joined forces to produce Harbour Town Golf Links at Hilton Head. For years he had ruminated about designing a world-class golf course in his hometown of Columbus, and he ultimately selected a rolling wooded site in the suburban town of Dublin for Muirfield Village Golf Club, which he intended would become a regular stop on the PGA tour. He acquired some 1,500 acres and planned a top-notch golf course complete with a large luxury housing development. Although he claims to have developed an interest in course design as a teenager, there is little doubt that his decision to build a PGA tournament-quality course was prompted in part by Arnold Palmer's purchase of the Bay Hill Golf Course near Orlando that he upgraded into a championship venue. Nicklaus was well aware that Arnold Palmer Enterprises was emerging as a leader in golf course construction, with more than a dozen courses already open, and many more under development. Once more the competitive juices began to flow.

Muirfield Village almost never got beyond the planning stage. After announcing his plans in 1968, the initial financing package fell through, and it was not until 1972 that he had a deal in place. Nicklaus concedes that the project almost failed due to his "naivety" about financing such an ambitious project. Even before any dirt was moved to sculpt what ultimately became an exquisite golf course, he readily concedes, "The project did come awfully close to taking me down the tubes. My financial picture then was nowhere near as strong as it would become later, but by 1971 I was personally carrying more than fifteen hundred acres of prime development property, every square inch of it nonproductive." After many delays, Nicklaus finally was able to play the symbolic initial round in October of 1974. In 1976, the inaugural Memorial Tournament – an invitational event – was played at Muirfield and it became one of the most prestigious stops on the tour outside the majors. Inspired by his success, and having learned a great deal about the complexities of the development business, Nicklaus concentrated much of his efforts on course design, leaving the financing and development aspects to those who hired him. Eventually, his company designed more than 200 courses located in some 30 states and 25 countries.

Just as their approaches to playing the game of golf were studies in sharp contrast, the personalities of Palmer and Nicklaus were revealed in their golf courses. Some technically inclined critics have suggested that Palmer tended to produce courses that required a draw off the tee, while Nicklaus, well known for his high fades, tended to design more holes that had a rightward tilt. What is clear is that the man who learned to play the game at the elite Scioto Country Club concentrated his efforts on elite courses that featured upscale housing developments. Palmer's company, in contrast, willingly took on projects that varied from inexpensive public courses all the way to the high end, such as the exclusive golfing venue of Old Tabby Links at Spring Island, South Carolina.

Palmer tended to be much less directly involved in the details of a specific project than Nicklaus, relying heavily upon his staff, who he expected to bring a project in on time and on budget. Palmer Course Design, emphasizing "playability and versatility," proved to be a steady money-maker. Although Nicklaus also had talented staff to do much of the detail work, he personally involved himself in each of the courses that would carry his name, walking the area multiple times to assure that the natural landscape would be emphasized. By varying the location of five separate tee boxes on each hole, he sought to provide unique challenges for golfers ranging from the average weekend player to the professional. "My number-one goal," he writes, "is to make the player use his mind ahead of his muscles – to control his emotions sufficiently to really think through his options before drawing a club from the bag." As Nicklaus's fame as a designer grew, the fees he could charge continued to increase. By the mid-1980s his standard fee was in the neighborhood of $1.5 million and, to his way of thinking, he had gotten the best of his rival when it came to creating true golfing environments.

The differences in their approaches to course design, reflecting their contrasting approaches to the game itself, were readily seen in the two courses with which they were initially most closely identified, Bay Hill and Muirfield Village. Bay Hill was built on the flat terrain of central Florida, and the individual holes, while attractive, are clearly designed for the power player; they featured wide fairways, few bunkers, and greens that are receptive to balls bouncing in from the fairway. Muirfield, on the other hand, had a feeling reminiscent of some of the great golfing venues: Augusta National, Shinnicock, Baltusrol, Oakmont. Most of the tee boxes were located above the sloping fairways, and the greens were well protected by bunkers and often elevated.

Even the two tournaments that are held at Muirfield and Bay Hill present a distinctly different ambience. The Bay Hill Classic (its name changed to the Arnold Palmer Invitational Tournament in 2008) is heavily underwritten by corporate sponsors; at the Muirfield Memorial, corporate signs and tents are barely visible, with the emphasis at this event being strictly upon the Augusta-like ambience that its designer had attempted to capture. Nicklaus best summed up the differences: "I don't really look at Arnold as a competitor in the golf course design business.

Arnold doesn't get into the design of the golf course. Arnold gets into the promotion of the golf course and does a damn good job of it. . . . If someone's interested in having a name on a golf course and the strength and promotion of it, Arnold's a good guy to have. But if they're interested in the quality of the facility and what they're trying to do with it, then they're looking at me."

Triumph in the Sunset

Some observers believed that Arnold Palmer's rapid decline as a tour professional resulted from his spending too much time on his business ventures, but the fact was that he began to lose his magic touch around the greens as he entered his 40s. The Senior Tour was inaugurated in 1980, and it got a major boost when Palmer agreed to take part. Like many professionals who had come to love the excitement and glamour of the regular tour, Palmer viewed the Seniors with considerable ambivalence. As he approached his 50th birthday in September of 1979, Palmer had come to accept that "I'd seen my putting touch go in the tank. . . ." To further complicate matters, he admitted to "having fits with my vision, wrestling with eyeglasses and finally growing accustomed to wearing contact lenses." So, in 1980, Palmer "managed to fend off an attack of the nerves," as he later wrote, to win the PGA Senior's Championship. He defeated Billy Casper in a playoff to win the 1982 US Senior Open, and that victory helped boost television ratings and was a major factor in making the Seniors Tour a modest success. Devoting more and more time to his flourishing businesses, Palmer cut back on his appearance at seniors events, winning the last of ten victories at the Crestar Classic as he approached his 60th birthday.

As Palmer entered the sunset years of his golfing career, Nicklaus entered his brightest phase. Despite his many difficulties in the world of business, Jack was able to keep a sharp focus on his game. He had already surpassed Palmer's seven majors with his 1970 British Open victory and the following year won his second PGA championship, making him the only person to have won each of the majors twice. During the 1970s Nicklaus was at the top of his game, winning a total of 38 tournaments, including eight majors. His fifth Masters championship in 1975 was undoubtedly one of the most satisfying of his many triumphs. Caught up in a dogfight with Tom Weiskopf and Johnny Miller on the final day, he drilled a long drive on the par 5 15th, thinking that he needed a birdie on this hole to maintain his one stroke lead. His ball somehow came to rest nestled precariously atop a little mound. He carefully calculated the distance to the pin at 246 yards and proceeded to hit a 1-iron that landed softly on the green and rolled just ten feet past the hole. He recalled 20 years later that this shot "may just have been the best full shot under extreme pressure I have ever hit." The ensuing birdie propelled him to a one stroke victory over Weiskopf and Miller. The tension on the final holes was palpable, but he recalled:

> To be out there in the middle of that is just the greatest fun. You're inspired, you're eager, you're excited. You almost want to break into a dead run when you hit a good shot. It's what you've prepared yourself for, what you've waited for, what keeps you ticking. To know you can look back someday and recall you were a part of something like that, well, that's just the greatest. I've never had more fun in my life.

It was altogether fitting that Nicklaus would win his final major at the 1986 Masters. He improbably did so at the age of 46 at a time when journalists were suggesting he had become the Olden Bear. He candidly admitted that he "was not the golfer of a decade earlier," and had not won a major since 1980, when he captured both the US Open and PGA. He had not won any tournament since he had taken his own Memorial in 1984. Entering the final day at Augusta, Nicklaus was four strokes off the pace but by the time he reached the back nine he had narrowed the gap and found himself caught up in a battle with Seve Ballesteros, Greg Norman, and Tom Kite. And then, as if in a time warp, he became once more the Golden Bear. He shot an eagle on 15 and dropped birdie putts on 16 and 17 to take the lead. When he took the lead, the roar of the crowd was overwhelming. Long gone were the snide barbs and catcalls. It was, Dave Anderson wrote in the *New York Times*, "a love-in. That was the way Arnold used to win, coming from behind. . . . Now Jack had his own army, so to speak, and it was incredible to watch it come together." On 18, he had to brush tears out of his eyes, as he recognized that he stood on the brink of pulling off one of the greatest victories in golfing history. He had a difficult 40 foot putt on the lightning-fast green, but he left the ball just four inches from the hole. He then tapped in for an astounding back-nine 30. He had shot an improbable 65 for the day.

Ed Pope of the *Miami Herald* watched this incredible event unfold, writing that "Nicklaus had become almost like Arnie. . . . He'd gotten past

Figure 5.2   Lining up a crucial putt at the 1973 Ryder Cup in St Louis. Arnold Palmer gives his friendly rival Jack Nicklaus the benefit of his reading of the line in the international competition that permitted them to become teammates. © Bettmann/CORBIS

the pudgy, smokey image he once had. . . . He'd generated so much good will, just like Arnie, and Jack loved it." Many in the gallery were wiping away the tears along with Jack as he made his way up the 18th fairway. "They were just as happy to see this happen, for Jack to end up like Arnold at Augusta."

Late in the 20th century, a distinguished panel of journalists named Nicklaus the "Golfer of the Century," selecting him over Bobby Jones, Ben Hogan, and, of course, Arnold Palmer. Nicklaus ended his career with 73 PGA tour victories, including 18 majors. Palmer won seven majors and a total of 62 tour events. When Tiger Woods burst onto the golfing scene near the turn of the new century, he paid the ultimate tribute to Nicklaus when he announced that his career goal was to exceed Jack's 18 majors victories.

Both Palmer and Nicklaus helped make the other a better golfer, as well as a more focused competitor. Despite the intensity of their competitive natures, they never permitted their rivalry to become embittered. Each developed a deep respect for the other, recognizing all the while that they were very different human beings. They paired up to win the Canada Cup and World Cup on five occasions during the 1960s and were teammates on Ryder Cup teams. They played innumerable exhibitions together. They flew on each other's airplanes, played cards, joked, and frequently dined together. They also endlessly needled each other with barbed comments. Early on, their wives became friends, often walking the course together on the final day as their husbands engaged in another duel. In short, the rivalry between Arnold Palmer and Jack Nicklaus was a healthy one because it produced a life-long friendship, forged under the heat of intense competition. Nicklaus notes that when he came on the tour, he looked to Palmer as the measuring stick by which to assess his own progress. "Even though he was also the guy I would be taking aim at, as a rookie pro the prospect of having such a man as a friend was most appealing." Palmer has a similar take on things, noting that, "Our rivalry . . . happened at a time when golf was just beginning to take deep root in the broader American sports psyche, and the intensity of our competition, as well as the distinct differences in our personalities, created tremendous natural drama and a fan interest in the professional game that had never been seen before."

He adds, "On the course there was – and still is – nobody I wanted to beat more. . . . And I'm certain Jack feels exactly the same way."

Familiarity breeds contempt. (Celtics' Kevin McHale about playing the Lakers frequently in NBA finals)

They're a bunch of thugs. (Lakers coach Pat Riley on McHale's violent foul of Kurt Rambis)

Nearly all of the great team rivalries in the history of American sports have thrived because of the proximity of the competitors. One of the most notable exceptions to this rule is the long-standing rivalry between the distant coastal cities of Boston and Los Angeles in the National Basketball Association. One statistic stands out: of the 62 league championships won between 1947 and 2009, the Celtics and the Lakers combined have taken more than half. On 11 occasions, they faced off in the championship series, nine of which went to six or seven games. Distance aside, all of the ingredients have been there to make the Celtics–Lakers rivalry red-hot – excellent coaches and great players who have come together to form dominant teams that set the standard for excellence in the NBA over five decades.

The two teams first tangled in the NBA finals in 1959 when the Lakers were still in Minneapolis. It was not much of a contest, as the Celtics romped to a four game sweep. That the Lakers made it to the finals was surprising enough, because they had fallen on hard times after they had won five of the first eight NBA titles of the small eight team league, dominating such teams as the Rochester Royals, the Tri-Cities Blackhawks, Fort Wayne Zollner Pistons, and the Syracuse Nationals. The Lakers enjoyed their early dominance because of the presence of the first truly great big man in American professional basketball: 6'10", 245 pound George Mikan. The strong center with thick eyeglasses blocked shots, dominated the backboards, and averaged 25 points a game.

In the spring of 1949, the Lakers defeated the Washington Capitals and their young coach Arnold Auerbach in the decisive seventh game of the championship series.

That Damned Cigar

After coaching the Tri-Cities Blackhawks during the 1949–50 season, Auerbach was hired by Boston Celtics owner Walter Brown who hoped to resuscitate a lackluster team that had just ended the season 22–46. A native of New York City, the new coach was strong-willed, aggressive, outspoken, and possessed of a fiery temper. He had learned the intricacies of man-to-man defense and set offenses on the playgrounds and in high school competition in Brooklyn, and then played guard at George Washington University where he was introduced to the potentials of the fast break offense.

Auerbach immediately changed the perennial losers by emphasizing a pressing defense and a fast break attack. His up-tempo offense was led by guard Bob Cousy, who he reluctantly acquired from the defunct Chicago Stags. Long-time Lakers radio announcer Chick Hearn believed that two things saved the struggling NBA in the early 1950s: Bob Cousy's "fancy passing" and the introduction of the 24 second shot clock that ended the slowdown offenses such as those run by the Lakers to accommodate the slow-of-foot Mikan. In Auerbach's first year, Cousy's ball-handling magic (no-look passes, behind-the-back passes, adroit dribbling), which many basketball experts (including Auerbach) had dismissed as "grandstanding," sparked an exciting offense that helped produce the Celtics' first winning season. Cousy became an instant favorite among fans, and attendance soared. The next year, Auerbach added sharp-shooting Bill Sharman to the backcourt, but the Celtics lacked strength up front and so they endured early departures from the playoffs. He solved that problem in 1956 by trading local favorite "Easy Ed" McCauley to acquire center Bill Russell. The future of the Celtics was assured.

Many of his players said that Auerbach's greatest strength was in motivating them, not in his mastery of the X's and O's. Focused intently upon winning, he did not play favorites and was quick to make personnel changes. His preseason workouts were legendary for the amount of running he required as he drove his team to be in top condition by opening day. Many of his players said that while they often played in fear of their demanding coach, they also appreciated his direct means of communication and ability to produce championship performances.

Opposing coaches, players, and fans were not of the same mind. The flamboyant redhead was the target of abuse on the road and he was generally disliked by his coaching peers. Typically, Al Cervi, coach of the Syracuse Nationals, dismissed Auerbach's winning record as the result of having better talent, ignoring the fact that he was also general manager in charge of personnel. Auerbach was not hesitant to take credit for his team's success, and enjoyed rubbing it in. When a game was safely in hand, he would sit back in his seat, take out an expensive cigar, unwrap it with ceremonial care, gently twirl it under his nose to savor the fragrance, emphatically light a match, and blow the smoke high into the air as if sending up a smoke signal proclaiming victory. Opposing coaches protested his arrogant routine as a put-down, which it was. "I thought it was funny," Bill Russell said. "It was part of what made us what we were. Ungracious? What's that got to do with it? Red never was gracious. Who cares about that? We certainly didn't."

Lakers coach Fred Schaus was certainly not gracious in his observations: "The success of the Celtics was not due to Auerbach, but to Bill Russell. I respect Red's ability to coach and judge talent, but not his attitude. Not too many people in the NBA liked it when he lit up the cigar, and when you lose to him in the finals four times, as I did, it can get to you. I don't like him. I just plain don't like him, and he knows it. The cigar wasn't necessary. I didn't admire some of the things Red said and did. It would have been nice to make him choke on that cigar." Celtics forward Satch Sanders got it right about Auerbach's signature moment: "Of course he was hated. He won all the time. You respected him, but there's not much love lost. And Red would rub it in. Blow that smoke."

Number Six

Bill Russell had led the San Francisco Dons to 55 consecutive wins and two NCAA championships. He stood 6'9" and was blessed with long arms, great jumping ability, and incredible agility. His shooting abilities were modest, and he even had difficulty dribbling the basketball. But he could rebound and block shots unlike anyone else. Russell was extraordinarily intelligent and possessed of an excellent memory. If an opponent beat him with an unusual move, Russell would file it away in his memory

Figure 6.1 Boston fans knew victory was assured when Celtics coach
Red Auerbach sat back and lit up one of his famous cigars. Here he puffs
contentedly in 1966 while sneaking a peek at the overhead scoreboard. When
the city fathers of Boston placed a life-size statue of Auerbach in a prominent
downtown location, his cigar was there for future generations to admire.
© Bettmann/CORBIS

bank and negate it the next time around. Russell dominated both the
offensive and defensive backboards, and his quick outlet passes ignited a
blistering fast break. Russell also turned the Celtics into the league's best
defensive team because he dominated the key. His teammates learned that
they could overplay their opponents to the outside, because if they drove
into the lane, Russell would reject their shots or force an off balance
attempt.

In signing Russell, Auerbach brought to Boston the city's first great
African-American athlete. In his rookie season, Russell was the only black
on the team, but he was joined in 1958 by his USF teammate and defensive whiz K. C. Jones. In 1960, Auerbach drafted forward Tom "Satch"
Sanders, the consummate team player and defender out of New York
University. The Celtics became one of the league's pioneers in promoting racial integration, paralleling the civil rights movement of the late

Figure 6.2 A titanic battle of basketball giants occurred in the championship series of 1969 when centers Bill Russell and Wilt Chamberlain matched up in the key. In this photograph, 6'10" player-coach Russell tosses a hook shot over the 7'3" Chamberlain. © Bettmann/CORBIS

1950s and early 1960s. By the mid-1960s, Auerbach frequently put an all-black starting five on the floor, openly defying the unwritten rule widely followed by many coaches that no more than three blacks should be on the court simultaneously. In 1966 he again broke down a major barrier when he named Russell the league's first African-American head coach in modern times. This appointment was a powerful statement that would only slowly be replicated in professional sports.

The Dynasty Begins

The impact of Auerbach's personnel moves immediately became apparent. Although his teams had made the playoffs each year, they usually made an early exit. Even the 1954–5 team, a fast-breaking bunch that became the first NBA team to average more than 100 points a game, had lacked the requisite force up front. When Russell joined the Celtics in December of 1956 after having led the USA team to an Olympic gold medal in Melbourne, they already had compiled a 16–8 record. But Russell added an important new dimension as he swatted away shots and rebounded with zeal. The Celtics won their first NBA title in the spring of 1957 when they defeated the St Louis Hawks 125–123 in a tense Game Seven that went two overtimes. It was a memorable victory, one that was highlighted by being one of the first NBA games to be televised nationally. The team had great balance, with Cousy and Sharman both averaging over 20 points per game at the guard positions, and forwards Tommy Heinsohn and strongman "Jungle Jim" Loscutoff providing valuable rebounds and timely scoring up front. Meanwhile, Russell dominated the paint.

The following year the Celtics continued their winning ways. Russell received his first of five Most Valuable Player awards, but the team stumbled in the finals against the Hawks when Russell suffered a severe ankle sprain in the third game. His lack of mobility enabled Bob Pettit to score 50 points to give the Hawks the championship in Game Six by a scant 110–109 margin. Russell's former college teammate at USF, K. C. Jones, joined the supremely talented backcourt in 1958 and the next season Auerbach drafted Sam Jones out of North Carolina Central. The "Jones Boys" provided invaluable back-up (and later replacements) for starters Cousy and Sharman as the Celtics rolled to a 52–20 season. After squeaking by Syracuse in a seven game playoff for the Eastern title, the Celtics were surprised that the heavily favored Hawks were not once more their opponents. Instead, it was an upstart team from Minneapolis that they confronted in the championship series. It was the beginning of professional basketball's great rivalry.

"More Moves than a Watch"

The Minneapolis Lakers were led by an exciting rookie forward, 6′5″ Elgin Baylor. After George Mikan retired in 1954, the team had fallen on hard times. Mikan was the first superstar in professional basketball, but his plodding style meant that the Lakers were forced to play a slowdown offense that was boring to the casual fan. The Lakers fell to the bottom of the league in 1955, fans quit buying tickets, and attendance plummeted. Owner Bob Short decided to make one last effort to save the franchise. He persuaded Seattle University junior Elgin Baylor to forgo his senior year with an offer of $22,000, at the time considered to be an outrageously high salary for a rookie. "If Elgin had turned me down, I'd have gone out of business," Short later said. Although Julius Erving and Michael Jordan received great attention for their acrobatic "hang time" as they soared to the hoop, Baylor was their equal; he just was not seen as often on national television. Chick Hearn, who broadcast the Lakers games for 40 seasons, said that Baylor "just might be the best player I ever saw. He was doing things that Dr J. made famous 20 years later, the hang time and so forth. But Elgin didn't have the TV exposure. Nobody did in those days." He had, Hearn once said, "more moves than a watch."

In addition to his prolific scoring, Baylor grabbed his share of rebounds, and his ability to hit open teammates with uncanny passes only made him more effective. In his rookie season, Baylor averaged 25 points, 15 rebounds, and four assists per game, providing the stimulus for one of the greatest turnaround seasons in NBA history. The Lakers upset the St Louis Hawks in the Western Division playoffs but lacked the personnel to handle the dominant Celtics. The Lakers lost the 1959 finals in just four games, but the rivalry had just begun.

In the opening game of his second season, Baylor scored 52 points against Detroit and a few weeks later hung 64 on the Celtics, setting a new single-game NBA scoring mark. In that game, the Celtics followed Auerbach's orders to foul Baylor every time he went down the court, but that only gave him a raft of free throws. The following season, the Lakers failed to adapt to the loss of long-time coach John Kundla and went into another slump, standing a dismal 11–25 at midseason. Attendance continued to plummet, and Bob Short was in a desperate financial situation.

It almost got much worse on January 18, 1960. After absorbing a road loss at the hands of the St Louis Hawks, the team's chartered DC-3 took off for Minneapolis at 8:30 p.m. after a long delay to repair a generator. The weather was problematical, with snow and sleet driven by a strong wind. After about 10 minutes aloft, the repaired generator quit working and the airplane had no electricity, and consequently no radio. Veteran pilot Vernon Ullman decided that air traffic over Lambert Field was too heavy to attempt a safe return to St Louis, so he flew northward attempting to chart his course by the stars. As the DC-3 plowed through the stormy night, the temperature in the cabin grew colder and the occupants much quieter. Ice began forming on the wings and then ice obscured the windshield. Ullman opened the side window and stuck his head out to try to get a glimpse of the stars. The normal two hour flight extended to over three. Ullman had no idea where he was, but he knew he was getting low on fuel. He decided he had to attempt an emergency landing and so he dipped down through the clouds and spotted lights of a small village. He buzzed the town, hoping that someone would turn on the lights at the airport, but tiny Carroll, Iowa – fully 150 miles off course to the west – had no airport. Co-pilot Howard Gifford walked back to the cabin and said, "Okay, buckle your seat belts, put your knees up, and say a little prayer. We're going in." Baylor recalled that he wrapped himself in several blankets and lay down in the aisle, thinking "If I'm going to die, I might as well be comfortable."

Ullman made several passes to find a landing spot, at one point barely missing some power lines, and then, with his head stuck outside the window to get a view, he cut the motor and deftly guided the aircraft into a field of uncut corn that fortunately contained three feet of fresh snow. The aircraft landed softly, as if gliding into a huge pile of marshmallows, and came to a stop as the frightened passengers erupted in cheers. As they happily walked the one mile into town, the town's combination ambulance/hearse rushed by en route to the crash scene.

Zeke from Cabin Creek

Following the 1960 season, owner Bob Short decided to move the Lakers to Los Angeles. The Cleveland Rams football team had moved out in

1945, and the Dodgers baseball team arrived there in 1958. Now came the Lakers, fleeing cold winters and apathetic fans, in hopes that they would get a warmer reception in sunny Southern California. The Lakers were the first NBA franchise to be located on the West Coast, and no one knew if Californians would support professional basketball. Short hoped that Baylor's sensational play alone would attract fans to the new 14,500-seat Los Angeles Sports Arena. For reasons unknown, Short decided to keep the name Lakers, although arid Los Angeles was not known for any lake, let alone 10,000 of them. Some wags thought that "Los Angeles Surfers" had a nice ring to it.

The relocated Lakers made one of their most significant decisions in franchise history even before they played a game in the Sports Arena. The club drafted Jerry West, All-American 6′4″ forward/guard from West Virginia. He had led the Mountaineers to the NCAA finals in 1959, and had been a standout member of the 1960 US Olympic gold medal team in Rome. When he first appeared in Los Angeles, West seemed to be anything but a future Hall of Fame player. He was shy, insecure, skinny, and spoke with a squeaky mountain twang that led teammates to call him "Tweety Bird." That nickname did not last, and was replaced by Baylor's more poetic "Zeke from Cabin Creek." West was not from Cabin Creek, which was a small hamlet located near his hometown of Cheylan, population 500. He hated the nickname, but it stuck. He would willingly sign autographs but adamantly refused to sign them "Zeke."

The Lakers also hired West's college coach, Fred Schaus, for their inaugural season in Los Angeles. He would guide the team to seven consecutive playoff seasons before moving into the front office. In their first season in Los Angeles, the Lakers lacked radio coverage and averaged only 3,000 fans. West required time to adjust to the team and the league and did not enter the starting lineup until midseason. Always his worst critic, the self-deprecating West made himself miserable by replaying over and over in his mind one of the few mistakes he had made in a game. Victories did not buoy him; defeats seemed almost too much to bear. As the initial season in Los Angeles drew to a close, Baylor and West began to mesh, feeding off of each other's strengths, propelling the team to a respectable 36–43 season and into the playoffs where they staged a surprising run all the way to the Western Division finals before losing to the heavily favored St Louis Hawks in seven games.

Throughout the rest of the 1960s, Jerry West and Elgin Baylor combined to form one of the most dynamic scoring and passing tandems in the history of the league. In his second season, West averaged 31 points, but insiders believed his defense was even more important to the Lakers' success. His jump shots and driving layups attracted the attention of the media and fans, but he also played excellent defense, becoming well known for his many steals. "He used to take the ball away from everybody," team statistician John Radcliffe recalled. "He knew how to time it just perfectly, taking it down low off the floor." Blessed with quickness and agility, West often seemed unstoppable. As he matter-of-factly put it: "I always thought that if we needed a basket, I could score. I didn't care who was guarding or what the defense was. I had nights where you just couldn't guard me. I was making them from everywhere." On January 17, 1962, with only 2,600 fans in the Sports Arena, he had one of those nights, lighting up the place with 63 points in just 39 minutes of playing time.

West ultimately became the public relations icon of the Lakers and even the entire league (the timeless red, white, and blue NBA logo of today is a replica of West in classic pose dribbling up court on a fast break). Tommy Heinsohn, star forward and later nine year coach of the Celtics, said West was "a freak. He had those long arms, and if you tried to match up with him and bring size into the situation, he would out-quick the guy. And if you matched up speed against West, he would shoot over the defender."

The Streak

Although the Lakers created plenty of excitement in their new home, even greater things were happening in Boston. Between 1957 and 1969 the Celtics appeared in 12 NBA finals, winning 11 of them. At one point they won eight consecutive championships. Highlighting that incredible streak was the fact that they met the Los Angeles Lakers six times in the finals, winning each contest. Those championship series created an intense, sometimes bitter, rivalry that gave the NBA a much-needed boost in the world of American professional sports. In Boston, the Celtics and basketball became as important during the winter months as hockey, and they played a major role in enhancing the national stature of the NBA. In 1960 and 1961, Boston defeated a strong St Louis Hawks team led by Bob Pettit and Cliff Hagan in the finals, and the following year they encountered the upstart Lakers.

In 1962, the Lakers turned what initially seemed a serious setback into a positive. Baylor started off the season racking up phenomenal single game scoring totals, but in December was called up for active duty by the Army. Throughout much of the season, he managed to play only in games on the weekend or occasionally when he could wrangle a pass out of Fort Lewis, Washington. He appeared in just 48 games the entire season, but instead of hurting the Lakers' title hopes, his absence enhanced them. West elevated his game and assumed leadership of the team. When Baylor did play, he had fresh legs and was a rebounding and scoring terror. He averaged 38 points a game, second only in the league to the amazing totals being racked up by Philadelphia center Wilt Chamberlain.

Despite Baylor's frequent absences, the Lakers compiled a 54–26 season record and defeated the Detroit Pistons in the divisional playoffs. The Celtics surprised many experts when they upended Chamberlain and the favored Philadelphia Warriors in the Eastern finals. The Warriors were led by the 7'3" Chamberlain, who had averaged 24 rebounds and a whopping 50 points a game. In one memorable game played in Hershey, Pennsylvania, he had traumatized the New York Knicks by scoring 100 points. Bill Russell was able to contain the overpowering Chamberlain just enough to enable the Celtics to pull out a 4–3 series win.

The Celtics won the first game over the Lakers at home by a 14 point margin, but the Lakers gained a home court advantage when they upset the Celtics in Boston in Game Two 129–122. Much to the delight of Bob Short, a roaring standing-room only crowd of over 15,000 greeted the Lakers in the Sports Arena when they returned home. The raucous crowd was rewarded with a high-scoring game that saw the lead change hands frequently. In one of the many memorable plays that dotted his career, West tied the game at 115-all with four seconds remaining and then stole the ball near midcourt and converted with a layup at the buzzer for a heart-stopping home team victory. An irate Auerbach contended that West could not have dribbled the 30 feet for the shot in just three seconds. "I had deflected the ball on the run," West said, and "I knew I would have enough time because I knew what the shot clock was." Thereafter, West was known in Los Angeles as "Mr Clutch." The Celtics won two days later and returned to Boston with the series tied at two-all. In that game, the well-rested Elgin Baylor went wild, bringing anguish to Boston fans when he scored 61 points, handed out assists for easy baskets when double-teamed, and grabbed 22 rebounds. "He had that wonderful, magical instinct for making plays and doing things that you had to just stop and watch," West said.

Trailing three games to two, the Celtics faced a hostile Los Angeles crowd, but they dominated in all phases of the game and won convincingly 119–105. The final game played in Boston on April 16 was one of the all-time classic NBA contests. The Celtics took a small early lead that they nursed until the fourth quarter. With the Lakers trailing 73–67, West scored on three consecutive shots to tie the game. Late in the quarter, the score was tied again at 88-all. By this time, three Celtics front liners, Jim Loscutoff, Tom Sanders, and Heinsohn, had fouled out, primarily in a futile effort to stop Baylor. The game went into overtime when Frank Ramsey missed a short driving shot on one end and Lakers guard Frank Selvy's eight foot jumper rimmed out at the buzzer. In overtime, guard Sam Jones scored five points, and the Celtics escaped with a 110–107 victory. This dramatic game – close until the end – set the tone for championships to come. Whether good, lucky, or both, the Celtics managed to slip by the frustrated Lakers by the narrowest of margins.

In 1963, the two teams met again in the finals, and this time the Wise Guys in Las Vegas made the Lakers a distinct favorite. It seemed that the Celtics were perceived as having gotten too old for a young man's game. That perception was fueled in large part by the announcement by Bob Cousy that he would retire at season's end. Auerbach, however, had drafted swingman John Havlicek out of Ohio State and added forward Bailey Howell to beef up the frontcourt, and in the "Jones Boys" he had already reshaped his backcourt in anticipation of the departure of Sharman and Cousy. Auerbach still had Bill Russell to wreak havoc on defense. On the eve of the finals, Auerbach took exception to claims in the Los Angeles newspapers: "Los Angeles is the Basketball Capital of the World? Los Angeles has been in the league two years and it's the basketball capital of the world?! [Obscenity!]"

The series once more featured close, hard-fought games that came down to the final few possessions. West and Baylor put up their points, and the Celtics were the same old Celtics, not nearly as old as Los Angeles reporters had made them out to be. After the first four games, the Celtics returned to Boston with a 3–1 lead, confident of victory. West and Baylor, however, combined for 75 points to quiet the Boston Garden, and when the teams returned to Los Angeles for Game Six, many experts affirmed that the aging Celtics were exhausted. When thousands of fans were unable to buy tickets, the Lakers management arranged for the game to be shown on closed-circuit TV. Just three years after fleeing Minneapolis, Bob Short's financially stressed club had inaugurated a new era of pay-per-view. The fans that paid $2.50 at local theaters and those 15,500 in the standing-room-only Arena, however, were to be greatly disappointed. Rookie John Havlicek went on a first half scoring spree and the Celtics led by 14 at half-time. In the third quarter, after Cousy went to the bench with a sprained ankle, the Lakers tied the score. With just two minutes remaining, Heinsohn scored on a breakaway to give the Celtics a two point lead, and a gimpy Cousy returned to milk the clock with some of his ball handling magic. The Celtics escaped with a 112–109 victory and their fifth consecutive NBA title. Cousy went into retirement in grand style, and the proud Celtics "celebrated" without the usual champagne spray in the locker room. After all, winning championships is what they routinely did: "Why celebrate?" As Heinsohn proclaimed to no one in particular, as Auerbach savored his post-game cigar: "We've won five in a row."

Auerbach was not about to let his team get too old. He never permitted himself to get sentimental about any player, even such an all-time great as Cousy. When any player showed signs of slowing, he was traded, released or asked to retire. The Celtics made history in more than one way in the 1964–5 season. They not only once more won the league championship, when they handily dispatched the San Francisco Warriors and Wilt Chamberlain in five games, but also, for 12 games in midseason, Auerbach put on the floor a starting lineup comprised of five African-Americans. When forward Tommy Heinsohn went down with a leg injury the day after Christmas, Auerbach inserted Willie Naulls in the starting lineup along with Russell, Sanders, K. C. Jones, and Sam Jones. Some feared that this time Auerbach had gone too far in offending the sensibilities of Boston's predominantly white fans. Auerbach would later claim that he was unaware of his pioneering move in starting five blacks, saying that he merely wanted to win games. His makeshift lineup proceeded to rack up 12 consecutive wins without a loss, and when Heinsohn recovered, he once more was back in the starting lineup.

The following season, the Celtics won a close seventh game in the divisional finals on Havlicek's last minute steal of an inbounds pass to deny the sure-shooting Hal Greer of the Philadelphia 76ers an open jumper that quite likely would have won the game for them. It was the most famous stolen pass in NBA history and became the signature call by long-time gravelly voiced radio announcer Johnny Most. His classic hyperventilating exclamation would be replayed innumerable times in Boston watering holes: "He stole the ball! . . . He stole the ball! . . . Havlicek stole the ball! Its all over!" That special moment in Celtic history remained the season's highlight, and the Celtics handed the Lakers yet another disappointment in a five game final. For the first time, Auerbach was selected as Coach of the Year, a bittersweet award since he and Boston fans had thought that previous awards had gone to the wrong man. Yet everyone knew that the abrasive, now balding, redhead was not a favorite of out-of-town voting sports writers. This time they had no viable alternative.

By the start of the 1965–6 season, the Celtics were riding high. Auerbach had managed to compensate for the retirement of Heinsohn by signing forward Don Nelson, and he inserted Willie Naulls into the regular starting lineup. Some muted comments about the all-black starting five were heard around the league, but no one could say that it was not a potent lineup. Because of his now legendary preseason-conditioning program, the team once more got off to its usual fast start, but by December the number of losses uncharacteristically began to mount. Auerbach, now approaching his 50th birthday, confided to friends that he seemed to lack his usual enthusiasm. He told the *Boston Globe*, "I haven't been getting myself up for games the way I should. I'm as guilty as anyone for not playing better. In some of the practice sessions – and games, too, for that matter – I've been much too relaxed and casual. I've been taking things for granted and when you do that you get beat." A players-only meeting was called, and the consensus was that while they believed themselves to be complicit in the downturn, they also believed that they were not getting the same commitment that they had come to expect of their head coach. Captain Bill Russell bluntly told him so. A few weeks later, Auerbach called a press conference to announce that he was retiring as head coach at the end of the season. He did it with his usual dramatic flair, challenging his opponents by saying, "I'm announcing it now so that no one can ever say I quit while I was ahead. I'm telling everyone right now – Los Angeles, Philadelphia, everyone – that this will be my last season, so you've got one more shot at Auerbach." He then hunkered down and coached his team into the finals once more.

It was only fitting that his Celtics would confront their Los Angeles rivals in their coach's last hurrah. The Celtics were gunning for their eighth straight title, but the Lakers had every reason for optimism. They had played well during the playoffs, and the team was in good health. Anticipating another hard-fought series, they took hope from the fact that the Celtics averaged 31 years of age. The Lakers promptly stunned the Celtics fans at the Garden in Game One, wining a high-scoring match 133–129. That road victory set the pattern for the series, in which the home team would lose four games. The championship appropriately came down to Game Seven at the Garden. With just two minutes left, the Celtics seemed poised to give Auerbach a big retirement gift as they sat on a ten point lead. At that point, Massachusetts Governor John Volpe – never one to miss an opportunity for public attention – walked in front of the Celtics bench and with much fanfare lit Auerbach's victory cigar. Not so fast. The cigar almost blew up in Auerbach's face when the Celtics committed four consecutive turnovers and the Lakers stormed back to within one bucket. K. C. Jones managed to run out the clock and the Celtics had their eighth consecutive championship, 95–93. The Lakers had been frustrated once more, and by the narrowest of margins.

Bill Russell Does Double Duty

After losing the first game of his final championship series, Auerbach announced that Bill Russell would take over as head coach the next season. Many interpreted the timing of the announcement as a motivational ploy. If so, it worked. Russell would be the first African-American head coach in the NBA and the first black head coach of any modern professional team. Auerbach left coaching forever, having won an enviable 67 percent of his games, and posting a 795–397 won–lost record. No professional coach has even approached his record of eight consecutive championships, although when Phil Jackson won his tenth championship in 2009 (six with the Chicago Bulls, four with the Lakers) he equaled Auerbach's career total. Once retired, Auerbach smoothly transitioned into the role of general manager, which he would hold for 20 more years.

Russell's first year as head coach yielded the inevitable – the streak of eight consecutive NBA championships ended with a 4–1 loss to the rejuvenated Philadelphia 76ers in the divisional finals. Russell's team was slowed by injuries, but even if completely healthy, they would have been no match for the 76ers. Wilt Chamberlain had returned to his hometown from San Francisco and now concentrated on defense and rebounding; although he still averaged 24 points per game, scoring responsibilities were now handed over to sharp-shooting guards Hal Greer and Chet Walker and forward Billy Cunningham. The Celtics nonetheless managed to win 60 regular season games in Russell's first year as coach, but Alex Hannum's 76ers put up a 68–13 record. In the fifth and final game of the divisional playoffs, the 76ers poured it on with a 24 point rout in the Spectrum as the raucous Philadelphia fans chanted, "Boston is dead! Boston is dead!" while the clock wound down.

Boston was anything but dead. The following season, down 3–1 to the 76ers in the divisional finals, Russell rallied his team to win the series. When the 1968 finals against the Lakers ended, the tenth championship banner was raised to the rafters of the Boston Garden.

Cut Down the Balloons!

The 1969 Lakers were determined and defiant when they once again confronted the now obviously aging Celtics in the finals. Media entrepreneur Jack Kent Cooke had purchased the team in 1965 from Bob Short and had set about infusing a new level of professionalism and accountability throughout the organization. He spared little expense to improve the franchise, and in return he demanded excellence. The Lakers under Cooke became the model organization in professional basketball. After Cooke and the management of the Sports Arena had a major disagreement, he simply financed the construction of a grandiose new facility designed to provide spectator comfort. He imperiously named the $16 million 17,500-seat facility located in Inglewood "The Forum." Its lavish design and décor soon had locals calling it "The Fabulous Forum." An imposing building, it featured 80 tall columns that gave the impression of a modern structure built in the great architectural tradition of ancient Rome. It opened on December 31, 1967, a fitting home for a well-managed franchise that was transforming professional basketball.

The 1969 finals provided one of the most memorable clashes in the series. Unlike previous meetings, the Lakers were the clear favorites. During the regular season the Celtics had shown cracks in their armor. Player-coach Russell had to sit out several games with a leg injury, and the Celtics barely made it into the playoffs with a lackluster 48–34 season record. K. C. Jones had retired after the 1967 season to be replaced by Larry Siegfried, and at age 36 Sam Jones had endured a long season beset by injuries and entered the playoffs hobbled. Russell had privately decided he would retire at the end of the season. He wanted to leave on a high note and expended every ounce of energy he could summon in the early rounds of the playoffs, pushing the Celtics past the 76ers and the surging Knicks by a narrow 4–3 margin and into the finals against the Lakers. Meanwhile, the Lakers' publicity machine had been proclaiming that they had the best guard, forward, and center in the league. In addition to veterans Jerry West and Elgin Baylor, the Lakers had acquired the much-traveled veteran Wilt Chamberlain to neutralize Russell in the paint.

Both teams won their first three home games. West came out on fire in the first game in Los Angeles, letting everyone know that he was out to avenge the four previous finals defeats he had suffered at the hands of Boston. He poured in 53 points, eclipsing Havlicek's 39, while Chamberlain and Russell battled to a standoff under the boards. Leading 2–0 in the series, the Lakers had to be contemplating a series sweep as they flew across country for Games Three and Four on the parquet floor. After the Celtics took Game Three, the Lakers apparently had Game Four in hand, holding on to a 88–87 lead with an out-of-bounds possession and just 15 seconds remaining. But Celtics reserve guard Emmette Bryant stole the inbounds pass. After a time out, an out-of-bounds play did not produce an open shot, and the ball ended in Sam Jones' hands as the clock wound down. He arched a desperate 18 foot jump shot over the leaping Chamberlain's outstretched fingertips. The ball hit the back of the rim, popped high in the air, and then improbably fell straight downward through the net. Series tied. "God's will," a devastated Jerry West groaned.

It naturally came down to Game Seven after the two teams traded home victories. Lakers owner Jack Kent Cooke could not help himself. He so fervently anticipated a Lakers championship that he had 5,000 purple balloons suspended above The Forum floor in large nets waiting to be released the moment the home team claimed their first championship in Los Angeles. But things did not go according to script; early in the fourth quarter Chamberlain sprained a knee and left the game limping, and Boston built up a 13 point lead. The Lakers surge fell short and the exhausted Celtics survived with their 11th championship in 13 years, 108–106. The suspended balloons were removed the next day.

Showtime

The rivalry cooled off during the 1970s, but returned with gusto in the 1980s. The Lakers won their first NBA championship in Los Angeles in

1972 but then faded with the retirement of Baylor and West despite the efforts of new head coach Jerry West. The Celtics, with the fiery Tommy Heinsohn now the head coach, captured two more titles in 1974 and 1976.

In 1980, the cross-continent rivalry moved into its most exciting era as two superstars entered the NBA. When Earvin "Magic" Johnson was drafted out of Michigan State by the Lakers and the Celtics nabbed Indiana State's Larry Bird, a new storyline was set for the old rivals. Basketball fans had a brief glimpse of the future when the two first met in the NCAA championship game in 1979, attracting a record national television audience.

Magic Johnson fit ideally into the frenetic fast-break style coached by Paul Westhead. He was thrilled to have the opportunity to play with his childhood hero, 7′2″ center Kareem Abdul-Jabbar. Their supporting cast included an impressive array of all-star talent: James Worthy, Michael Cooper, Jamal Wilkes, and Byron Scott. Johnson ran the floor with breathtaking efficiency, dishing the ball off on lightning-fast breaks or taking it to the hoop himself with authority. In leading the Lakers to the NBA title in his freshman season, Johnson sparkled in Game Six of the finals in Philadelphia. With Abdul-Jabbar out with an injury, he ran the offense, sometimes even posted up at center, and even played on the wing where he drilled jump shots. His unerring no-look passes to open teammates stunned the 76ers as the Lakers won a romp. One Philadelphia writer was mesmerized by this virtuoso performance: "He brings the ball up the court, sets up the plays, runs the fast breaks. His height gives him an advantage over other guards, and his ability to determine in an instant how a play might develop – by now it's a reflex – allows him to take maximum advantage of his teammates' extraordinary quickness."

Johnson's performance anticipated what soon became known in Los Angeles as "Showtime." In the 1981–2 season, 11 year journeyman forward Pat Riley assumed the Lakers' head coaching position and took advantage of Magic Johnson's special talents by heavily emphasizing a wide open offense and a suffocating pressure defense. The result was another championship in Riley's first year. However, the Celtics were now preparing to challenge with a team that included a powerful frontcourt consisting of Cedric "Cornbread" Maxwell, Robert Parrish, and Kevin McHale. The team revolved around the skills of the new 6′9″ wingman Larry Bird, whose selfless blue-collar image as a hardworking player who used every ounce of his energy and every trick in the book to win captured the imagination of fans everywhere. The Celtics had won their

Figure 6.3   Lakers center Kareem Abdul-Jabbar throws up one of his famous sky hook shots over Celtics center Dave Cowans in the championship series of 1982. Celtics forward Kevin McHale is on the right. © Steve Lipofsky/Corbis

14th NBA championship in 1981 under veteran coach Bill Fitch and their 61–21 regular season record constituted a 32 game improvement over the previous season.

Dr Jerry Buss had purchased the Lakers from Jack Kent Cooke in 1979. He had made his fortune in real estate but became a full-time sports entrepreneur. Buss placed great emphasis on building team identity. Public relations and extensive promotional campaigns were launched to reflect the Southern California mystique. He insisted upon fielding teams that would always be capable of challenging for the NBA title, but with a unique Southern California touch. His vision was a high-tempo offense featuring the sleight-of-hand ball handling of Johnson and monstrous dunks by the high-flying Michael Cooper and James Worthy. He launched the Lakers Girls, a team of 20 curvaceous dancing cheerleaders whose frenetic dance routines spiced up timeouts and half-time, and he lured Hollywood stars with complimentary front row seats. Their presence added to the elaborate mixture of show business and sports set against the luxurious backdrop of The Fabulous Forum. Such stars as Doris Day, Dinah Shore, Dyan Cannon, and Pat Boone along with many others added a special Hollywood glitz to the games. Actor Jack Nicholson became a fixture on the front row. "Put a guy like Jack Nicholson in the front row, and people will come to see the game and the star," Chick Hearn observed. Head coach Pat Riley added a finishing touch. Sporting hand-tailored Armani suits and Gucci shoes, with his black hair styled to perfection, Riley's image standing in front of the Lakers bench put an emphatic exclamation mark on Showtime.

Turning Up the Heat in Boston

Just as Jerry Buss found the right man to run his team in Pat Riley, Red Auerbach selected the popular K. C. Jones to lead the blue-collar Celtics. The quiet Jones brought to the team a leadership style that meshed well with a team that prided itself on its work ethic. The Celtics shunned the flashiness and glitter that personified the style of their West Coast rivals. By the mid-1980s the consensus of basketball experts was that this was the finest team in Celtics history. The low-key Jones was the anti-Riley – quiet and reserved – but able to handle the egos of his highly paid stars. Unlike predecessor Bill Fitch, he was not a master of intricate coaching strategies; instead, his strength lay in his ability to communicate with and motivate his team. The Celtics even resolutely refused to create their own version of the Lakers Girls, instead letting the dreary ambiance of the Garden quietly underscore their connections to working-class New Englanders as Larry Bird and company went about their labors.

These two talented teams met in the 1984 championship series. It was the first meeting since the classic of 1969. After the Lakers romped to a 137–104 blowout win in Game Three at The Forum, Larry Bird told the press (and his teammates) that he was disgusted with their effort. "We played like a bunch of sissies," he complained. The next day the Los Angeles newspapers egged on the Celtics by essentially declaring the series over, even naming James Worthy as the MVP. Kevin McHale took Bird's criticism to heart. In the second quarter of Game Four at The Forum, when burly Kurt Rambis went up for a layup, McHale whacked him across the neck, dumping him in a heap on the floor. McHale explained the joys of physical intimidation: "The Lakers were just running across the street whenever they wanted. Now they stop at the corner, push the button, wait for the light, and look both ways." McHale's takedown spurred the Celtics to a 129–125 win as they tied the series at two games apiece. Pat Riley could only fume publicly: "They're a bunch of thugs," but privately he vowed that his team would never again be physically intimidated. The ante had been raised.

Auerbach, officially the Celtics president, but still the wily game psychologist, was up to his old tricks, and he worked on playing with Pat Riley's mind. Game Five became famous as the "Heat Game." It was hot and humid in Boston in early June, and inside the Garden the temperature reached 97 degrees. The Lakers, accustomed to playing in the air-conditioned confines of The Forum, wilted and were jeered by Boston fans as they sucked on oxygen masks. At half-time in the sweltering Lakers locker room, Riley discovered heat was being pumped in through the vents! Auerbach's doing? Who knows, but Riley thought so: "I thought he [Auerbach] was the man behind everything," he snorted. Auerbach was cheerfully noncommittal. After the Lakers evened the series at The Forum in Game Six, the Celtics asserted their home court advantage. Late in Game Seven, Cedric Maxwell sensationally stole a Magic Johnson pass on a fast break to stymie a furious Lakers comeback: Celtics 111–102. Much to Riley's torment, Red Auerbach puffed on several cigars and sipped champagne late into the night.

The two teams squared off again in 1985. Despite having the home court advantage and devastating the Lakers in the opening game 148–114 – a blowout known as the "Memorial Day Massacre" – the Celtics could not hold off a determined team led by Abdul-Jabbar, Johnson, and Worthy. The Lakers won in six games. Pat Riley felt that he had finally gotten the best of Auerbach because his team played with so much "passion." Jerry Buss let the world know that the weight of eight straight losses to Boston in the championship series had finally been lifted: "It can never be said that the Lakers have never beaten the Celtics." Of course, Celtics fans pointed out that it took the Lakers more than two decades to get to that moment.

The Lakers won their fourth championship of the 1980s when they overcame the Celtics 4–2, but the following year they barely held on in Game Seven against the Detroit Pistons to garner their own back-to-back championships. Riley departed two years later, following a season marked by acrimony in the locker room. Some observers believed a players' revolt ended Riley's reign. Others believed that general manager Jerry West, always a believer that basketball was a players' game, felt that Riley strayed from his earlier strategies and put too many clamps on instinctive play. Still others simply concluded that Riley believed the time had come for a fresh start as he took his act to the New York Knicks.

Decline and Despair in Beantown

The major change in the rivalry occurred in 1985. Auerbach announced his retirement and was acclaimed as one of Boston's living legends. His name was placed on a Celtics jersey and lifted to the rafters, and a life-size bronze statue, complete with the ubiquitous cigar, was placed in Quincy Market near historic Faneuil Hall. And much to the disgust of some of his peers, the NBA named its Coach of the Year Award the Red Auerbach Trophy. (He later tweaked Pat Riley, who won the Coach of the Year award in 1990, by noting that every time his old nemesis looked at the award, he would see Auerbach's image.)

In 1986, still involved in overall team policy, Auerbach orchestrated the drafting of a multi-talented 6'8" prospect he believed would replace Larry Bird as team leader. Len Bias was a gifted All-American at Maryland. After greeting the Boston media and signing a lucrative contract, Bias returned home to College Park, went to a party, and within 12 hours was declared dead of a drug overdose. Auerbach, who had scouted Bias for several years, was devastated.

The Bias tragedy seemed to condemn the Celtics to two decades in the wilderness. Auerbach withdrew from day-to-day involvement to take up a consultant's role. In the ensuing years, several coaches, general managers, and a large cast of players came and went. Losing seasons followed mediocre seasons, highlighted by a few early playoff departures. Bone spurs in his feet and a chronic back condition reduced Larry Bird's effectiveness and he retired in 1992. Tragedy continued to plague the once-lucky Celtics. In January of 1993, Johnny Most, the long-time radio voice of the team, died of heart failure at age 69; in June, Auerbach underwent emergency six hour quintuple bypass surgery. That same summer, co-captain Reggie Lewis collapsed while playing in a pick-up game and died of cardiac arrest. An autopsy identified the cause of death as a genetic heart condition.

Even the opening of the modern 18,500-seat Fleet Center in 1995 failed to provide the team a boost. Two seasons and 116 defeats later, the celebrated Rick Pitino took over as coach and general manager amidst a flurry of optimistic publicity. Just four years later, with a 102–146 record, under intense criticism for failed player transactions and embroiled in a deteriorating relationship with the hypercritical Boston sports media, Pitino resigned and returned to the college ranks.

The Celtic's fortunes finally began to turn in 2004 when new ownership hired former guard Danny Ainge as general manager. He began to systematically rebuild the franchise. Doc Rivers was hired as coach based upon a successful run with the Orlando Magic. Ainge had inherited forward Paul Pierce and not much else, and so he methodically built the team through the draft. Before the 2007–8 season, Ainge went for broke and acquired center Kevin Garnett from Minnesota and guard Ray Allen from Seattle. The stage was set for a reprise of the Lakers–Celtics post-season drama.

The Age of Jackson

While the Celtics struggled unsuccessfully to find the right combination in the 1990s, the Lakers rebounded quickly from the dissolution of the juggernaut of the 1980s. They even managed to overcome the psychological blow suffered in 1991 when Magic Johnson announced that he had contracted the HIV virus. He retired, served as head coach briefly in 1994, attempted a short-lived return to the court in 1996, and then retired permanently. Following the 1996 season, the Lakers acquired center Shaquille O'Neal (7′1″, 325 pounds, size 23 shoe) as a free agent from Orlando and traded center Vlade Divac to Charlotte to get the rights to 18-year-old Kobe Bryant. Equally important, general manager Mitch Kupchak hired Phil Jackson as head coach. Utilizing the talents of Michael Jordan, Scottie Pippen, and a host of other talents, Jackson had won six NBA titles with the Chicago Bulls. He proceeded to work his special magic in Los Angeles. It was no small challenge, however, because he needed all of his persuasive skills to get his talented but egocentric superstars to buy into his team concept built around a complex motion offense he called "The Triangle."

Those three championship seasons were filled with an ongoing melodrama as Jackson found it necessary to massage the fragile but immense egos of Bryant and O'Neal. Neither superstar could quite appreciate the contributions of the other. After achieving the stunning "Three-peat," the Lakers fell from their lofty perch, due largely to errors of their own making. In 2003–4, the increasingly acerbic verbal jousting between Bryant and O'Neal became a major distraction. The Lakers managed to make it to the finals in 2004 but were ambushed by the Detroit Pistons. After protracted deliberations and negotiations, Kupchak decided to keep Bryant rather than O'Neal and the perturbed center opted to accept a trade to the Miami Heat where a multi-year $100 million contract awaited.

Jackson also departed, apparently exhausted from the celebrity-driven madhouse that the Lakers had become. Rudy Tomjanovich, well known as a "players' coach" during a long stint in Houston, replaced Jackson. As Tomjanovich prepared for his initial season in Los Angeles, the Lakers suffered an enormous distraction when sensational allegations of sexual assault were brought in a Colorado court against Kobe Bryant. Following months of saturated media coverage, the plaintiff dropped the charges on the eve of trial and just before the Lakers began fall camp. Tomjanovich departed midway through the season due to health problems, and not surprisingly the Lakers fell to a 34–48 record.

In the wake of this media carnival, Jerry Buss convinced Phil Jackson to return for the 2005–6 season. A more mature Kobe Bryant proved eager to demonstrate that he could lead the Lakers to a championship without Shaq, and bought into Jackson's offensive schemes. By 2008, the Lakers were once more ready for a title run, having added 7′0″ center Pau Gasol as the final piece to the puzzle. They powered their way into the NBA finals by upending defending champions San Antonio. Awaiting them were the resurgent Celtics.

Reprise of a Rivalry

The Celtics happily returned to the finals for the first time in more than 20 years, and did so in style after cruising to a 66–16 regular season record. Ainge had assembled a solid team built around forward Paul Pierce, but it was the acquisition of center Kevin Garnett and guard Ray Allen that rekindled the glory days of the 1980s. The first game in the series in the renamed TD Banknorth Garden in Boston produced a bizarre episode. Midway through the third quarter, Pierce went down in pain with an apparently serious knee injury. With 19,000 raucous fans suddenly quieted, he was carried off the floor and taken to the locker room. The apparent loss of Pierce threw a pall over the Boston faithful. As it turned out, the injury, however painful initially, proved to be relatively minor. Pierce improbably returned during the final quarter and finished the game with 22 points, sparking a last quarter drive as the Celtics won 98–88. Led by the recovered Paul Pierce, in Game Two the Celtics jumped out to a 2–0 advantage despite Kobe Bryant's 30 points.

Some members of the media speculated that Pierce had engaged in a cheap motivational tactic, but that criticism lacked credibility. Although the Lakers won their first home game on the strength of Bryant's all-around play, they could not hold off the visitors in Game Four as the Celtics' stifling defense proved to be the deciding factor. The Lakers managed a narrow win in Game Five at the Staples Center, but they had to win two games in Boston. That proved to be too much to ask as the Celtics forced 18 turnovers off a tenacious defense; they pushed out to a 25 point lead midway through the third quarter and won going away. Paul Pierce was a virtual unanimous selection for MVP.

Despite the vast amount of pre-series hype that flooded the media before the 2008 finals, once the games began, the suspense and tension that had been commonplace during the 1980s was definitely missing. Boston fans were genuinely enthusiastic – it had been two long decades since their team's last appearance in the finals – but the response in Los Angeles was surprisingly muted. Red Auerbach was no longer around to needle the Lakers. Also, Garnett and Allen were in their first season in Boston and, while their acquisition was crucial to making it into the finals, they had little connection to the Celtics tradition.

Hopes for a rematch in 2009 were not realized. A season-ending knee injury to Garnett severely crippled the Celtics and they lost in the second round of the playoffs to Orlando, who proved unable to handle the Lakers in the finals as Kobe Bryant put on a clinic with his shooting and all-around play. With his tenth NBA title as a head coach, Jackson surpassed Red Auerbach, whose total of nine championships had once seemed untouchable. Kobe Bryant was the runaway favorite in the voting for Most Valuable Player, and he relished knowing that he had led the Lakers to the championship without the towering presence of Shaq O'Neal over-shadowing his every move.

The Bull and the Butterfly

The Never-Ending Rivalry Between Joe Frazier and Muhammad Ali

It's hard to be humble when you're the greatest. (Muhammad Ali)

One of these days I'm really gonna show the world who is the greatest. (Joe Frazier)

For the past several decades, the once thriving sport of boxing has been on the ropes, its stature reduced by the shenanigans of corrupt promoters, a precipitous decline in fan interest, and a corresponding reduction in the number and quality of fighters. Put off by the likes of Mike Tyson and Donald King, the deaths that occur periodically in the ring, the confusion created by conflicting associations, new weight divisions ("junior lightweight," "cruiser weight"), and multiple reigning champions, many fans have tuned out, perhaps attracted by the new violence of mixed martial arts.

In a real sense, boxing has never regained the popularity that it enjoyed when Muhammad Ali and Joe Frazier captivated the boxing world with their emotionally charged bouts between 1971 and 1975. They were unquestionably the two greatest boxers of their era, whose epic battles became a centerpiece of boxing history. It is also beyond question that they truly did not like each other and that their titanic battles were fueled by true animosity and hatred.

Boxing would never be the same after their final bloody slugfest, proclaimed by Ali as the "Thrilla in Manila."

That Ali won two of the three bouts is almost irrelevant. Pulitzer Prize-winning journalist David Halberstam aptly wrote after Manila, "Technically the loser of two of the three fights, Frazier seems not to understand that they ennobled him as much as they did Ali, that the only way we know of Ali's greatness is because of Frazier's equivalent greatness." Halberstam correctly concluded that these two great fighters ended their bouts with "no identifiable winner or loser."

The Man from Beaufort

Because of the massive media coverage that Ali commanded, Joe Frazier seemed to operate mostly in the shadows of his hated adversary, acting at times like a prop on Ali's stage. Frazier deserved better. His life story suggests that his accession to the heavyweight crown and his ability to fight Ali to a standstill was the accomplishment of a man of substance and character overcoming major obstacles.

Ali sometimes portrayed his own childhood as one of hardship and discrimination but, compared with Frazier, his early years were relatively pleasant and supportive. Frazier had to struggle mightily to overcome the extreme poverty into which he was born; his limited education in the segregated rural south greatly reduced his options as an adult.

Joe Frazier was born on January 12, 1944, the 12th of 13 children of sharecropper Rubin Frazier and his wife Dolly. His mother had quit school after the fourth grade to work full time in the fields for 50 cents a day. His father scraped together a subsistence living for his large family, working variously as a sharecropper, bootlegger, junk dealer and casual laborer. As a child, "Billy Boy" Frazier lived with his family in a sharecropper's shack stuck on a ten acre plot of infertile soil in the low country of South Carolina near the port of Beaufort. By the time he was seven, he worked long hours in the fields, picking vegetables. Billy Boy dropped out of school after the eighth grade.

As a young boy he watched the Wednesday and Friday night fights on television, especially admiring Sugar Ray Robinson, Archie Moore, and Jersey Joe Walcott. "We admired Rocky Marciano and those white fighters," he later recalled, "but lookin' at the black fighters, men that made it all the way, there was your hope, your chance, right in front of you!" He made punching bags out of feed sacks, stuffed them with rags and sand, hung them on tree limbs, and spent hours punching away while imagining himself fighting in Madison Square Garden. "I'm going to be the next Joe Louis," one sister remembered him saying. He never gave up on that dream.

At the age of 15, he married Florence Smith, who would bear him six children (he also acknowledges four sons born out of wedlock). Following an argument with two sons of an influential white landowner, Frazier judiciously decided to leave town in a hurry and rode the bus to New York City. Unable to find steady work and being played as a sucker by unscrupulous employers, he relocated to Philadelphia, where he had relatives, and hoped his luck would change.

His luck indeed did take a turn for the better. He found a full-time job in a meat packing plant where he worked from 1961 until 1964. He made enough to send for his wife and their first child. The 5′11″ Frazier had permitted his weight to pile up to 230 pounds. In January of 1962, he joined the Police Athletic League gym, determined to get into boxing shape. Veteran boxing coach Yancey "Yank" Durham had a good reputation for training amateur boxers, but his immediate reaction was that "he looked like a fat kid with no skill who would soon give up. Then he kept comin' back and comin' back after a hard day's work. He had character and persistence, which I'll take over raw talent every time." Durham began to work with the 17-year-old, and Frazier doggedly stuck to his arduous daily routine, from which he seldom deviated: up at 5 a.m. to put in five miles of roadwork, off to work a long day at the packing company, and then to the gym to undergo Durham's tough regimen. His weight leveled off at a muscular 205 pounds. At the meat packing plant, Frazier took to practicing his combination punches by pummeling the sides of beef hanging in the refrigeration rooms, a gimmick that actor Sylvester Stallone made famous as the hardscrabble fighter Rocky Balboa in the original *Rocky* movie.

Durham molded Frazier into a promising amateur who won the Middle Atlantic Golden Gloves heavyweight championship for three consecutive years. "I've had plenty of other boxers with more raw talent," Durham told a reporter, "but none with the dedication and strength." Frazier reached the finals of the US Olympic trials in 1964 only to lose to 295 pound Buster Mathis. When Mathis was injured, Frazier replaced him on the Olympic team and won the Gold Medal at the Tokyo games over favored Hans Huber of Germany. In the semi-finals, he broke his left thumb but fought through the pain to win the Gold.

On his return to Philadelphia, Frazier launched his professional career, bankrolled by several local investors who put up $20,000 so that he could focus his full attention on his chosen profession. Durham and the Cloverlay Group of investors ("clover" for luck, "overlay" for good odds) sent him to Los Angeles to work with experienced trainer Eddie Futch. Frazier's new trainer had been in the fight game since the 1930s and was recognized as one of the best teachers in the game. Frazier found Eddie Futch to be a teacher he could trust while Yank Durham continued as manager.

Smokin'

Frazier developed a relatively unsophisticated boxing style, one that he liked to call "smokin'." He disdained the tactics of bobbing and weaving, of dancing in and out, of flicking light jabs. Rather, from the opening bell he went for the kill, throwing his best punches. He was willing to take hard blows in order to get close enough to deliver his own. Smokin' was a style not given to nuance or artistry as he continually stalked his opponents. Frazier's punches packed a wallop and, in the parlance of the sport, he had a "good jaw." He would use his right hand to set up his best shot, a lethal left-hand uppercut that Futch had carefully crafted. His aggressive, always advancing style gave his opponents little opportunity to maneuver and even less time to think as they found themselves forced on the defensive by the relentless approach of their impassive foe. Norman Mailer described Frazier's style thusly: "He clubbed opponents to death, took a punch, gave a punch, took three punches, gave two, took a punch, gave a punch, high speed all the way, always working, pushing his body and arms, short for a heavyweight, up the middle, bombing through on force."

From his technical knockout of Woody Goss in his first professional fight in 1965, Frazier climbed rapidly up the heavyweight rankings. By 1967, he remained undefeated and had become a fighter to be reckoned with. In that year, Muhammad Ali was stripped of his heavyweight crown after his refusal to accept induction into the Army, which left the heavyweight division in disarray. With several potential challengers worthy of title consideration, the World Boxing Association set up an eight man elimination tournament that included such prominent fighters as Jerry Quarry, Jimmy Ellis, and Floyd Patterson. Frazier turned down an invitation but continued to gain experience against quality opponents. In 1968, he won the New York State version of the heavyweight championship with an 11 round TKO over Buster Mathis and successfully defended that title five times. By 1970, he had built an unbeaten record of 26 victories (21 by knockout) over highly regarded fighters such as Oscar Bonavena, Eddie Machen, George Chuvalo, and Jerry Quarry. He then met champion Jimmy Ellis in Madison Square Garden in February of 1970. Ellis had once beaten Cassius Clay in a three round amateur bout in Louisville and had risen to the WBA title under the guidance of trainer Angelo Dundee. Frazier dropped Ellis to the canvas several times with his signature left hook. After his man absorbed brutal punishment for five rounds, Dundee threw in the towel.

Frazier had risen to the top of his tough profession without much fanfare or controversy. Outside of the ring he was modest, allowing his record to speak for itself. This reticent persona was, of course, the polar opposite of Muhammad Ali, who had shaken the traditional boxing world to its foundation with his unpredictable, controversial, and outlandish behavior. In retrospect it seems that these two very different but very proud men were destined, at some point, to meet in the ring. Despite Frazier holding the title, the attention of the boxing world was focused on Ali.

"I Am the Greatest"

At the time his crown was wrested from him by boxing's ruling elders in 1967, Ali had already come to be recognized as one of the greatest of all heavyweight champions. The American public first encountered the voluble Cassius Clay in Rome during the 1960 Olympics. He was bright, opinionated, and dripping with self-confidence. This self-assured 18-year-old was a striking example of the new generation of African-Americans who no longer were willing to sit deferentially on the sidelines, silent and obedient, while meekly accepting the racial status quo. Clay returned from Rome with the Gold Medal draped around his neck and he prepared for a professional career.

He was born Cassius Marcellus Clay, Jr, on January 17, 1942. His father worked as a painter – houses and signs – and his mother Odessa made certain he was raised in the Baptist faith. From all indications, his parents provided a warm and nurturing environment. Early on, young Cassius evidenced a precocious nature, learning that unusual behavior would attract attention. "I've been an attraction ever since I've been able to walk and talk," he once commented. "When I was a little boy in school, I caught on to how nearly everybody likes to watch somebody that acts different. I always liked to draw crowds." By the time he was 12, Cassius had had a few minor brushes with the local police. Officer Joe Martin believed Cassius could be steered in the right direction and introduced him to a local boxing gymnasium, where he became an enthusiastic learner. There he came to the attention of trainer Angelo Dundee, who at the time was working with the up-and-coming light-heavyweight (and future champion) Willie Pastrano. "There was something special about him even then," Dundee recalled. "Something about the way he moved, like the song says. Something about the way he talked. He really learned a lot." Clay won both the national Golden Glove and Amateur Athletic Union championships as a prelude to his triumph in Rome. On returning to Louisville, he entered the professional ranks supported by a group of wealthy white Louisville investors.

Dundee guided him through a progression of professional matches. He won his first professional fight in Louisville against Tunney Hunsaker on October 29, 1960. The following year he won all eight of his bouts, including knockout victories over highly regarded Alex Miteff and Willie Besmanoff. Boxing critics could not believe his style, which was to carry his hands very low while using his quickness to avoid punches. He also began to create a public persona that deviated from the norm expected of fighters. He proclaimed himself "the prettiest" and "the greatest," and before his February 1962 fight with Sonny Banks, Clay made his first of several predictions in the form of a simple rhyme: "The man must fall in the round I call. Banks must fall in four." And indeed he did. Before he fought former light-heavyweight champion Archie Moore in late 1962, Clay told a press conference, "Don't block the aisle and don't block the door/You will all go home after round four." Sure enough, he put Moore away in the designated round. Even when he was wrong, he had an excuse. After he knocked out Don Warner in the fourth round, instead of the predicted fifth, he told reporters that he had to subtract one round because Warner had refused to shake hands before the bout!

Shocker in Miami

By the early 1960s, interest in boxing was on the wane. But here came a handsome and talented young heavyweight who made for good copy. By late 1963, Clay had won 19 consecutive fights, 14 by knockout. This set up a championship match in February of 1964 in Miami with the imposing Sonny Liston.

The sullen and violent Liston seemed too formidable a foe for the young Clay. Liston possessed an intimidating 36–1 record and had demolished Floyd Patterson with a ferocious knockout punch in the first round of their 1962 bout to claim the heavyweight title. In a rematch nine months later he once again scored a knockout in round one. Liston had a reputation as a powerful predator in the ring, capable of doing permanent injury to opponents. His threatening scowl and his lack of social or cultural refinement enhanced the perception of him as a dangerous assassin. Liston's life story reinforced that image: he had done hard time in the Missouri state prison for armed robbery, and several vicious assaults dotted his record. To further darken the picture, a series of recent news reports alleged that he still lived on the dangerous side, drinking heavily, driving recklessly, and using his fists on helpless victims.

Clay seemed to be hopelessly overmatched against this ruthless ex-con with the long rap sheet. Liston did not attempt to sugarcoat his reputation, at one point telling a reporter, "A prizefight is like a cowboy movie. There has to be a good guy and a bad guy. Only in my cowboy movies, the bad guy always wins." It was not surprising, then, that the California boxing commission refused to sanction the fight because it believed it to be "a dangerous mismatch." Other boxing experts publicly announced their opposition to putting the young boxer in harm's way. Even former champion Rocky Marciano expressed his fear that he faced serious injury at the hands of Liston. Promoters finally secured permission to hold the fight in Convention Hall in Miami.

Incredulous reporters watched Clay train for the fight in Miami, where he dazzled them with his wit and daffy poetry. During his training sessions, he spent a great deal of time working on his footwork and throwing light jabs. His strategy, Dundee told reporters, was "Float like a butterfly, sting like bee." In the weeks leading up to the fight, he more than confirmed the validity of his new nickname, "The Louisville Lip." Veteran boxing writers looked on in bemusement as Clay needled the impassive Liston with a barrage of verbal assaults, suggesting that the champion was "ugly" or "a slow ugly bear," among other things. Clay had begun this comic form of psychological warfare as an amateur, publicly insulting his opponents before the fight and barraging them with trash talk during it. As prominent sports historian Professor Randy Roberts has observed, Clay's act was a product of the rich verbal tradition of trading insults, sometimes to rhymed verse, that had long existed in the urban black community. Thus, Cassius Clay gave the white reporters an in-depth introduction to a part of black culture that they neither understood nor appreciated. "Maybe I'm old fashioned," one such reporter wrote on the eve of the Miami fight, "but I always thought a fighter had to prove himself with his fists, not with his mouth." But, as Professor Roberts concludes, "In Clay's world, a man had to prove himself with both."

Thus Clay was in top form the morning of the fight, when at the weigh-in he seemingly went berserk, shouting insults at Liston, his face quivering with emotion. "You're a bear, an ugly bear! I'm gonna whup you sooo baaaad! You're a chump, a chump!" he shouted at the scowling, if not bewildered, champion. Clay even stuck out his tongue at Liston. Some onlookers concluded that Clay had been overcome with fear of his opponent and had lost control of his senses. No wonder he was a prohibitive 7-to-1 underdog and that many Las Vegas sports books had even refused to make a line on the fight because it was deemed so lopsided. Clay's outburst, however, was merely part of a psychological assault he had waged upon earlier opponents.

From the opening bell, Clay dominated the plodding Liston. Clay did indeed float like a butterfly and repeatedly stung his opponent with crisp jabs and powerful counterpunches. Clay's quickness negated Liston's vaunted power, and soon he was dropping his hands to his sides, daring Liston to connect with the unprotected jaw. As Liston futilely flailed away, Clay began to taunt the champion, tattooing his face with jabs. By Round Four, the 8,300 spectators in Convention Hall and the estimated one million watching on a primitive closed-circuit television network recognized that they were seeing a new champion being crowned. In less than 15 minutes, Clay had completely demoralized his supposedly invincible opponent. At the end of Round Six, Liston slumped hopelessly on his stool, his face carved into a bloody mess. When the bell clanged for Round Seven, Liston remained seated and Clay exuberantly danced around the ring, shouting at reporters: "I told you so! I told you so! I'm the Greatest!" It was a stunning victory, one that reinforced the view of boxing aficionados that there was indeed, beneath all of the violence and cruelty of this blood sport, a "sweet science." Clay's win was a magnificent triumph of style and intelligence over brute force. He had entered the ring as a 7-to-1 underdog and emerged as a modern day David who had slain his Goliath.

A Muslim Champion

However stunning the outcome of his fight against Liston might have been, it paled in comparison to the shock that Clay delivered to a baffled cluster of white reporters the next morning. In response to a question regarding rumors that he had become connected with Malcolm X and Elijah Muhammad's Nation of Islam, the new champion confirmed that he had left his Christian faith and was now a true believer in "Allah and peace." Islam, he said, "is a religion and there are 750 million people all over the world who believe in it, and I'm one of them. I ain't no Christian." In Chicago, Elijah Muhammad told a national convention of the Nation of Islam, "I'm so glad that Cassius Clay was brave enough to say he was a Muslim. Clay whipped a much tougher man and came through the bout unscarred because he has accepted Muhammad as the messenger of Allah." Shortly thereafter, Elijah Muhammad said that he had given Clay a new name: Muhammad Ali (Muhammad for "worthy of praise" and Ali after an ancient warrior who had been related to the Prophet Muhammad). The new heavyweight champion renounced his "slave name" of Cassius Clay and requested that everyone, including very resistant white reporters and their editors, use only his new name.

Equally significant was his statement that he would not be the same type of passive champion as Joe Louis, whose hard work and straightforward disposition had endeared him to the American people. He was going to be his own man: "I know where I'm going," he said quietly but defiantly, "and I know the truth and I don't have to be what you want me to be. I'm free to be what I want."

Contrary to widespread skepticism, his dedication to his new religious faith was sincere. It was a decision that cost him millions of dollars in product endorsements and produced a torrent of criticism from white America. Mainstream boxing writers, predominantly white and conservative, turned on him with a vengeance. Joe Louis publicly criticized him and Billy Conn said, "He is a disgrace to the boxing profession. I think that any American who pays to see him fight after what he has said should be ashamed." Even Dr Martin Luther King, Jr, weighed in: "When Cassius Clay joined the Black Muslims and started calling himself Muhammad Ali, he became a champion of racial segregation and that is what we are fighting against." Throughout the ferocious blowback, Ali was unmoved by his critics and instead emphasized that his new faith valued marital fidelity, and a life free from drugs and alcohol. Most of white America, and especially the mainstream media, opted instead to focus on the fearsome rhetoric articulated by militant spokesmen in the emerging Black Power movement.

Ali did nothing to soften his image, and after he easily dispatched Liston in Lewiston, Maine, in a 1965 rematch, he turned his attention to former champion Floyd Patterson. Before their November 1965 title bout, Patterson objected repeatedly to Ali's embrace of the Muslim faith, saying that he intended to "take back" the crown for Christianity. At one point he compared the Black Muslim movement to the Ku Klux Klan. "I have nothing but contempt for the Black Muslims and that for which they stand. The image of a Black Muslim as the world heavyweight champion disgraces the sport and the nation. Cassius Clay [he pointedly refused to refer to his opponent as Muhammad Ali] must be beaten and the Black Muslim's scourge removed from boxing. I believe the Muslim preaching of segregation, hatred, rebellion, and violence is wrong. Clay is disgracing himself and the Negro race." The championship bout in Las Vegas became a battle between the Cross and the Crescent.

The fight itself generated additional controversy. From the beginning of Round One it was apparent that Patterson was hopelessly outclassed and a nagging back injury only slowed him down further. As Ali easily slipped Patterson's sluggish punches, he peppered his opponent with stinging blows and a running commentary of insults. To many at ringside, Ali seemed to be taking pleasure in tormenting, even torturing his opponent. *Life* magazine called the fight a "sickening spectacle," and many fans and reporters condemned Ali for purposely prolonging the fight just to humiliate and punish his opponent. Of the few reporters on the scene who defended Ali's performance was television commentator Howard Cosell, one of a small number in the mainstream media who now referred to the champion as Muhammad Ali.

Ali successfully defended his title five times in 1966 in what some called "The Palooka of the Month Club," knocking out four of his opponents and winning a 15 round decision over George Chuvalo. In February of 1967, he defeated Ernie Terrell by a decision and then knocked out Zora Foley in New York City on March 22. That would be his last title bout for four years. When not defending his title, Ali had been busily seeking a deferment from military duty. In 1961, he had been classified by his draft board as 1-Y, which meant that he had scored too low on intelligence tests to serve in the Army, and in 1964 he had been retested with the same result ("I always said I was the greatest. I never said I was the smartest," he quipped). But after President Lyndon Johnson committed the United States to a major military effort in Vietnam, the quotas of draft boards increased and so too did Ali's draft status. In 1966, he was reclassified 1-A, fit to serve.

His announcement that he would not accept induction into the United States Army set off an emotional national controversy. His much-repeated comment, "I ain't got no quarrel with them Viet Congs," drew derisive attacks. Veterans' organizations noted that Joe Louis had volunteered for military duty immediately after Pearl Harbor; Ali was either a coward or the dupe of a radical sect. Others pointed to the irony of a man whose profession was fighting but who refused to fight for his country. Overlooked in this public fury was the fact that he could most likely have negotiated an offer to join the military in a non-combatant role, perhaps giving exhibition bouts to entertain the troops and assisting in recruiting (as Louis did during the Second World War). Instead, he announced, "I have searched my conscience and find that I cannot be true to my belief in my religion and accept [induction]." Thus in Houston on April 28, 1967, he refused induction into the Army, was promptly arrested, and a four year legal and political battle ensued.

The wheels of justice in the United States normally turn slowly. Not so in this case. First came the precipitous action of the New York State Boxing Commission. Without even a pretext of a hearing, it stripped him of his title within hours of the public spectacle in Houston. Other state boxing bodies followed in short order. The United States Department of Justice moved with incredible speed. Just ten days after his arrest, Ali was indicted and his trial commenced six weeks later in a Houston federal courtroom. Judge Joe Ingraham gave detailed jury instructions that virtually assured a verdict of guilty for having violated the Selective Service Act. The judge then threw the book at the former heavyweight champion, giving him the maximum sentence permitted: five years in jail and a $10,000 fine. For good measure, he ordered Ali to surrender his passport so he could not travel abroad to fight in order to pay his bills.

Ali's speedy conviction drew widespread praise, perhaps best summarized by a comment by congressman Robert Michael of Illinois: "While thousands of our finest young men are fighting and dying in the jungles of Vietnam, this healthy specimen is profiteering from a series of shabby bouts. Apparently Cassius Clay will fight anyone but the Viet Cong." Ali, however, remained steadfast in his decision: "Why should they ask me to put on a uniform and go ten thousand miles from home and drop bombs and bullets on brown people in Vietnam while so-called Negro people in Louisville are treated like dogs? If I thought going to war would bring freedom and equality to twenty-two million of my people, they wouldn't have to draft me, I'd join tomorrow. . . . I either have to obey the laws of the land or the laws of Allah. . . . So I'll go to jail."

Ali managed to stay out of prison as his lawyers appealed his conviction. Denied the right to fight, he earned money on the college speaking circuit. As the years went by, however, public support for the war ebbed to the point in 1970 where it barely hovered above 50 percent. Ali now had an increasing number of supporters come over to his side. Thus, the New York Boxing Commission decided to reissue his license, and on June 21, 1971, the United States Supreme Court overturned his conviction on a narrow legal technicality.

With many questions now making the rounds as to whether the long layoff had reduced his skills, Ali resumed his boxing career in September of 1970 with a series of easy tune-up exhibitions and then scored knockouts over Jerry Quarry and Oscar Bonavena. He had, however, lost three-and-a-half years from his fighting prime. He seemed rusty, and perhaps a tad slower, but close observers noted that he still had the same verve and determination. And, awaiting him was a match with heavyweight champion, Smokin' Joe Frazier.

The Fight

It was called simply "The Fight." It was what boxing fans had been anticipating for years: a clash between two undefeated heavyweights, one the champion, the other having lost his title at the hands of the New York Boxing Commission. Frazier–Ali in Madison Square Garden was a promoter's dream. The profit potential in the new technology of closed-circuit television had convinced two well-connected entrepreneurs, Jerry Perenchio and Jack Kent Cooke, to promote the fight. They were new to the fight game, having made their mark as investors in entertainment and sports (Perenchio was a major producer of films and television shows; Cooke owned the Los Angeles Lakers). Having willingly agreed to pay each fighter an unprecedented purse of $2.5 million, the pair lined up 360 theaters and auditoriums in the United States for their closed-circuit production, selling more than 1.5 million seats at prices ranging from

Figure 7.1 Muhammad Ali and Joe Frazier mix it up at a New York City press conference in December of 1970 where they signed a contract for their March 8, 1971, fight in Madison Square Garden. Ali often provoked pre-fight episodes such as this one to stimulate interest in his fights as well as to "get into the head" of his opponents. © Bettmann/CORBIS

$12 to $50. The fight was also carried via satellite to 35 foreign countries, where it was watched by roughly 300 million people. It was estimated that Cooke and Perenchio pocketed $15 million for their efforts. One veteran fight promoter acknowledged that Perenchio and Cooke had changed the rules, probably forever: "The fight game will never be the same. They're running this thing like a circus. You don't hear anything about the fight. Its nothing but money, money, money."

Actually, there was a great deal to hear about the fight. It was, for boxing fans, a classic match-up of two gifted heavyweight champions with sharply contrasting styles, both seemingly at the peak of their talents. But this fight was much more. It was a morality play to be acted out in the ring. In the eyes of many Americans it was a contest between the forces of good and evil, but with the terms defined differently by different people. For young Americans who had opposed the war in Vietnam, and especially for the millions of African-Americans who believed that Ali had been persecuted by a repressive white establishment, Ali would carry into the ring their hopes for redemption. Conversely, others viewed the dark skinned Frazier as the new "Great White Hope," whose lethal left hook they hoped would silence the bigmouth who had spoken out against the war in Vietnam, who had become the nation's most visible draft resister, and who had, for much too long, taunted white America.

Frazier was not prepared emotionally or intellectually for the cultural battle into which he was thrust. He was the consummate career fighter, simply a decent but unsophisticated man, a hard-worker who exuded little charisma. He became the best hope for those who wanted to bring Ali down. Frazier had not dodged the draft (earning an exemption as a parent), he refused to criticize the war, and he steadfastly insisted on calling his opponent "Clay." He came to symbolize much more than he intended. In the days leading up to The Fight, publicists for Madison Square Garden issued statements that emphasized Frazier's Americanism: "Not since the days of Joe Louis and Ray Robinson and Floyd Patterson has a black man brought so much dignity to boxing." They had no comparably kind words for Ali. Frazier seemed baffled by the ferment as he became a symbol for causes he only vaguely understood, especially when he was derisively tabbed the "white man's champion" by Ali and his supporters. Frazier never could match Ali's verbal virtuosity, nor could he fully comprehend the manner in which he was being depicted and manipulated. He simply wanted to ply his trade. "The thing I want most," he said plaintively as their meeting approached, "is to fight Clay and to settle this thing."

For many Americans, Ali had been too outspoken, too controversial, too brash. He had long attempted to humiliate his opponents with sexist and racist names ("little girl," "Uncle Tom," "baby rabbit") in part to hype ticket sales but more deeply to satisfy his own sense of importance. At times his verbal thrusts were humorous and telling, but as the years went by they increasingly took on a crude, cruel, and tasteless quality. His decision to become a Black Muslim and change his name was deeply troubling to mainstream America, and when he rejected military service he challenged traditional assumptions. That he did so at a time when the Civil Rights movement had reached its dramatic crest, and had seemingly morphed into disturbing outbursts of urban rioting, did nothing to reassure conventional thinkers about his radicalism. Frazier, in their view, had avoided the draft legitimately. He had fought his way from obscure poverty to the title against a substantial list of challengers, and he had done it the American way as pioneered by Joe Louis – by avoiding controversy and by following a staunch work ethic.

Thus did both fighters carry with them into the ring the conflicting dreams and hopes of millions of supporters who believed that their man was the one on the side of truth and righteousness. But Ali also recognized the obverse: "People will come to this fight because I'm undefeated and unscratched. People want to see me whipped – because I'm arrogant and because of the draft, because of my religion and because I'm black." That said, the supreme irony of the standoff between the Muslim and the black man now carrying the incredible burden of "The New Great White Hope" was that the deep emotional issues in which they had become embroiled would not be resolved, but only exacerbated, by the powerful emotions unleashed by The Fight.

Round One, New York City

In the weeks leading up to The Fight, Ali had unleashed an unrelenting attack upon his opponent, and this time nasty racial overtones were front and center. Unlike other fights, there was no hint of humor in his rhetoric. For starters, in concert with his fans, he claimed that he was the real champion and Frazier an imposter. It was a fight, he said, between "the champ and the tramp." But his major verbal blasts carried with them a paradox that not many at the time perceived. Frazier, the son of impoverished black South Carolina sharecroppers, a man who had diligently worked to improve himself, was according to Ali an "Uncle Tom." That cruel racial thrust came, in fact, from the son of a Louisville family that owned its own modest home and had the advantages of a regular paycheck.

Frazier had successfully defended his title when he knocked out journeyman Bob Foster in Round Two in November in Detroit, which was viewed as a tune-up for what many were already referring to as yet another "Fight of the Century." Meanwhile Ali had to go 15 ragged rounds in December in Miami before winning a decision over Oscar Bonovena. Frazier trained diligently, and he and trainer Eddie Futch quietly developed a strategy based on Futch's observation that Ali had a tendency to drop his right hand before throwing a right uppercut. Frazier's few pre-fight comments had none of the soaring rhetoric of Ali, but they did resonate a quiet confidence: "I'll whip him good. Clay's easier to hit in the body than anywhere – sticks his head back and his body out. And I'm a body puncher."

On March 8, 1971, Ali entered the ring bedecked in red velvet trunks with matching tassels on his shoelaces that danced when he moved, while Frazier wore green and gold trunks, and no designer tassels. Before the referee called them to the center of the ring for instructions, Ali bounded around the ring, tassels flopping, purposely coming close to bumping the impassive Frazier. At one point he shouted into the press row, "No contest!" No contest!" A sellout crowd of 20,455 jammed Madison Square Garden; ringside seats had gone for an unprecedented $150. People around the globe gathered before their television screens and in theaters in anticipation. Many a celebrity was sighted at ringside, including local politicos and former Vice-President Hubert Humphrey and Senator Ted Kennedy. Movie stars included Burt Lancaster, Dustin Hoffman, and Woody Allen. Singer Diana Ross was there, along with Frank Sinatra who had somehow wangled a gig as a "photographer" for *Life* magazine. Hugh Hefner was up front with girlfriend Barbie Benton. Among the literary crowd, novelist/essayist Norman Mailer was also on *Life's* payroll, commissioned to write an in-depth analysis for the next issue; Budd Shulberg was on special assignment from *Playboy*, and William Soroyan for *True*. The tension was palpable as the opening bell rang. Ali's biographer Thomas Hauser writes, "The eyes of the world were focused on a small square of illuminated canvas, which had become one of the great stages of modern times. Never before had so many people watched and waited for a single event. Tension, anticipation, and excitement were everywhere."

Unlike so many championship fights, this one lived up to its billing. It was a brutal slugfest from start to finish. Ali had predicted a Round Six finish, but the fight was just getting cranked up at that point. In the early rounds Ali danced about, flinging jabs and counterpunches, while Frazier, true to form, waded into his opponent smashing him in the torso with punishing blows. Ali soon settled into a flat-footed approach, his legs no longer able to float him like a butterfly for 15 rounds. Frazier believed, "Kill the body and the head will die," and so he took Ali's best shots as he waded in to deliver his crushing punches to Ali's body. In the middle rounds the crowd began shouting "Ali! Ali!" as he seemed to gain momentum, but Frazier regrouped and the battle went on. In Round 11, Frazier detected what Eddie Futch had predicted: Ali dropped his right hand in preparation for throwing his famous uppercut. Frazier recognized the move and nailed him with a powerful left that sent Ali staggering onto the ropes. That one punch changed the fight's momentum. In Round 12 Frazier folded Ali like an accordion with repeated shots to the head and body. Ali wobbled on rubbery legs back to his corner where he was greeted by a bucket of water thrown in his face by his trainer and cheerleader Bundini Brown trying to revive his fighter.

The final rounds were a standoff as the tired fighters continued to pound each other. The fans were now shouting in a near frenzy. Finally, at the 2:34 mark of Round 15, Frazier ended any doubt as to the winner. He once again landed a powerful left hook to Ali's jaw, sending him sailing backwards onto the canvas, his bright red tassels dancing high above his head as he landed. Ali courageously regained his feet at the count of four and held on until the final bell.

The fight was indeed close, despite the late knockdown, but Frazier was declared the winner on all three cards. Ali's fans claimed the judges had been subconsciously swayed by public opinion. The knockdown, however, was the final embarrassment in a long night for Ali. His braggadocio had been trumped by the understated 27-year-old defending champion. "I always knew who the real champion was," Frazer said quietly, his two swollen eyes framing a smile. In fact, Frazier had not only bested Ali in the ring, but he had bested him in the pre-fight prediction game as well. "Clay is good," he had said a week before the fight, "but he isn't good enough to escape."

Ali quietly told one visitor to his locker room, where he lay in considerable discomfort, that "I got whupped." Indeed he had, and with a badly swollen jaw he had also been temporarily silenced. A trip to the hospital confirmed that the jaw had not been broken. Actually, Frazier's face, swollen and twisted in pain, indicated that the winner had also absorbed major punishment, but Frazier had always fought toe-to-toe, willing to absorb his opponent's best blows in order to land his own. He never claimed he was a gifted boxer or, like Ali, boasted that his face was "beautiful" and unmarked by his opponents. Years later, Ali later would quip, "My jaw told me he won. He hit me so hard it shook my kinfolk in Africa." But in the days following the fight, he was in no mood for laughter.

Weeks after The Fight, speculation naturally began to circulate about a rematch. For the time being, Ali told reporters that his loss had not devastated him: "Just lost a fight, that's all. There are more important things to worry about in life. Probably be a better man for it. News doesn't last that long. Planes crash, ninety people die, it's not news a day after. Presidents get assassinated, civil rights leaders get assassinated. The world goes on. You'll all be writing about something else soon. I had my day. You lose, you don't shoot yourself. I'm going to have to make the best of it." And, as if to launch a new prediction: "I'm taking a whipping home with me. I got to win next time."

The first meeting between the two men would be considered by some boxing fans to be one of the most exciting and hard-fought heavyweight championship fights in history. Ali's supporters tried to convince themselves that he was still the *de facto* champion. Ali's plan to regain the crown was derailed when Frazier surprisingly lost his title to George Foreman in Kingston, Jamaica, in January of 1973. The 25-year-old Foreman completely dominated the lethargic champion, knocking him down six times in the first two rounds. Now Ali had to deal with two foes.

Ali fought a series of exhibitions in 1972 but interspersed among these bouts were some legitimate adversaries: Mac Foster, George Chuvalo, Jerry Quarry and Joe Bugner. Although he won these fights, it was evident that some of his quickness had eroded. This might explain why he was beaten by the lightly regarded Ken Norton in March of 1973. Norton lacked experience but he had Eddie Futch in his corner, and Futch knew Ali's tendencies better than anyone. In the second round, Norton pinned Ali on the ropes and smacked him with a straight right hand that broke his jaw. Nonetheless, Ali fought on through intense pain, not giving any indication of the break. According to the scoring cards, he and Norton were even when they entered the final Round 12, but Norton dominated in a flurry to win a major upset. Ali had to undergo surgery to repair the jaw and the surgeon later said, "I can't fathom how he could have gone on the whole fight like that." Ali's medical doctor and corner man, Ferdie Pacheco, knew: "Underneath all that beauty, there was an ugly Teamster Union trucker at work." The New York City tabloid columnist Jimmy Cannon, who had long berated Ali for his multiple perceived sins, exuberantly proclaimed, "He's a loser now!"

Round Two

Six months later, the jaw had healed and a well-prepared Ali defeated Norton by a close decision in a rematch in Los Angeles. He then set his sights on Frazier to earn the right to take on Foreman for the title. A week before "The Fight II," scheduled for January 28, 1974, Howard Cosell interviewed the two men together in an ABC television studio and asked them to comment on a tape replay of their epic first bout. They had been trading public insults for weeks, with Ali especially upset that Frazier refused to use his Muslim name: "I still call him Clay; his mother named him Clay. If you've been around this guy long enough, you can have a lot of hate in your heart when the bell rings." Ali, for his part, had gotten under Frazier's skin by calling him "ignorant."

As the two men sat side-by-side in the ABC studio with Cosell and the tape rolling, Frazier noted that "Clay" had to visit the hospital after their first fight. Ali retorted, "You ignorant Joe." Ali's brother Rahman jumped on the stage shouting and rushed toward Frazier. Ali grabbed Frazier in what he later claimed was a friendly bear hug, but Frazier was in no mood for camaraderie and shoved Ali to the floor. Soon all three men were scuffling in a heap. At that point the scrum ended. Feelings were hurt, feathers ruffled, and the real fight was still a week away.

The rematch might have been tinged with hostility, but it lacked the drama of their initial bout. This time Ali was able to avoid the bull rushes by Frazier as he connected with jabs and combinations throughout. Ali dominated much of the fight, but Frazier began a rally in Round Seven, which he sustained through to Round Nine. Ali effectively responded during the final three rounds and claimed a unanimous decision. He had managed to avoid Frazier's potent left hand, and he had earned a shot at George Foreman plus an opportunity to reclaim his long-lost title.

"The Rumble in the Jungle"

What Ali called the "Rumble in the Jungle" was the first major fight to be promoted by the former Cleveland numbers racketeer and ex-con Don King. He got Foreman and Ali to agree to split a $10 million purse. One minor technicality existed: King did not have the money. He proceeded to fast-talk the president of Zaire (now the Democratic Republic of the Congo) into sponsoring the fight. President Mobuto Sese Seko envisioned (incorrectly it turned out) using the fight to publicize his country and stimulate foreign investment. All did not go well on the public relations front for the ambitious president: an early poster injudiciously proclaimed the fight as "From the Slave Ship to the Championship" and had to be scrapped; then Ali told a bunch of reporters that unless they accepted his prediction of victory, "Mobuto's people are gonna put you in a pot, cook you, and eat you." After a lecture on political correctness from the Zaire foreign minister, Ali agreed not to infer again that his high-paying host was head of a nation of cannibals.

Ali spent several months in Zaire training for the fight, getting his body accustomed to the heat and humidity that he would encounter in the outdoor stadium. The serious money was on Foreman, who had dismantled Frazier. Most experts believed that Ali had lost his quickness and would be unable to avoid Foreman's sledgehammer punches.

Ali came into the fight armed with a new tactic that he and trainer Angelo Dundee had devised to counter Foreman's power. Beginning in the second round, Ali lay on the ropes, protecting himself with his arms, permitting Foreman to bang away at his body, sometimes forcing Ali into a clinch, occasionally flicking jabs and counterpunches to Foreman's jaw. The tactic was designed to wear out the champion in the hot and steamy arena. By the fifth round, Foreman had thrown hundreds of punches, most with little effect, and he was visibly tiring. Further, Ali's counterpunches had produced substantial swelling around the eyes. Ali would later call this unusual tactic "rope-a-dope," and it worked spectacularly well. In Round Eight he nailed the exhausted Foreman with a hard right hand and the champion spun around across the ring and collapsed in a heap, unconscious. Seven years after he had been stripped of the championship and ten years after trouncing Sonny Liston, once more Muhammad Ai was the world champion. In his latest victory, he had unquestionably demonstrated the importance of strategy and psychology. And, for good measure, he had contributed "rope-a-dope" to the lexicon of American popular culture.

Round Three: "Thrilla in Manila"

In 1975, Ali decided to reap the financial benefits of the title, defending successfully against a string of unimpressive challengers. He knocked out Chuck Wepner and Ron Lyle and won a 15 round decision in Kuala Lumpur over Joe Bugner. This set up his final match with Joe Frazier. It would be another Don King production, staged in a large arena on the outskirts of Manila.

Both men understood that they were on the downside of their careers and that this would be their last battle. The rancor between the two was palpable, with Ali once more irritating Frazier, this time by correcting his grammar at press conferences. He also came up with a new moniker for his adversary. Playing upon an historical racial stereotype, he called Frazier an "ugly gorilla." At a press conference he even held up a black toy gorilla. This sorry episode, and others of similar bad taste, hurt his opponent more deeply than anything his fists could accomplish. Baseball star Reggie Jackson was on hand for some of these taunting sessions and later recalled, "Joe Frazier's a hard-working, honest, decent man. He's a proud man. There's a great honor about Joe. . . . Muhammad Ali ridiculed Joe; he humiliated him in front of the world. . . . This time he stepped over the line – and he did it several times . . . calling him ignorant. He took the English language and ripped Joe to death with it. And Joe couldn't match wits; he didn't have the verbal skills. So his response was to get more angry and more bitter. Muhammad was pretty hard on Joe, and it was as bad as ever in Manila." Frazier did not hold back: "It's real hatred. I want to take his heart out. If I knock him down, I'll stand back, give him a chance to breathe, to get up, so I can knock him down again."

The arena's air conditioning failed but the fight went on before a crowd of 27,000 in extremely hot and humid conditions. Ali scored early, landing powerful shots to his opponent's face that seemed to stagger Frazier. Joe continued to wade in, taking more punishment, attempting to unleash his killer left hand. Ali tired and Frazier controlled the middle rounds while Ali went to the rope-a-dope. Round after round, both fighters wearily battled on, taking turns pummeling each other. Finally, in Round 12, the bout turned in Ali's favor when he connected with a left hand that knocked Frazier's mouthpiece into the crowd and buckled his knees. Ali won the next round in a rush and then, in the decisive Round 14, he hit Frazier at will. Frazier's eyes were nearly closed from swelling. Frazier could barely see his opponent as the round ended. Manager Eddie Futch recognized as much: "His left eye was completely closed; his right eye was closing. It had been a grueling fight, and that's when fighters get hurt, when they get hit with good clean punches they don't see and still don't go down. I didn't want Joe's brains scrambled." The exhausted and wounded Frazier pleaded to continue but Futch decided to end the bout.

Things might have turned out much differently had Futch waited a bit longer. Ali returned to his corner after the 14th a beaten man. He slumped onto the chair, held up his gloves and told Dundee, "Cut 'em off." Dundee refused and Ali slumped even more, seemingly unwilling to return for another three minutes of hell. Then Futch signaled from the other corner

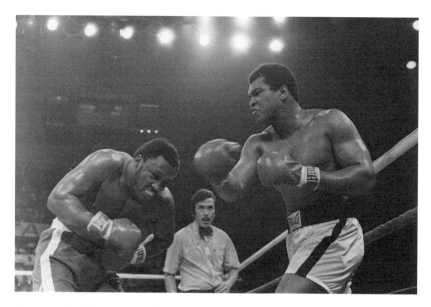

Figure 7.2 Muhammad Ali lands a blow to the head of Joe Frazier in the tenth round in Manila on October 1, 1975, in what many boxing experts believe to be one of the most compelling bouts in the history of the sport. Frazier's manager threw in the towel after his fighter's eyes swelled shut following the 14th round. The referee is Carlos Padilla. © Bettmann/CORBIS

to the referee to call the fight and both Ali and Dundee broke into tears. Had Dundee acted immediately upon Ali's request, the distinct possibility that Frazier would have been declared the winner existed. Frazier had plaintively told Futch, "I want him," but he was too exhausted to do anything but slowly shake his head when Futch insisted on ending the brawl. Ali later admitted he had wanted to quit: "Frazier quit just before I did. I didn't think I could fight anymore." Moments after he was declared the victor, Ali rose, his legs wobbly like a bowl of jelly, and then slowly slumped to the canvas. No one ever knew if he had actually lost consciousness or merely had been overcome by the emotions of the moment.

Both men had to be helped to their dressing rooms, where they lay bruised and swollen, dehydrated and exhausted, emotionally and physically spent. Both men could barely talk. Frazier could not see anything but dim shadows through his puffy eyes. Ali's ringside physician, Ferdie Pacheco recalled later that it took Ali weeks to recover from the effects of the fight. "It was the toughest fight I've seen in my life." Ali concurred, ruefully acknowledging, "It was the closest I've come to death."

Final Rounds

Both men were voted the Boxer of the Year by the Boxing Writers Association for their valiant efforts in Manila. Frazier was finished. He lost by a five round TKO to Foreman in 1976 and retired, while a markedly slowed Ali defended his title six times against less-than-stirring challengers before he lost a lopsided decision to Leon Spinks in Las Vegas on February 15, 1978. For that title defense, he appeared overweight and out-of-condition, and not much enthused about being in the ring. He joined Frazier in retirement, but both men missed the excitement that surrounded the sport to which they had devoted more than 20 years of their lives. They made the mistake of trying to turn back the clock, but their comeback attempts were sad. Ali took a frightful beating in 1980 when he challenged new champion, Larry Holmes. It was followed up by a desultory performance against Trevor Berbick the following year. Frazier's furtive comeback effort was even more disheartening, when he shuffled to a ten round draw with the unknown Jumbo Cummings in Chicago in 1981.

Frazier moved permanently into retirement in Philadelphia, enjoying his gig as a nightclub singer. His act was appropriately named "Smokin' Joe and the Knockouts." He now owned and operated the boxing gym and building that Cloverlay had acquired for him during his championship days. There he greeted visitors and trained young fighters (including his son Marvis, whose 21 fight professional career ended in 1987 by a knockout at the hands of Mike Tyson). He also owned a restaurant and operated a limousine service. He and Florence divorced in 1985, and he struggled through various legal and business setbacks while battling hypertension and a serious case of hepatitis. He watched with pleasure as several of his children graduated from college and pursued successful professional and business careers and oversaw the Smokin' Joe Frazier Foundation. Compared with the recurring sad tales of many ex-professional boxers, Frazier handled his post-ring life quite well.

It was not long after Ali retired that the effects of absorbing blows to the head for 25 years began to evidence themselves in the form of slurred speech and halting steps. He suffered from tremors and poor balance.

The once loquacious Ali could no longer float like a butterfly, and he had difficulty speaking. Almost overnight, he had become an old man. In the ancient parlance of the fight game, he was "punch drunk," but his physicians diagnosed his condition as an advanced form of irreversible brain damage caused by Parkinson's disease. Ali's deteriorating condition produced an outpouring of concern and admiration, and he became one of America's most beloved public figures, widely hailed as a courageous man who had doggedly stuck to his beliefs in the face of enormous public vilification, eventually to be exonerated by the changing tides of history.

Over the ensuing years, the two men vacillated between reconciliation and a renewal of hostilities. They appeared together at black tie dinners and posed amicably for the requisite photographs. But beneath the veneer of good will, the open wounds still festered. Ali apparently felt no ill will but was frustrated by the icy indifference of his former foe. It appears that Frazier never forgave his adversary for all of the hurtful things he

Figure 7.3 Gallant foes in repose. Despite this amicable scene, captured on film in 2002 at the NBA All-Star game in Philadelphia, Joe Frazier was never quite able to forgive Muhammad Ali for his many stinging comments made prior to their three fights, many of which questioned Frazier's intelligence.
© Reuters/CORBIS

had said. In particular, he still smarted from the indirect apology the wounded Ali offered up in his dressing room through his son Marvis in Manila ("Tell your father all that stuff I said about him, I didn't mean it. Your father is a helluva man."). It was not accepted: "Why not be man enough to say what you feel to me, to my face?" Frazier asked. "He couldn't bring himself to do the right thing." When Ali had the honor of lighting the Olympic flame at Atlanta in 1996, Frazier told a *New York Times* reporter, without any hint of humor, he wished he could push him into the burning oil. Ali's cruel verbal thrusts had gone too deep. He admitted that he had little compassion for the ailing Ali: "Nope. I don't. I don't give a damn. They want me to love him, but I'll open the grave-yard and bury his ass when the Lord chooses to take him. . . . Clay always mocked me – like I was a dummy. . . . Now look at him: he can hardly talk and he's still out there trying to make some noise." And, for good measure, "He's a ghost and I'm still here. Now let's talk about who *really* won those three fights."

8 Friendly Foes
Chrissie and Martina

Together, match by match, final by final, Chris Evert and Martina Navratilova changed women's tennis forever. I watched their rivalry with pride: two remarkable athletes, fierce competitors – and good friends. (Billie Jean King)

American tennis will probably never again have the opportunity to enjoy the likes of the rivalry between Chris Evert and Martina Navratilova. Their skill and athleticism was a sight to behold, and they each played with a tenacity that refuted all of the clichés about women athletes, that ladies should "play nice." At a time when such male tennis stars as Jimmy Connors, Bjorn Borg, and John McEnroe were in their prime and attracting unprecedented public attention to tennis, the quality of their play elevated women's tennis to an equal stature. Evert and Navratilova met on 80 occasions in sanctioned tournaments, 14 times in the finals of a Grand Slam. In head-to-head competition Navratilova held a narrow 43–37 edge. For nearly 15 years, one or the other was ranked as the Number One player in the world. In examining this special rivalry at its peak during the mid-1980s, Frank Deford appropriately described them as a "pair beyond compare."

Their rivalry was not only marked by the unusually high number of times they met, but by the sharp contrasts in backgrounds, personalities, and styles of play. Evert came out of the traditional mold, playing cautiously from the baseline, resolutely returning shot after shot, preferring to wear down her opponent with long rallies, eventually producing an unforced error. She never developed much of a power game. Consequently, her serves were of pedestrian quality, at best, and only on rare occasions did she charge the net for a decisive volley put-away. Raised in a middle-class American family, Evert's public image was that of the distinctly feminine "girl next door." Throughout her career, she enjoyed the enthusiastic support of American tennis fans and a fawning media, while Navratilova was perceived as the outsider whose strong physique, controversial personal life, and tennis game built on strength and power seemed both fascinating and troubling. After years of less-than-stellar commitment to her game, Martina changed her attitude and embraced a rigorous conditioning regimen that propelled her to the top of women's tennis.

The most intriguing part of this fierce rivalry was that they managed to remain friends off the court, and they often joined forces to make a fearsome doubles team. Their competitive natures naturally produced moments of tension but, all in all, this has to be considered a rivalry between two mature athletes who appreciated the many positive attributes of the other.

Women's Tennis and the Struggle for Equality

Evert and Navratilova came onto the tennis scene at the right time. Up until the 1960s, women's tennis was a sport of the affluent amateur. The best women players during the formative years – Helen Wills, Alice Marble, Doris Hart, Althea Gibson – played as amateurs. That situation began to change during the 1960s as the United States Tennis Association (USTA) sanctioned professional tournaments that included a women's division. However, the USTA was definitely not committed to equal opportunity for women. Tournament officials seldom assigned women's matches to the prestigious center court, and prize money remained significantly smaller than that offered to men. Nonetheless, most women players during the 1960s were simply pleased that they were now offered opportunities to compete and grateful that they were even included in a growing number of tour events that offered very modest prize money.

That change occurred simultaneously with the rise of the women's rights movement. But it was one woman, Billie Jean King, who led a determined effort to improve the lot of the first generation of women professionals. Her stature buttressed by US Open and Wimbledon championships, King aggressively challenged the second-class treatment women professionals received from the male-dominated USTA and local tournament officials. She formed the Women's Tennis Association and assumed its leadership, applying public pressure for equal prize money and the end to other discriminatory practices. She convinced leading tobacco company Philip Morris to finance an all-women's professional circuit named after its female-oriented product – the Virginia Slims Tour. In 1973, bowing to increasing public criticism, the USTA announced that the US Open prize money would be equal.

The Girl Next Door

The first major beneficiary of Billie Jean King's crusade was a young lady who had grown up on the public tennis courts of Fort Lauderdale where her father, a former college tennis star at Northwestern, taught the game and supervised the tennis complex at Holiday Park. From the time his daughter was five years old, Jimmy Evert patiently taught her the fundamentals of the game, putting her through long and demanding drills. These tedious sessions developed muscle memory that would provide the basis for her future success. Over the years, Chrissie Evert developed the patience and control that would amaze future spectators and frustrate her opponents. She also learned to hit each shot with a different pace and different spin. She became a master of the baseline game and would stick with it throughout her long career. Many an opponent who charged to the net would watch helplessly as Chrissie whistled a winning passing shot down the line. When her opponents decided to play her game from the baseline, she relied on her superior abilities of concentration, patiently maneuvering her exasperated opponent out of position or producing an unforced error after a long rally. Chrissie later commented that, "When I was a youngster I was a little robot. Wind her up and she plays tennis."

The skills that carried her to the heights of women's tennis were learned on the clay courts of Holiday Park. By the time she reached the age of ten, Jimmy Evert had crafted a future world champion in his own image. Because she was so small, young Chrissie took to hitting her backhand with both hands, and that technique became one of her signature strokes on tour. She began to win local tournaments when she was eight and within two years Chrissie was defeating players much older than herself. She became the national 16-and-under champion, and in 1970, in a tournament in Charlotte, she shocked the tennis world by beating highly ranked Margaret Court 7–6, 7–6. Spectators became enthralled as she drilled precise shots deep to the corners and passed Court when she dared to venture to the net. That victory led to an invitation to the 1971 US Open in Forest Hills.

In this premier event of American tennis, Evert virtually overnight became a household name, her blonde ponytail bobbing up and down as she relentlessly wore down more experienced players. She seemed to have poise beyond her years, appearing unperturbed when she lost an important point and showing no emotion when she hit a winner. Spectators were amazed that such a slight young lady could hit such precise shots with such power as she mowed down several established players to reach the semi-finals. Her magic run ended with a 6–3, 6–2 loss to top-seeded Billie Jean King, but she had moved with incredible speed to the top tier of women's tennis.

Evert selected her 18th birthday, December 12, 1972, to announce that she was turning professional. Her timing was absolutely impeccable. She joined the initial Virginia Slims tour that sponsored seven tournaments and $300,000 in prize money. Two years later the prize money had jumped to $775,000, and television producers learned that women's tennis made for good ratings. Journalist Grace Lichtenstein wrote later about just how radical the Slims tour seemed at the time and that the women were seeking recognition as elite athletes in their own right, independent of the men. Stanford graduate and tour member Julie Heldman took note of the fact that they were challenging "the false tenets of femininity that had plagued me and so many other girls. As a kid growing up in the 1950s, I accepted the concept of women athletes as freaks. I had been taught that to want to become an athlete of any kind was unacceptable. Girls were passive, non-competitive, dependent. The notion of a sexy woman athlete was a contradiction." Heldman realized that throughout her life she had been "programmed to quit." All through high school and college, as she pursued her love of tennis, she kept being asked, "When are you going to quit?" After college and having turned professional, the questions became, "When are you going to quit, get married, and have kids?"

Even Chrissie Evert at her prime was sometimes criticized for her gritty play. She was, writers noted, too "determined," too "cold," too "calculating" on the court, and she was given the cruel nickname of "The Ice Maiden" who intimated her opponents with "The Stare." Evert later wrote of these difficult times as a teenager playing on the cutthroat professional circuit with adults: "If I wasn't that warm, it's because I was petrified of people." Her early success at age 16 produced jealously and bitterness among many of the older women, who saw this upstart deprive them of some of what little prize money was available. When she defeated the veteran Mary Ann Eisel in a close match at the 1971 US Open after holding off six consecutive match points in the second set, she was greeted in the locker room coldly by a group of sullen women. They were upset that she had defeated one of the tour's regulars and generated such enthusiasm for her own play among the 10,000 fans. This treatment continued as Evert began to pile up one victory after another. Finally, Billie Jean King intervened and told her petulant colleagues that Evert was for real, and that the excitement she was generating was good for everyone. "Hey, Chrissie's good for women's tennis, Let's give her a chance. Let's take advantage of the publicity."

King was right. Evert's sudden emergence was good for women's tennis, as she did indeed generate an enormous amount of interest. In her first three years on the pro tour, she won an astounding 23 tournaments. She represented a new generation that was set apart from the anger and militancy associated with the women's movement of the 1960s and, in the world of tennis, embodied in the pugnacious personage of Billie Jean King. She was a cute teenager, quiet and reserved to the point of acute shyness, ever polite and courteous to the media, fans, and her opponents. By 1975, Evert had accomplished a great deal on the court, but perhaps her greatest achievement was that she had become a top-ranked star player while maintaining her image as the likeable girl next door. She was not outspoken or angry, she had no burning social or political agenda, and she had maintained her feminine identity while unremorsefully pounding the daylights out of her opponents.

Evert moved with stunning speed into the top five in rankings. At Wimbledon in 1972 she lost in the semi-finals to Aussie Evonne Goolagong, but the following year she made it to the finals before bowing to King. At the French Open she lost in the finals in 1973 to Margaret Court 6–7, 7–6, 6–4, but won her first Grand Slam event on the red clay the following year over Russian Olga Morozova 6–1, 6–2, and weeks later triumphed again over Morozova at Wimbledon. Her victory at Roland Garros in the suburbs of Paris was part of a remarkable winning streak of 125 consecutive tournament matches played on clay between 1973 and 1979. She won her first US Open in 1975 in three sets over the popular Goolagong. At the age of 20, Chris Evert had become the top-ranked woman player in the world.

Challenge From Behind the Iron Curtain

The best thing that happened to Evert's rising tennis stature was the arrival of Martina Navratilova as a major challenger in 1975. The husky lass from

Czechoslovakia provided a startling contrast to the pristine image that Chris exuded, and she soon became a threat to Evert's dominance of the women's circuit. Martina idolized Evert when she was in her early teens and mounted a poster of Chris in her room. In 1973, she was thrilled to be invited to the United States to play on a six week mini-tour. While in Akron, she exchanged greetings with Evert, who was playing backgammon on the club patio with her younger sister Jeannie. The smile and a few words from Evert thrilled Martina: "I thought, 'She's so nice.' . . . I was excited, I was mesmerized. Chris was a perfect blonde goddess who was challenging Billie Jean King and Virginia Wade. Before I even met her, she stood for everything I admired about this country: poise, ability, sportsmanship, money, style."

Like Evert, Martina Navratilova grew up in a supportive family environment. Her family had owned a substantial house and a 30 acre plot of land in the Prague suburb of Revnice, but lost it when the Communist regime took over in 1948. Her family continued to live in the house, but now were relegated to a small apartment and forced to share the building with other families. Born in October 1956, her parents divorced when she was three. However, her mother remarried in 1962 and Martina became close to her stepfather Mirek Navratil and took his name (the "ova" is added in the Czech language to denote female). Her grandmother and mother were both capable tennis players, but her mother preferred skiing. Martina took to both sports as a young child, learning to ski during the winter months and play tennis when the snows melted. She began swinging a sawed-off racquet before she was four. By the time she was five, she had mastered hitting a ball against a wall and volleying with herself, often keeping the ball in play for several minutes. Mirek duly noted the sharp crack of the ball coming off the racquet and was impressed with her consistency and accuracy. One day he took her to the local municipal courts, an experience Martina never forgot: "The moment I stepped on that crunchy red clay, felt the grit under my sneakers, felt the joy of smacking the ball over the net, I knew I was in the right place. Mirek was at the net and I was between the service line and the baseline. I could have hit with him all day. I had all the energy and patience in the world."

By the time she was seven, Mirek was transporting her to local tournaments on the back of his motor scooter. When she was nine, Mirek convinced the popular Czech singles player George Parma to take her on as a student at his indoor Sparta Club courts in Prague. Parma decided to develop her game around the serve and volley because it best fit her physique and psyche. For several years she rode a commuter train from Revnice into Prague twice a week after school, and she thrived under Parma's instruction. By 1972, she was one of the leading juniors in Czechoslovakia. Her tennis future now lay in the hands of the powerful Czech Tennis Federation that oversaw the considerable number of Czechs who were capable of competing internationally.

The invasion by the Soviet Army in 1968 made a lasting impression on the 11-year-old Navratilova. The efforts of president Alexander Dubček to provide his people with "socialism with a human face," were seen as threatening to Moscow, and so in came the tanks in August, stifling Dubček's efforts at creating a minimal level of democratic government. She was old enough to recognize tyranny and felt deeply the anguish the incursion generated among her parents and neighbors. She joined her friends in a concerted passive resistance movement, at one point giving false directions to Soviet tank commanders and, when they were not looking, writing freedom slogans on their armor. "It was just depressing to see everything," Martina later recalled. "The countryside was being ruined by those frigging tanks that came out of nowhere. Our lives were changed for good – well, not for 'good,' but forever. And I just remember being absolutely livid and feeling helpless and mad at the same time. And there was nothing you could do. Being an 11-year-old girl, what can you do?"

What she did was throw herself into her tennis, dreaming of someday playing at Wimbledon. Speaking about the terrible psychological impact of the Soviet invasion and the suppression of freedom across her country, Martina recalled, "Wimbledon was the only dream you were allowed to have." Her emotional reaction to the suppression of Czechoslovakian nationalism did not die, and when she began to travel abroad, always after having to struggle with Czech bureaucrats who put roadblocks in her path, the thought of defecting to the United States began to germinate in her mind. When she first visited the United States in the spring of 1973, she was immediately struck by the openness, optimism, and freshness of American life. She was blessed with an aptitude for language and readily developed a facility with English. What appealed to her most was American food, especially the fast food variety. She put on 20 pounds during her visit as she enjoyed a constant repast of cheeseburgers and fries, fried chicken and ice cream sundaes.

The attraction of the West did not die when she returned to Revnice. The post-invasion crackdown by the new Communist government extended to its athletes. Because authorities feared the embarrassment of a defection, tennis players were routinely accompanied by government supervisors. Their passports were seized on their return, as was any prize money won at tournaments outside the Iron Curtain. Beginning with her first trips, Martina could not disguise that she was enthralled with the culture of the West. Concerns about her loyalty intensified among Czech officials as she moved up in international rankings. It was apparent that she not only liked American food – and indeed she did – but also the American lifestyle. Rather than fork over her winnings upon returning home, she spent them on fashionable clothing and expensive jewelry in upscale American boutiques. She also made friends easily, one among them being Shari Barman, a tour player from Los Angeles. Her father was a successful businessman, and Fred Barman helped Martina devise strategies to keep her winnings out of the hands of the Czech government. With her prize money growing in 1974, she no longer needed to survive on the $17 a day allowance permitted by the Czech authorities. She began to stay in comfortable hotels because she enjoyed the amenities and it was a way of snubbing her own government. Her parents became concerned for her safety, warning her at one point to curb her newfound exuberance for the American lifestyle. "You can't do whatever you want," her concerned mother scolded. "Why not?" Martina responded.

By 1975, Martina had become a tennis player to be reckoned with. After losing several matches to Chris Evert, she finally defeated her 3–6, 6–4, 7–6 in a quarter-final match in a tournament in Washington, DC, and two weeks later, she knocked off in succession Margaret Court, Virginia Wade, and Evonne Goolagong in the US Indoor Championships. She later lost to Evert in a semi-final match in Philadelphia but the next day found herself playing with Evert, at her invitation, in doubles and spending time hitting with Chris to help her get ready for the finals. The two women had discovered that they had much in common, and a friendship was improbably taking hold. "I used to turn to Chris for a lot of help and advice in those early years in America," Martina recalled, "and she was always so understanding." The influential *Boston Globe* sportswriter and television tennis commentator Bud Collins was not quite so friendly. Taking note of Martina's extra poundage, he dubbed her, women's tennis's "Great Wide Hope."

Despite her inattention to her physical condition, and her disinclination to practice with much enthusiasm, Martina rose rapidly to high rankings on the basis of her immense natural talent. In 1975, she was seeded

Figure 8.1 Martina Navratilova takes a typical diving lunge at a Chris Evert passing shot during the Virginia Slims tournament in Madison Square Garden in March of 1984. © Bettmann/CORBIS

second behind Evert at the French Open, where they also were entered as a doubles team. They managed to win the doubles, giving Martina her first Grand Slam title, and they plowed through their respective brackets to meet in the singles finals. Navratilova won the first set in seemingly easy fashion, 6–2, but that only made Evert more determined than usual and she stormed back to win decisively 2–6, 6–2, 6–1. Navratilova flew back to Czechoslovakia, expecting a hero's welcome, but instead she was subjected to a barrage of questions about her refusal to stay with the other Czech players in a cramped Paris apartment, selecting instead a high-class hotel. For a time, officials threatened to deny her permission to play at Wimbledon – her long-time dream – but then relented. As she departed for Wimbledon, having gained the necessary permissions, she and her family secretly contemplated that she might not return home. These were weighty issues for a teenage girl who had virtually no significant personal relationships established in the West.

Defection

Martina's early career, while filled with promise, did not take off nearly so smoothly as Chris's – after 36 tournaments, she could claim just two singles championships, in sharp contrast with Chrissie's 36 wins in her first 49 tournaments. But Navratilova never set her sights any lower than catching Evert, who was just two years older but light years ahead of her in the rarified atmosphere of big-time tennis. Navratilova had the overriding problem of her growing unhappiness with the treatment she was receiving from the Czech government. In 1974, her parents had been permitted to accompany her to Wimbledon, and they seriously considered seeking asylum as a family at that time. But the pull of the mother country and the uncertainties that her parents contemplated about their own defection led to a decision to return to Revnice.

Martina came to the realization that if she was going to make the break, she would have to do it herself. On one hand, she was confident in her ability to earn a good living playing tennis; on the other hand, it was difficult for a teenager to overcome the ties of family attachments. She made the fateful decision while practicing before the 1975 US Open. She had received increasingly severe warnings that her behavior outside of Czechoslovakia was unacceptable, with indirect warnings that she might be denied future visas if her conduct did not improve. With her mind thus distracted, she got thoroughly embarrassed by a lesser player, Dianne Fromholtz, in a warm-up match. "I was in such an emotional state it was pathetic," she would later write in her autobiography. "I was so depressed, I didn't know what was happening." As she left the court in Westchester Country, she made the decision. "This can't go on, I told myself. Every time you go home, you're going to wonder if they'll ever let you out again. It's time to make your move." Back in her hotel in the city, she called Fred Barman who arranged for a meeting with the FBI and began to work out arrangements for a defection with the Bureau of Immigration and Naturalization. As the tournament unfolded, Navratilova played well despite the international drama that was building. She defeated Margaret Court in the quarter-finals and then had to face her ultimate rival in the semi-finals. Chris played with her usual consistent determination and won a close match 6–4, 6–4. Evert now held a commanding 11–2 margin over Navratilova.

As planned, Martina went into hiding at the end of the tournament. She fully understood that she was not going to see her parents for a long time, if ever. To defect from a Communist country in the depths of the Cold War was to acknowledge that you could not go home again. She had this fact drummed into her by Mirek shortly before she had departed for the last time in July. "If you do defect," he told her, "all future telephone conversations back home would be monitored. Stay there. Don't come back, no matter what we say."

American authorities were pleased to have such a high profile defection. She was given FBI protection and her application for citizenship sailed through the bureaucracy. At age 19, she was free, and would soon become an American citizen. She was also earning large amounts of American dollars that she no longer had to share with the Czech government. That she had second thoughts about her decision was to be expected, and for months it weighed heavily upon her. Although she made many friends through her tennis associations, she was nonetheless alone in a semi-foreign country, with no family and no home. Homesickness was a natural result. She had studied English with determination, but then again she longed to hear her parents' voices in their native tongue and to learn what was happening back in Revnice. She compensated by eating plenty of cheeseburgers and fries and by going shopping in high-end stores where she displayed all of the symptoms of a compulsive shopper. By year's end, the *New York Times* wrote, "The Czechoslovak-born star has become a walking delegate for conspicuous consumption," taking due notice of her many fancy outfits, fur coats, expensive jewelry, and "the usual status-symbol shoes and purse that round out the wardrobe. She owns a $20,000 Merecedes Benz 450SL sports coupe. She is fluent in American slang." And for good measure, "As an undisciplined gourmet, she is overweight."

Her undisciplined lifestyle began to weigh on her – literally – as the months went by. Increasingly conscious of her excess weight and frustrated by her inability to play up to the level of Chris Evert, her game went south. Consequently, Navratilova failed to win a single title in 1976. When she returned that August to the place where her defection had taken place, the US Open in Forest Hills, the immensity of what had transpired finally hit home. Out of condition, and naively believing that she did not have to practice during the weeks before the Open, she was roundly defeated before a contemptuous crowd by journeyman Janet Newberry. Embarrassed and distraught, her emotions, pent up for a year, spilled over as she left the court. Tears streamed down her face, and she stuffed a towel over her head to cover her embarrassment. Her whole body shook with emotion. Martina recalled this pivotal incident, when she found herself "rocking back and forth, moaning and crying." She remarked: "So much had been expected of me, so much had happened to me, and now I felt that the whole world was crashing in on me . . . I don't think I had any control over myself at the time." A sympathetic Newberry told Bud Collins, "I never saw anybody so miserable, so totally out of control." Fred Barman spirited her out the back way to avoid the press, and he later wrote, "This whole year Martina had been like a kid taking her first trip to Disneyland. Here's a kid who was imprisoned just a year ago." Navratilova left New York in an emotional shambles, not staying to watch Chris Evert win her second straight Open title over Evonne Goolagong in a match that was decided 8–6 in the third set. Beyond all of the other emotions that had churned within her, Navratilova now came to realize that she could no longer suppress the fact that she was attracted to other women.

Navratilova in Search of Herself

Earlier that year, Martina had been introduced to the 32-year-old professional golfer, Sandra Haynie and over the following months they communicated with increasing frequency. The 19-year-old asked for advice on dealing with the pressures of the tour, her seeming lack of a killer instinct in close matches, even her persistent weight problem. The day after her emotional breakdown, Navratilova boarded an airplane with Haynie and moved to Dallas where the two women bought a house together and began a close personal relationship. Haynie provided Martina with a sense of stability that enabled her to move past her emotional distress.

Haynie had won her share of golf tournaments, including the US Open and PGA championships, and, although she was not a tennis player, was able to help Martina deal with her emotional swings on the court, to help her concentrate full attention on each point, and to teach her how to prepare for matches psychologically. Haynie also got her to control her emotional outbursts that produced extravagant spending sprees. Martina signed on with a reputable agent, Marvin Demoff, to gain even more control over her finances. That said, her well-publicized relationship with Haynie and future female companions would severely limit her ability to attract endorsement contracts.

Under Haynie's influence, Martina began to practice with greater intensity and she began to lose weight. In the first year that they shared a house in Dallas, Martina's weight fell from 167 to 144 pounds, which contributed to better results on the tennis court. Although their relationship became a source of much comment, the openly lesbian Haynie cared not a whit, and Navratilova finally had the sense of contentment that she had lost when she left her parents to become an American citizen. In 1977, she began to play with more consistency, and tournament championships began to accumulate.

Thus did a more confident, mature, and emotionally stable Navratilova begin to enjoy the success that so many had predicted. She won 37 consecutive matches to begin her breakout year of 1978. She realized that she was now ready to achieve an ambition she traced back to when she was nine years old: to win Wimbledon. In London, she worked her way through a tough draw, having to defeat the teenage sensation Tracy Austin in the fourth round. In the semi-finals against Evonne Goolagong Cawley, she bounced back after losing the first set to win the final two sets 6–4, 6–4, and then came face-to-face with a player who had defeated her consistently, top-seeded Chris Evert. Navratilova had won but four of the 24 matches they had played up to this pivotal match, and she seemed in a daze in the first set, unable to handle Chris's usual combination of precisely placed cross-court and down-the-line shots. But early in the second set, one of Evert's cross-court shots caught Martina in the side of the head, and, although the shot was not hit intentionally, it seemed to shake Navratilova out of her stupor and she proceeded to win the set 6–4.

The third and final set was a classic. Evert won four straight games to go up 4–2, and it seemed that she was on the brink of winning another important match with her steady play. But she uncharacteristically missed a forehand that enabled Navratilova to break serve and pull back to 3–4. Martina drew upon her new reserve of energy as she rushed the net, forcing Evert to hit ever more precise passing shots under severe pressure, but Evert remained her tautly focused self and managed to hold serve to take a 5–4 lead.

This match established what many tennis fans had been anticipating, a fierce rivalry between two women whose lifestyles and tennis games were virtually polar opposites. The day before the match, both were pressed by the media to explain how the two could be, from all appearances, good friends off the court as well as doubles partners on it, and still deal with the pressures of facing each other in the finals. With Evert on the verge of another Grand Slam title, Martina seemed to move to a higher level of play, hitting her serves with such tremendous force that Evert had difficulty in getting a racquet on them, slashing across the court to return Evert's baseline shots and ending each point with a ferocious, well-placed volley. At one point during this amazing burst of inspired tennis, Martina won 12 of 13 points. She evened the match at five-all by winning her serve at love, then broke her opponent at 15–40 to take the lead, and served out the match by hitting a hard low half-volley for the winning point that handcuffed Evert. As the two embraced at the net and walked off the court together, it was difficult to tell who had won and who had lost. Evert, deeply disappointed, nonetheless seemed genuinely happy for Martina. At that moment, however, Martina recognized just how bittersweet her triumph was. Her parents were not there to share in her joy. "I'm not sure how they'll find out," she said. "Since I defected three years ago there hasn't been a word about me in the Czech newspapers. Tomorrow they'll probably say that Chris Evert was playing somebody."

Evert: Number One

Navratilova's breakthrough victory at Wimbledon did not change the pecking order of women's tennis. She lost to Evert three more times that same year, as Evert retained her Number One world ranking. Actually, for a brief time, both had to contemplate the challenge being mounted by the latest teenage phenomenon, the charming Californian Tracy Austin. To most observers, Austin's efficient baseline game, played without the slightest hint of emotion, brought to mind a teenage Chrissie Evert. In 1979, the 16-year-old Austin sent shock waves through women's tennis when she snapped Evert's six year string of 125 consecutive wins at the French Open. Evert was devastated: "I felt like it was the end of an era." Evert's sensibility that she was losing control was intensified when she lost to Navratilova once more in the Wimbledon finals 6–4, 6–4. To most observers, the actual match was not nearly as close as the score, since Martina was in control throughout. Both women had to be concerned when Austin proceeded to defeat Navratilova in a close 7–5, 7–5 semi-final match at the US Open and then beat Evert decisively in the finals, 6–4, 6–3. Austin's future seemed boundless: she was just 16 and had won two Grand Slam events.

Evert's decline was attributed to her adjustment to marriage. Chris had tied the knot with the handsome English tennis star John Lloyd in 1978 and the pair struggled with their respective tennis careers as they often had to live apart on their tours. Evert took a sabbatical from tennis in early 1980 to deal with her options, ultimately vowing to return to the tour with both Austin and Navratilova looming as her primary adversaries. At the same time that Evert was dealing with the complexities of mixing marriage with a professional career, Navratilova's personal life had changed. She and Haynie had drifted apart, and the impulsive Martina began a new relationship with the feminist novelist Rita Mae Brown in a sprawling 20-room mansion on the outskirts of Charlottesville, Virginia. Neighbors duly noted that Martina had seven luxury automobiles parked in and around the five-car garage. This brittle relationship soon dissolved in a raft of bitter arguments, but for a time it caused Navratilova once more to lose focus on her tennis.

After her break from tennis, Chris Evert returned to her winning ways, determined to regain her Number One world ranking. She decisively defeated Navratilova in the semi-finals at Wimbledon, ending Martina's streak of 19 consecutive victories in singles matches. Martina's troubles continued with a fourth-round loss to Hana Mandlikova at the US Open, and many tennis experts offered the opinion that her days in the sun were numbered. On the other side of the draw, Evert met her nemesis Tracy Austin in the semi-finals. Evert had been told that she could not win if she attempted to outstroke Austin from the baseline, but that is precisely what she set out to do. After her service had been broken twice, the crowd began to sense that Evert was in deep trouble. Behind 4–0, Chris decided to go on the attack, hitting drop shots and lobs, and uncharacteristically charging the net to smash winning volleys. She still dropped the first set 6–4, but the momentum had changed the match and her unexpected burst of aggression had unsettled Austin, producing a rash of unforced errors. Evert won the next two sets in convincing fashion, 6–1, 6–1. Her three set victory in the finals over Hana Mandlikova was almost anticlimactic, although it restored her to the Number One ranking. Austin would not remain for long on the tour, and instead of becoming Evert's major rival, that distinction fell to the struggling Navratilova. Austin, like other female teenage tennis sensations, had placed too much stress upon her still maturing body. Debilitating back and leg injuries limited her play in 1981 and three years later her physical ailments forced her retirement from competitive tennis at age 24.

For the time being, Evert had managed to balance her marriage and her tennis. However, she later said, "When it came down to it, I was married to my tennis. Tennis was how I identified myself." Commenting on her marriage to Lloyd, which ended in divorce in 1987, she observed, "Maybe my priorities were wrong, but I'd always fit things into my tennis, not the other way around."

Meanwhile, Navratilova was caught up in another frenetic lifestyle that saw her once again going on spending sprees. She also fell into several brief, emotionally charged relationships and even acquired a substantial number of pedigree dogs. As her tennis began to suffer, she bounced from one tennis coach to another. Despite living life in the fast lane, Navratilova could not avoid the brutal fact that, in 1981, Chris Evert had won 11 major tournaments while she had taken a mere two. Even such a close observer as Billie Jean King had begun to publicly speculate that Martina did not have the self-discipline and maturity to become a perennial champion. Many had predicted her career was rapidly coming to a premature, hapless ending.

Team Navratilova

Martina's decline definitely seemed to be on the cards in March of 1981 when she entered a clay court tournament at Amelia Island, Florida. During the middle of a match with Kathy Rinaldi, she noticed the flaming red

Figure 8.2 Nineteen-year-old Chris Evert, ponytail and all, hits her patented two-handed backhand from the baseline in the finals of the Rome Open tournament in 1974. Her opponent in this match was the unheralded teenager from Czechoslovakia, Martina Navratilova. Evert won convincingly 6–3, 6–3. © Bettmann/CORBIS

hair of women's basketball star Nancy Lieberman in the stands, and they had a pleasant conversation in the VIP tent afterward. According to both women, they were immediately attracted to each other and they talked long into the wee hours of Saturday night, even though Navratilova was scheduled for the singles final against Evert. The result was the most embarrassing loss in Navratilova's career: Evert defeated her 6–0, 6–0 in a match that lasted less than an hour. Martina was distraught and even apologized to the fans for her sloppy play during the trophy presentation. Although some say that this defeat forced Navratilova to reassess her training methods and face up to the negative influence of her roller-coaster emotions, she merely said that her long evening with the engaging Lieberman was "not the optimal way of getting ready for a match." But that chance meeting did lead to profound changes in Navratilova's life and the way she approached tennis. It also would be the pivotal moment in which she began to realize her goal of ousting Chris Evert from the top rung of women's tennis.

Lieberman forced Navratilova to examine herself critically. She had accompanied Martina to the French Open in June of 1981 and was appalled by Martina's lack of dedication to her conditioning and match preparation, bluntly accusing her of being lazy and unprofessional: "I couldn't imagine putting myself in front of the whole world and practically setting myself up to fail . . . I could see that Chris Evert wanted to win and Martina just wanted to play. Chris saw Martina as her rival. Martina saw her as her friend. Martina wanted to be nice." Lieberman had become the top women's basketball player by taking no prisoners, by forcing herself to refine her skills by competing on the concrete courts of Harlem against skilled male players. After early exits at the French Open and Wimbledon, Martina invited Lieberman to move in with her and to take over her conditioning and match preparation. Navratilova did not know it, but Lieberman planned to remake Navratilova's physique and mental outlook, to make her the top woman tennis player in the world.

Lieberman changed Navratilova's diet to eliminate the junk food, and put her on a grueling physical conditioning regimen that Martina later confessed made her feel real physical pain for the first time in her life. She ran steps, she ran long distances, she ran sprints. She learned to stretch and she began to lift weights. She played basketball. And for the first time in her adult life, she hit tennis balls with a purpose for three hours a day. Lieberman also worked to make Martina mentally tough, forcing her to understand that a champion at the highest level had to do more than defeat one's opponent, but want to destroy her. "It's not just about winning – it's about how you win," she said, telling Martina that she needed to increase her aggressive play, to put away volleys as if pounding out a large exclamation point. She oversaw the restructuring of Martina into a powerful tennis machine that would intimidate and obliterate opponents.

Lieberman used every opportunity to convince Martina that Chris Evert was not her friend; rather, she was the enemy. Lieberman demanded a new confrontational approach to her matches with Evert. Perturbed as this new image began to coalesce, Evert came to call it, "The Kill Chris Strategy." What had been a cordial, even friendly, rivalry became much cooler, much more intense.

There thus emerged what came to be known as Team Navratilova. She no longer approached tournaments as a social event, but seemed to come prepared to go to war. Her earlier image of the "Great Wide Hope" was replaced by the image of a powerful woman who carried not a pound of excess fat on her ripped body. She definitely set a new standard on the women's circuit for physical conditioning. Her entourage became the talk of the tennis world and included Lieberman in the lead roles of physical trainer and psychologist. She also hired a nutritionist, a masseuse, and a new tennis coach. That coach was one of the most controversial people in the sport, the formerly male tennis professional Richard Raskind. With a mediocre record on the tour, Raskind underwent a sex-change operation in 1975 and then won the right to compete on the women's tour as Renee Richards. The new coach was dumbfounded by Navratilova's lack of understanding about tennis strategy and, especially, the preparation required prior to playing an opponent. "I couldn't believe how little Martina knew about playing tennis and how faulty her strokes were," she recalled. "She's very intelligent, but she's not an abstract thinker, *per se*. She was playing on talent and instinct." Martina quickly took to the new approach as she and Richards went over the detailed scouting reports on opponents and prepared a strategy to attack each one. Martina admitted how abashed she felt when she realized just how lacking her knowledge was.

Thus a new Martina Navratilova was prepared to challenge Chris Evert. That opportunity came in the semi-finals of the US Open at Forest Hills in September 1981. She seemed to be a different player. Unlike many previous matches where she seemed to lose focus, nothing seemed to distract her as she won the first set 7–5. Spectators noticed Martina's intensity, and the way she concentrated on every point. Evert naturally became more determined and the second set turned into a veritable war. Even the standing ovations from the capacity crowd of 18,000 after every particularly stirring point did not seem to break their concentration. The match was a marvelous display of both raw power and incredible finesse, as both players made one breathtaking shot after another. Ultimately, Evert won the set 6–4. To knowledgeable viewers, this was the moment when Navratilova would most likely find a way to lose. However, she had become a different player; she did not lose her focus even when a fight erupted in the stands and play had to be stopped while security removed the pugilists. With the second set tied at 4–4, and Navratilova serving, she fell behind 15–40, but rallied back with a booming ace and powerful ground strokes to go up 5–4. In earlier times, Evert would most likely have been serving for the match. Instead, she faced a determined opponent who became even more aggressive. Navratilova proceeded to win the game and take the third set. The rivalry certainly took on a new hue when Evert's last desperate lob sailed long.

Navratilova's victory was especially meaningful to close observers of women's tennis, but the emotion that it drained from her was evident in the finals against Tracy Austin. After winning the first set 6–1, Navratilova made several unforced errors that permitted Austin to win the final two sets in tie-breakers. She had resolutely fought off three match points in the third set, but a horrendous double fault gave the match to Austin. Nonetheless, Martina had won over the crowd, who sensed that they were finally witnessing the type of player many had anticipated for more than half a decade. Evert had taken due notice that Martina had become a much more determined and confident player. That person was on display when they met in the finals on the grass at the Australian Open in December of 1981. Navratilova had not won a Grand Slam tournament for more than two years, and by this time the combined efforts of Lieberman and Richards were evident as she and Evert pushed each other into the last stages of the third set in the finals. With the score tied at five-all, Navratilova broke Evert's serve in a flurry of volleys and then served out the match to win 6–7, 6–4, 7–5.

Navratilova: Number One

That decisive Australian Open match turned the tide in the Chrissie–Martina rivalry. Martina now was firmly in command of her emotions and the result was a dazzling display of domination that left Evert well behind. Between 1982 and 1986, Martina won 12 Grand Slam tournaments and captured an incredible 70 championships in the 84 tournaments she entered. Her combined match record for this period of absolute domination was 427–14. Chris Evert played her heart out and won five more Grand Slam titles, including three on her favorite surface, the red clay of Roland Garros. After losing to Martina 6–3, 6–1 in the 1984 finals in Paris, Evert defeated her in three sets in both the 1985 and 1986 French Open finals. On grass and hard court surfaces, however, Evert could no longer match the strength and speed of Navratilova, and she had to be satisfied with the runner-up trophy after losses to Martina at Wimbledon in 1982, 1984, and 1985 as well as at the US Open and the Australian Open in 1985. Their matches became the hottest ticket item in tennis and at Grand Slam finals the galleries were filled with the rich and famous. As Nancy Lieberman said, "It brought out the casual fans, brought out men, not just women. It was soap opera. It was drama."

And drama there was. In the mid-1980s, Navratilova was at the height of her physical prowess. Her new image as the physical conditioning freak did not sit well with many who held more traditional images of the ideal female tennis champion. Her openly lesbian lifestyle prevented her from being accepted with the admiration and affection that engulfed Chrissie. Although she proclaimed herself to be bisexual, Navratilova had never sought to hide the fact that she had a succession of lesbian relationships. She made certain that her female companions were seen with her in public and she gave them prime box tickets to her matches. Her entourage also became a focus of comment for the gossip columnists. It was large and its composition was always in flux as various characters came and went. Although Lieberman and Richards were constants, she was forever hiring a wide variety of health and fitness specialists to accompany her on the tour. They might be, at any given time, weight trainers, acupuncturists, massage therapists, and avant-garde dieticians touting unconventional fruit and vegetable concoctions. Martina's diet changed drastically, as she moved away first from red meats, then from chicken and fish. At one point she even stopped consuming dairy products. She became a committed vegetarian, and during one long stretch, joined the ranks of vegans, subsisting on uncooked vegetables and fruits. She became, one amazed reporter said, "the bionic tennis player."

Lieberman's emphasis upon Martina disliking – "hating" perhaps might be too strong a word – her most fearsome opponents as a means of psychologically preparing her for major matches naturally chilled the renowned friendship between Navratilova and Evert. The *New York Times* sports columnist George Vecsey reported that he met many people who sided with Chris in this situation. "I think Martina disturbed people on a psychological level even more than she did on a physical level," he said. "For years, some people still treated her like the Commie defector. Other times, it was as if there was this fear she was going to seduce some-body's little girl . . ." She was, to many, the muscular lesbian, an image to be feared. Rumors abounded – incorrectly – that she was taking large doses of steroids. Certainly most corporate sponsors felt that way: Martina seldom picked up a check for endorsing commercial products – her pro-motional contract with the Japanese automobile manufacturer Subaru being the major exception – while Chris's feminine image was widely sought for a wide range of products aimed at women. At one match, a man shouted out to Evert, "Come on Chris, I want a real woman to win!" And, after losing several consecutive matches to Martina, Chris said, perhaps only half in jest, that Martina should play on the men's tour, "and leave us alone."

The membership of Team Navratilova remained a controversial, con-stantly changing group of offbeat individuals, but was also growing larger. In 1985 at Wimbledon, Navratilova had to rent two houses for her entourage. In 1983, Renee Richards (the former Richard Raskind) left the group to return to her profession of New York City ophthalmologist. Replacing her as coach was Mike Estep with whom Martina had played in 1975 as part of the Boston Lobsters in the short-lived World Team Tennis. He proved to be a steadying influence, especially after Leiberman departed the scene in the wake of a series of disagreements. As the 1983 US Open loomed, she leaned heavily for support upon the steady Estep as she once more prepared for the possibility of meeting Chris in the finals. During the year she had won all five encounters with Evert, but she knew that Chris would be revved up for the match. Significantly, they had now become tied at 19-all in their championship matches, and so Martina recognized that she was on the cusp of achieving her long-standing ambition of surpassing her one-time idol. She was not about to let that opportunity pass, and she won convincingly in straight sets, 6–1, 6–3, despite having the match interrupted briefly when an airplane few low overhead pulling a banner that read, "Good Luck Chrissie." Martina felt complete redemption, telling the post-match press conference, "If I don't win another tournament in my life, at least I can say I did it all." It was, the press related, the most complete defeat Chris had ever absorbed in a Grand Slam match. Most writers concurred that Navratilova had finally surpassed Evert.

During the press conference, however, the familiar criticisms of Navratilova were raised. At one point, she was asked if she thought her crushing victory was "unfair," an obvious reference to the role Team Navratilova played in preparing her both physically and mentally for the match. This time she was not defensive: "Look. The other women can do everything I do, all the line drills, the quarter-mile runs on the track, the full-court basketball games. If they want to, they can do it. I've put in the work. I'm a size eight, same as Chris. The only thing that's big about me is my feet. So how is that unfair? How?"

The rivalry continued and, after Lieberman departed the scene, the rift between the two women healed. But, on the court, Chrissie had been firmly displaced as Number One. Chrissie was approaching her 30th birthday, but her marriage to John Lloyd was on the rocks and heading for divorce. It was generally conceded that even though she had begun to emulate some aspects of Martina's conditioning program, including weight lifting, she could not match Martina's gift of genetics, which naturally made her an exceptional athlete. She could not completely revamp her game and abandon her natural space at the baseline; nor could she develop a booming serve that was one of Martina's greatest weapons. Even one of Chris's best friends and supporters, Billie Jean King, admitted that, "Martina is so head and shoulders above everybody, a baseliner can't beat her anymore. Chris is going to have to change her style, and its kind of late for her to do that." Her view seemed all too accurate. At one point Martina won 15 straight sets from Chris while winning ten consecutive matches. "She wasn't just beating me," Chris admitted, "she was killing me."

Friendly Rivals to the End

Although Evert still was dominant on clay, her days of dominating on grass and hard court were essentially over. Her final two Grand Slam victories came in the 1985 and 1986 French Opens with close three set wins over Martina, but Martina continued to dominate elsewhere, winning the Wimbledon and US Open singles titles in 1986 and 1987. Evert married the Olympic downhill skier Andy Mill in 1988 and retired from the tour the following year. She wrote in *Sports Illustrated* that she had always planned "to play beyond my prime, to find out what my prime was."

After confronting the rising tide of new challengers – Steffi Graf, Gabriel Sabatini, Monica Seles, and Arantxa Sanchez, as well as a seemingly bionic Martina – she decided the time had come to retire and build a new life with Mill as a housewife and mother. Of Martina, she wrote, "I'll miss playing her. My biggest thrills came in beating her, yet when I lost to Martina, I was disappointed but never devastated. If I couldn't win a tournament myself, I wanted her to win." Martina was as generous in her comments, "Even when she beat me, and I'd be sitting in the locker room depressed, she'd come over to cheer me up. . . . Not only did we bring out the best in each other, but we brought it out for years longer than if either of us had been alone at the top. If she had never gotten there, I might have long since left the sport."

Chris and Mill had three children, but their marriage ended in divorce in 2006. In June of 2008, she remarried, this time to Australian golfer Greg Norman, but they separated the following year. Martina was not interested in a conventional domestic life, and she continued to pursue her tennis career long after her rival had retired. She won her last Grand Slam at the age of 33 when she swept by the American Zina Garrison 6–4, 6–1 at Wimbledon in 1990. It was her ninth singles championship at the All-England venue. She continued to compete with the new generations of players, losing to Monica Seles in the 1991 US Open after turning back Steffi Graf in the semi-finals. Her final appearance in a Grand Slam final was at Wimbledon in 1994, where she lost to Conchita Martinez in three sets. She soon thereafter retired from singles but continued to play doubles, winning the 2003 mixed doubles title at the Australian Open and Wimbledon with partner Leander Paes, a doubles specialist from India. The victory in the Arthur Ashe Stadium in New York came at the age of 46, making her the oldest player to win a major event. Her final appearance came at Wimbledon playing doubles in 2006 when she was 50.

In 1984, when she finally had pulled even with Evert in their personal duel, Martina matter-of-factly told a reporter, "Professionally speaking, I'd like to be the greatest women's tennis player of all time." From the perspective of a quarter century later, that seems to be her destiny.

"Dearest Enemies"
Ohio State-Michigan Football

This is not a game. This is war. (Woody Hayes)

You grow to hate Ohio State. It's like good versus evil. (Don Dufek, Michigan defensive back, 1973–5)

As the clock ticked off the final minute of play in 1968, the Ohio State Buckeyes owned a 44–14 lead and had the ball inside the Michigan five yard line. Instead of ordering quarterback Rex Kern to kneel down and run out the clock, coach Woody Hayes reinserted first-string fullback Jim Otis into the game with instructions to run his favorite play, "Robust 26," an off-tackle power slant. After Otis bulled into the end zone, Hayes called for a two point conversion attempt. Although the play failed, it served its purpose of rubbing salt into deep wounds. Asked afterward by a reporter why he went for the two point play, Hayes snarled, "Because I couldn't go for three."

Hurry Up

At the end of the 2009 season, Michigan held a commanding 57–43–6 lead over Ohio State in a rivalry that dates back to 1897. That margin is deceptive, however, because Michigan defeated Ohio State 13 times before Ohio State administrators decided to get serious about football. Michigan embraced football long before Ohio State because of the determination of president James B. Angell to use a winning football team as a means of increasing the school's national visibility. Appointed president in 1871, Angell served until 1909 and during that long tenure turned a small state university into one of the nation's leading public academic institutions.

Campus records indicate that the game had been played on campus since 1879, but no one paid much attention. That changed in 1901 when Angell appointed 30-year-old Fielding Yost to coach the Michigan Eleven. Yost had played the game at West Virginia, where he earned a law degree but found himself drawn to football. After one year coaching stints at Ohio Wesleyan, Nebraska, Kansas, and Stanford, he arrived in Ann Arbor brashly predicting, "Michigan isn't going to lose a game." For a surprisingly long time, he proved to be a man of his word.

Yost emphasized speed and precise execution, shouting to his players as he put them through their drills, "Hurry Up! Hurry Up! If you can't hurry, make way for someone who can!" The Wolverines went undefeated during his first season while outscoring their opponents 550–0, and then annihilated Stanford 49–0 in the first Rose Bowl. After 55 consecutive victories, they finally lost to the Chicago Maroons 2–0 in the season finale in 1905. During this span, Yost's teams outscored the opposition by 2,821 points to 42, leading to his nickname of "Point-a-Minute Yost."

Yost racked up five Western Conference championships between 1901 and 1906 and drew much attention by winning four of five games against Amos Alonzo Stagg's exalted Chicago Maroons. He also dominated Ohio State: Michigan held a 12–0–2 mark over the Buckeyes when the series was temporarily suspended after the 1912 game. Regents Field was inadequate for the large crowds that Yost's teams attracted, and he convinced seed magnate Dexter Ferry to make a donation of $30,000 so that a 14,000-seat stadium would be in place for the 1902 season. By the time Yost retired, it held 42,000. After dominating the young conference, Michigan withdrew in 1907 because of reform efforts that were perceived to be anti-Yost and anti-Michigan. The Wolverines played as an independent until returning to the conference, now popularly called the Big Ten, in 1918.

Chic

Only after joining the Western Conference did Ohio State officials decide to upgrade their football program. They appointed Dr John Wilce, a former star fullback for the University of Wisconsin, as head coach. Eleven coaches had come and gone in Columbus since the Buckeyes began playing in 1890 against the likes of Kenyon, Oberlin, and Ohio Wesleyan. For years the Buckeyes had played on a vacant lot near the unpaved

Figure 9.1   A young Fielding Yost poses at the Michigan practice field circa 1902. He established the winning football tradition at Michigan with a 165–29–10 record. As athletic director he oversaw the construction of the "Big House" in which the Wolverines play to this day. (Bentley Historical Library, University of Michigan. Fielding H. Yost, box 8, Portraits)

North High Street before ramshackle wooden bleachers that held, perhaps, 300 spectators.

By 1916, Wilce had the Buckeyes on a winning path and football fever began to take hold in Columbus. Much of the enthusiasm was generated when Wilce corralled a potential star, who turned down overtures from Notre Dame and Michigan, into attending his hometown university. Charles "Chic" Harley had enjoyed a sensational career at East High in Columbus. Weighing just 145 pounds, the 5′10″ halfback played sparingly in his first game on the varsity team as Ohio State overwhelmed Oberlin 128–0 (to this day, still a school record). The following week at Illinois against Bob Zuppke's much-vaunted team, Harley began to build his superstar reputation with a spectacular 60 yard touchdown run in the fourth quarter to tie the score. He then calmly kicked the winning extra point. The following Saturday, a crowd of over 12,000 converged on Ohio Field to get a glimpse of the famous sophomore against Wisconsin. Chic did not disappoint as he passed over and ran through and around the Badgers. His spectacular 80 yard run, in which he eluded several open field tacklers, sparked a 14–13 upset win.

On his elusive runs Harley seemed to lope down the field, changing speeds to confuse tacklers and shrewdly slowing down to set up a block. A *Columbus Dispatch* writer explained: "He'd loaf along hoping to string out his field of tacklers so he could meet them one by one. If he could he was gone. And so he was." One of Harley's classmates at Ohio State was journalism major James Thurber. Writing in 1940, now a famed essayist for the *New Yorker*, Thurber recalled watching Harley perform his gridiron magic: "If you never saw him run with a football, we can't describe it to you. It wasn't like Red Grange or Tom Harmon or anybody else. It was a kind of cross between music and cannon fire, and it brought your heart up under your ears."

Late season victories over Indiana and Northwestern gave Ohio State its first conference championship and an undefeated 7–0 season. In the process, Chic Harley had almost single-handedly ignited football frenzy in Columbus, never to go away. The *Dispatch*'s enormous headline the next day proclaimed, "Ohio, Champs of the West!" and the lead story was altogether prescient: "November 25, 1916, will go down in athletic history as beginning a new epoch in Ohio State football."

America's entrance into the Great War in Europe muted football enthusiasm in 1917, but Harley led the Scarlet and Gray to an 8–0–1 season and a second consecutive conference title. Crowds continued to overflow Ohio Field and new bleachers were erected, bringing seating capacity to 14,000. Harley spent 1918 in the military, but when he returned for his senior year in 1919, Buckeye fans exuded a newfound confidence: Maybe, just maybe, this was the year that they could finally beat Michigan. The Wolverines had rejoined the Western Conference in 1918 after a ten year run as an independent. Wilce focused the attention of his squad squarely on the October 25 game in Ann Arbor. The two teams were not exactly rivals – yet – because a rivalry requires a modicum of balance in victories, and after 15 games with the Wolverines, Ohio State remained winless.

For years, Ohio State fans had referred to the lauded Wolverines as "our dearest enemy," although Michigan fans viewed Ohio State as merely a tune-up for big games with the likes of Chicago and Minnesota. The Buckeyes rolled into Ann Arbor undefeated, accompanied by thousands of fans. Throughout the afternoon, Chic Harley's right foot kept Michigan penned up deep in their own territory. He booted 11 punts, averaging 42 yards. Midway through the third quarter, the triple-threat back broke loose on a stellar 42 yard run around end for a touchdown

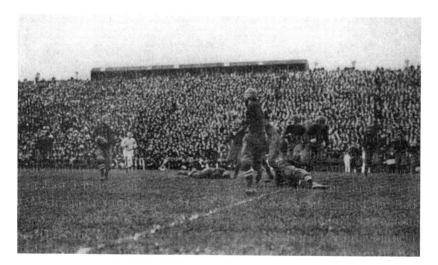

Figure 9.2 Chic Harley is on the loose against Michigan in 1919 at a packed Ferry Field. The much-acclaimed Buckeye halfback helped produce Ohio State's first ever victory over the Wolverines in this October classic. (Bentley Historical Library, University of Michigan. *Michiganensian*, 1920, vol. 24, p. 327)

to take the lead. When a desperate Michigan went to the air late in the game, Harley intercepted two passes.

The scoreboard read Ohio State 13, Michigan 3. "Harley's change of pace, straight-arming, and shifting of the hips as he shook off three tacklers in making his run for a touchdown was as pretty a piece of work as I ever saw a player do," a chastened Fielding Yost said to the press afterwards. "Harley threw off my best tacklers when making that run." For the only time in his career, Yost visited an opponent's locker room to congratulate the victors, bringing a special message to Chic Harley: "You are one of the finest little machines I've ever seen."

On that sunny October day in 1919, college football's most compelling, most enduring rivalry was born.

The Horseshoe and the Big House

Enormous crowds overran Ohio Field for the final games of the season to get a last glimpse of the famous senior. Harley's final game definitely did not go according to script: disconsolate fans wept as Illinois upset the Buckeyes 9–7. After his last desperation pass fell incomplete, Harley left the field, tears streaming down his cheeks. He bravely told the press that he alone was to blame for the loss in his final game. "Like the dawn he came," read the purple prose next morning in the *Ohio State Journal*, "Like the night he departed. It is natural. It was true to the inevitable."

More than 20,000 fans had witnessed this poignant moment, and the size of the crowd was not lost on President William Oxley Thompson and athletic director Lynn St John, who told the Board of Trustees that 55,000 tickets could have been sold for the Illinois game. The Trustees thereupon made the only decision possible in a town now obsessed with football. A motion was passed authorizing St John to build a new stadium sufficient to accommodate anticipated future crowds. Comments at the time were that the stadium, and the winning team everyone now expected to play in it, would put the university on the map.

St John moved with considerable speed lest the momentum slip away with the departure of Chic Harley. He audaciously unveiled the updated plans for a cantilevered double-decked stadium that utilized the latest in structural steel and reinforced concrete design. Open at the south end, it would become known as "The Horseshoe." This radical design concept would, he gushed, provide unobstructed views for 63,000 spectators who would be placed closer to the field than in any other stadium. The Trustees were duly impressed, in part because the stadium would dwarf Michigan's Ferry Field.

Ground was broken in August of 1921 on the west edge of campus adjacent the Olentangy River. Considerable talk about naming the enormous structure Chic Harley Field floated across town, but nothing came of it. It became, and remains to this day, Ohio Stadium. Even the optimistic Lynn St John had to be flabbergasted when a standing room crowd of 71,138 paid its way into the new monument, which triumphantly proclaimed that big time football had become a cornerstone of Ohio State University. Fielding Yost and his team, however, refused to cooperate with the celebration and shut out the Buckeyes 19–0, ending their three game winning streak against the Wolverines.

As he surveyed the enormity of the "House that Harley Built," Yost began to think big thoughts. Ohio State had caught the imagination of football fans everywhere with the construction of one of the nations' biggest stadiums. Ohio State was now competitive with his powerful squads. Yost had assumed the duties of athletic director in 1922, and became a man possessed: He would replace Ferry Field with a stadium bigger and better than the one in Columbus. Within a year he was talking up a 72,000-seat stadium to be constructed on the southeast corner of campus. Unlike St John, however, he ran into considerable opposition from anti-football faculty, skeptical alumni, and cautious Board of Regents members. Yost, however, was not just a football man, but a successful lawyer and entrepreneur to boot.

It took all of his persuasive skills to win over the skeptics. Yost raised $950,000 from donors to launch construction of an enclosed rectangular football stadium. Michigan Stadium, later to be informally called "The Big House," opened in the fall of 1927 and Yost was delighted when 84,000 paid to see Ohio State fall by a decisive 21–0. Even in its first season, the 72,000 permanent seats were insufficient and temporary wooden seating was added on the concourse.

Football Between the Wars

By the time Yost became athletic director in 1922 he was already hearing criticism of his coaching skills. He had inexplicably lost three straight games to Ohio State and that simply was unacceptable to spoiled

Michigan fans. He was learning that the value of a big time college coach was no greater than the previous Saturday's score. Yost quickly adapted to the new trends in the game and rededicated himself to winning championships and beating Ohio State. Between 1922 and 1926 his teams compiled a 28–2–1 record and captured the conference championship each year. His teams no longer scored a point-a-minute, but during these years they outscored their opponents on average 25 to 2. In 1923, sports writers voted his undefeated team national champions.

After taking the 1924 season off to concentrate on the new stadium, Yost returned to coaching in 1925 and built his offense around quarterback Benny Friedman and end Bennie Oosterbaan. Michigan had college football's first famous passing combination. In 1925 and 1926, they led Michigan to 7–1 records and two more conference titles. Yost then made the irrevocable decision to concentrate on his athletic director's duties and appointed Elton Wieman head coach. Harry Kipke replaced him in 1929. Yost remained as athletic director until he retired in 1942. His overall coaching record at Michigan was a resounding 165–29–10. He had won six national championships and ten Big Ten titles.

The Graveyard of Coaches

Although Michigan became a national football power during the early years of the 20th century and vigorously maintained its stature as an elite program to the present day, its student body, alumni, and fans generally managed to maintain their perspective on football and The Rivalry. Perhaps that was because Ann Arbor was located near Detroit, home to professional baseball, football, hockey, and basketball teams, all of which helped drain away emotions. By the 1950s, Michigan also had to contend with Michigan State, a serious foe located nearby in East Lansing. In Columbus, there was only Ohio State football. At Michigan, a strong liberal arts and humanities tradition placed political and economic issues – and political activism – at the center of campus life. The same was not the case on the Land Grant campus in Columbus. In the 1960s, the Ann Arbor campus naturally became a national center for student anti-war and social protests. Tom Hayden, editor of the student newspaper *Michigan Daily*, famously became the founder and leader of the Students for a Democratic Society, while Ohio State's Board of Trustees expected its administration to discourage student protest activities. Given the different academic and social climates of the two institutions, the Big Game assumed a much greater do-or-die emotional level in Columbus than in Ann Arbor.

The high expectations of Ohio State fans were evident by the end of the Chic Harley era. Dr John Wilce was a superb football coach, and during his tenure he produced winning seasons and conference championships. But he was not immune to scathing criticism from unforgiving boosters whenever the team played at less-than-perfection. When the Buckeyes lost in a shutout to Michigan on the day Ohio Stadium was dedicated in 1922, he was cruelly vilified. This loss was but the first of six consecutive defeats in the Big Game. By 1928, it was obvious that he had to go. He was replaced by "Sad Sam" Willaman, a former Buckeyes star. Willaman's teams won 70 percent of their games, including beating Michigan three times, but fans never became excited about the coach or his teams. In 1933 and 1934, the Buckeyes lost only one game each season, but unfortunately it was to Michigan. Tiring of the constant pressure, he resigned before being told to leave.

Athletic director St John brought in highly acclaimed Francis Schmidt as the new head coach. Schmidt had turned heads with a five year record of 45–5–5 at Texas Christian and enjoyed a reputation as an offensive whiz. Schmidt was a curious choice for conservative Columbus. He was loud, profane, raucous, and unpredictable, both on and off the football field. He paced, ranted, and raved throughout practices and games, profanities spewing in all directions, and he loved to flummox opponents with unusual formations and trick plays. Over the years, his teams used an early version of the I-formation and a spread punt formation (now called the "shotgun"), and they often tossed two or even three laterals on plays from scrimmage. As his teams flourished in his initial seasons, OSU fans praised his "razzle-dazzle" offense.

Schmidt's bizarre behavior was overlooked because he won his first four games against Michigan. Shortly after being hired, he became an instant Ohio hero when he responded to a question about whether he feared Michigan: "Well, shucks, beat Michigan? Why not? Those guys put their pants on one leg at a time like everybody else." Schmidt's comment made headlines all across the state, and his team thrashed the Wolverines 34–0. Grateful Columbus businessmen raised money to create the Gold Pants Club in order to award each of the triumphant players a small gold replica of a pair of the traditional yellow Michigan football pants. It is a tradition that continues to this day.

Things were not going so well in Ann Arbor. After undefeated seasons in 1932 and 1933, the Wolverines lost most of their top players and fell to a 1–8 record in 1934, despite the play of a rugged center from Grand Rapids. His team's dismal record notwithstanding, Gerald Ford was named first team All-American. When he became President of the United States, Ford would arrive at social events with the band playing, at his request, the Michigan fight song "Hail to the Victors!" His number 48 is one of five jerseys retired by the football program.

Francis Schmidt was the toast of Columbus until the Buckeyes lost three straight games to Michigan between 1938 and 1940. Michigan's legendary All-American halfback Tom Harmon had a lot to do with those losses.

Figure 9.3 One of the three numbers ever retired by the University of Michigan was number 48, once worn by their All-American center Gerald Ford. Ford turned down an offer to play professionally, flirted briefly with a career in coaching, and instead opted to attend the Yale School of Law. © Bettmann/CORBIS

Schmidt's bizarre behavior suddenly became a pressing issue in Columbus. In 1940, Harmon ("Old 98") intercepted three passes (running one back for a touchdown), rushed for 139 yards, scored two touchdowns from scrimmage, and passed for two more as Michigan trounced the Buckeyes 40–0 before a stunned crowd of 90,000 Ohio State fans. No one doubted that Harmon deserved his Heisman Trophy, but many Ohio fans believed that Schmidt deserved to be shown the door. Schmidt resigned before getting fired and departed to coach Idaho University, having captured two conference championships and compiled a 39–16–1 record during his seven year tenure in Columbus. That apparently was not enough for the Ohio faithful: Francis Schmidt had lost three straight games to Michigan.

Tom Harmon's exploits exceeded in every way those of Chic Harley. His breathtaking play underscored the coaching of Fritz Crisler, who arrived in 1938 after a successful run at Princeton. Crisler stayed ten seasons at Michigan, winning 71 games and losing just 16. He capped off his career by leading the Wolverines to a 10–0 season in 1947 that included a 21–0 shutout of Ohio State and a 49–0 wipeout of Southern California in the Rose Bowl. Beyond his winning record, the popular coach made a lasting contribution to the Michigan tradition – he put his players in the winged helmets, leaving a unique stamp on Wolverine football.

Within a span of 12 years, three coaches with winning records had been let go at Ohio State, and the school became known as the "graveyard of coaches." Following Francis Schmidt's resignation, much to Lynn St John's irritation, a tidal wave swept across the state supporting the unlikely prospect of naming a high school coach without any college coaching experience as the new savior. St John wanted an experienced college coach and Don Faurot of Missouri emerged as his man, but St John could not dampen the feverish support that coalesced behind 32-year-old Paul Brown. At Washington High in the small mill city of Massillon, Brown had compiled a stunning 58–2 record between 1935 and 1940. His legend as a strategist and motivator was further enhanced by his skills in mobilizing community support and in his organizational skills that seemed not to overlook a single detail.

The campaign on behalf of the "Massillon Miracle Man" was not subtle. The Ohio High School Football Association not only endorsed Brown, but also informally suggested members would steer top recruits to other schools if someone else were selected. With all three Columbus daily newspapers openly supporting Brown, St John finally caved in to the onslaught. Football had become the driving force on the Columbus campus, with the community at large controlling an important university personnel decision.

Nonetheless, Brown was an excellent choice. Cerebral, unruffled, superbly organized, Brown was the anti-Schmidt. He also understood his major task, telling alumni groups, "We'll prepare all season with the thought in mind that we'd rather beat Michigan than any other team on the schedule." He tackled recruiting with his usual zeal for organization, dividing the state into sections with an assistant coach coordinating activities with local boosters. The intent was that not one blue-chip Ohio high school prospect would get away. Come his first spring practice, the squad he inherited was stunned by the intensive classroom work: coaches would explain plays and the players would have to create their own diagrams and notes rather than peruse a playbook handed out to them. Once they got on the practice field, they were put through meticulously scripted sessions. Brown's first game in the Horseshoe was, by chance, against Don Faurot's Missouri Tigers, and the Buckeyes won 12–7. The following week the team traveled by train to Los Angeles where they overwhelmed Southern California 33–0. Only a narrow loss to Northwestern marred the resurgent Buckeyes' season record before they met Michigan in Ann Arbor. The resultant 20–20 tie against 13 point favorite Michigan pleased most Buckeye fans, and Brown and his players celebrated on the field as if they had pulled off a major upset. In 1942, before the war effort drained away most of his squad, Brown's structured system produced a 9–1 record. Quarterback Les Horvath threw three touchdown passes as Ohio State defeated Michigan 21–7, and when several top-ranked teams fortuitously lost late in the season, Ohio State was voted national champion for the first time.

Brown coached the Great Lakes Naval Station football team as his contribution to the war effort. During his absence, assistant Carroll Widdoes was given the reins. In 1944, the caretaker coach posted a 9–0 season that ended with an 18–14 victory over Michigan as senior quarterback Les Horvath was named Ohio State's first Heisman winner. Widdoes coached the Buckeyes to a 7–2 record in 1945 but, after losing to Michigan 7–3, he opted to move on to coach at Ohio University in Athens where the pressure was considerably less intense. Instead of returning to Columbus after the war, Brown greatly disappointed Ohio State officials and fans by accepting the head coaching position of the newly created Cleveland professional team at a hefty salary of $25,000; ecstatic Cleveland fans voted to name the team the "Browns." St John turned the team over to assistant Paul Bixler. After a lackluster 4–3–2 record and a 58–6 drubbing in Ann Arbor, Bixler departed for the head job at Colgate.

In one of his first decisions, new athletic director Dick Larkins appointed former Ohio State All-American end Wes Fesler (letterman in 1928–30) as head coach. Despite great promise, the handsome former Phi Beta Kappa graduate never could please the unforgiving fans. His initial season was disastrous (2–6–1) and soured fans to the point that three winning seasons, one Big Ten title, and a 17–14 Rose Bowl victory over Pappy Waldorf's California Golden Bears in 1950 could not calm the troops. His greatest sin, however, was presiding over four straight losses to Michigan, the last of which occurred in the most bizarre game ever played by either school.

The Snow Bowl

Wes Fesler's fate turned on what became known as the "Snow Bowl." Going into the November 25 game at Ohio Stadium in 1950, Fesler's future seemed to hinge on defeating Michigan. Because his teams had lost the three previous games, the boosters were restless and ornery. Bennie Oosterbaan's team, although considered to be the weaker of the two, like Ohio State had lost only one conference game. The weather was expected to be cold and cloudy. However, much to the surprise of everyone, a heavy snowstorm blew into Ohio during the night and five inches of snow had fallen as game time approached. By kickoff time – delayed two and a half hours as the grounds crew cleared the field – near-blizzard conditions existed and the snow hammered down throughout the game. The temperature hovered at a mere 10 above zero and mean 25–40 mph winds whipped through the open end of the Horseshoe. Athletic directors Crisler and Larkins discussed canceling the game, but the decision was made to go forward (Larkins did not want to refund 87,000 tickets; Crisler thought the conditions might help his team pull an upset). Attendance was announced at 50,000, but most observers thought that number to be exaggerated by at least a factor of two and most of those who had shown up had departed by the third quarter. Even in Columbus, there are limits to the dedication of its football fans.

The game was a farce. The falling snow obscured the yard markers and sidelines, and the bitter cold made it virtually impossible to hold onto the ball. Snaps from center sailed wildly and players could not gain footing on the frozen, snow-covered turf. Attempted passes were buffeted in strange directions by the winds. It became apparent that the best strategy was to be on defense. "Having possession of the ball today is a liability," Oosterbaan concluded. Ohio's famed All-American, halfback Vic Janowicz, soon to be named Ohio State's second Heisman winner, was playing his last game. Even he was stymied: his 13 yard pass completion to end Tom Watson proved to be biggest ground gainer of the game. Janowicz managed to kick a short field goal through the swirling snow in the first quarter and Michigan scored a safety on a blocked punt that rolled out of the end zone.

The game turned on a yet another blocked kick. With 47 seconds left before half-time, Fesler ordered a punt on third down with his team penned deep in its own territory. Michigan's Tony Momsen split the blocking and Janowicz's punt boomed off his shoulder pad. Momsen recovered the ball in a pile of snow in the end zone and the Buckeyes slouched to the locker room to get warm trailing 9–3.

Even before the second half kickoff, the second-guessing had begun. Critics said that Fesler should have run two plays to run out the clock and taken a 3–2 lead into the locker room. During the second half the weather worsened and neither team could move the ball. Both of them jockeyed for field position on the ice-covered turf, sometimes punting on first down. The game ended as the second half began, with Michigan ahead 9–3. Game statistics were bizarre. The teams had combined for a record of 45 punts. Ten fumbles were lost. Michigan passed nine times with zero completions, and Janowicz connected on three of 18 attempts for a grand total of 25 yards. "It was a nightmare," Janowicz told the press. "My hands were numb. I had no feeling in them and I don't know how I hung onto the ball. It was terrible."

Irate Buckeye fans did not give Fesler a pass due to the incredible conditions. He was denounced as the dumbest coach in the history of the game for his decision to punt on third down late in the second quarter. A few weeks later, with Michigan preparing to travel to Pasadena and the Rose Bowl, where they would defeat California, Fesler announced his resignation to accept a job in real estate. His physician was reportedly treating him for severe depression and exhaustion. Ohio State's loyal fans had only a long winter to look forward to (the Michigan streak now standing at four), and the sting of knowing that the Wolverines had beaten the Buckeyes out of a trip to the Rose Bowl without having made a single first down.

Less than two month's after his resignation, a surprisingly refreshed Fesler announced that the life of a realtor was not for him and that he was accepting the head coaching position at Minnesota.

Woody and Bo

Immediately after Fesler's forced resignation, a cry for the return of Paul Brown to Columbus spread across Ohio like a prairie fire. Once more, high school coaches trumpeted his candidacy, and all three Columbus daily newspapers predicted his impending return. Flush boosters agreed to pony-up $100,000 to pay Brown a salary too big for him to turn down.

The frenzy surrounding the selection of a new coach underscored the enormous importance otherwise normal Ohioans placed on OSU football. The Athletic Board and athletic director Dick Larkins, however, were still furious with Brown for not returning to Ohio State after the war. They were also impressed by the interview they had with the young head coach at Ohio's Miami University, Wayne Woodrow Hayes. They knew that he had out-recruited Fesler for some top Ohio high school prospects, and they were intrigued by his erudite comments that tied American history (and especially military history) to his coaching style. Hayes exuded confidence and demonstrated an unquestioned mastery of the art of coaching, earning him the Board's endorsement. President Howard Bevis and the Trustees, however, remained under strong pressure from influential Brown supporters.

The issue came to a head at the January meeting of the Board of Trustees. The Athletic Board had strongly recommended Hayes, but the Trustees were determined to have the final say. They found themselves deadlocked between the two candidates, at which time Trustee – former governor and now US Senator – John Bricker arrived after a delayed flight from Washington. A hard-right Republican, Bricker saw in Hayes a soulmate: he liked the reports he had received about Hayes' emphasis on team discipline, his deep Ohio roots, and his reputation as someone who absolutely hated to lose. Bricker explained to the Board that Hayes would constitute a dramatic change from the laid-back Fesler, and his comments carried the day. The Trustees voted unanimously to confirm Hayes.

The Trustees voted to give Hayes a one year contract with a non-binding verbal commitment of five years – not exactly an overwhelming vote of confidence – and so he knew that he had little time to solidify his position. After commanding a destroyer escort in the South Pacific during the war, Hayes had assumed the head coaching position at Denison University in 1946, where at one point his team won 19 straight games. He moved on to Miami University in 1949 and in his second season the Redskins went 10–1 and upset Arizona State in the Salad Bowl.

From the day he arrived on the Ohio State campus, Hayes changed the way things were done. He zealously oversaw his players' academic performances and implemented a rigorous off-season conditioning program. He installed a simplistic offense that used the forward pass sparingly and emphasized a power running game. He relied on raw power and good execution rather than finesse and deception. His favorite play, about which he could rhapsodize for hours, was "Robust 26," right or left, the fullback smashing off tackle behind beefy linemen. Critics dismissed his vanilla offense as "three yards and a cloud of dust," but he preferred a more lofty description: "a crunching, frontal assault of muscle against muscle, bone upon bone, will against will."

It would take four years for Hayes to earn the confidence of most fans. He drove his assistant coaches hard, holding long and often tempestuous meetings and film sessions. He was famous for his temper tantrums, sometimes throwing the projector against a wall amid a torrent of foul language. His practices were much more physical than players had experienced under Fesler, and he ended each practice with his dreaded "gassers," six fast laps around the field. Players collapsed during training sessions and he was even reported to have physically attacked players while in one of his rages. "How would you like it," one player asked, "with 82,000 fans screaming at you while you're on the field and that bull ranting and raving at you when you came off it?" A near mutiny occurred his first season at Illinois when the team locked him out of the locker room to escape another profane pre-game exhortation. Despite his manic efforts, his first three seasons were no more than marginally acceptable (4–3–2, 6–3, 6–3), and many a "Goodbye Woody!" banner was seen fluttering in the breeze around Columbus.

His endeavors were rewarded in 1954 when he had his own recruits on the field. The Buckeyes compiled a regular season 10–0 mark and romped to a Rose Bowl victory over Southern California. His offense was sparked by another scatback out of Columbus, Howard "Hopalong" Cassady. The national championship effectively silenced Hayes' critics. It was a team that *Cleveland Plain Dealer* writer John Dietrich called "the most inspiring team in Ohio State history – a tight-fisted, hard-hitting crew playing the game as it was meant to be played." Cassady, the sensational running back many believed had saved Hayes' job, became the third Buckeye to win a Heisman. Many old timers compared his running to that of Chic Harley.

Hayes seemed to have his pick of Ohio's best high school players, and he operated an effective statewide recruiting network that relied heavily on the involvement of wealthy boosters. National championships came again in 1957, 1968, and 1970. His teams carried off 13 Big Ten titles and endured only two losing seasons. In his 28 seasons, Hayes compiled a record of 205–61–10. After winning only one of his first three games with Michigan, he delighted Buckeye fans by going on a dominating run, winning 11 of the next 13 games.

Success on the field mitigated the bizarre conduct that his critics believed should have led to censure or dismissal. As his teams racked up one win after another, his legions of supporters grew exponentially, and they were quick to spin his questionable antics into laudable behavior rationalized as extreme dedication. He became famous for his controlling, demanding, domineering coaching style. He prowled the sidelines during games like a man possessed, ready to erupt in a furious outburst at any moment. Referees as well as his own players were lambasted for perceived mistakes. He clashed with Iowa coach Forest Evashevski before a game over the length of the grass on the Iowa field, pushed a camera into the face of a photographer in Los Angeles after a bitter loss, and punched another LA reporter in the nose. He became famous for breaking sideline downs markers, for throwing or breaking team equipment, and not infrequently pointedly stomping on his own eyeglasses in a rage (in one season, the unofficial count was 12). More often than aides could recall, he sported black eyes from having punched himself in the face during an explosion of anger. If Hayes had not won on the field, such behavior would have produced a quick dismissal. But beating Michigan and posting winning seasons, it seemed, covered most sins in Columbus.

One of his most famous battles, however, occurred off the field in 1961. After an 8–0–1 season, a 28–0 shutout of Michigan, and a national number one ranking, the OSU Faculty Council shocked Buckeye fans and their coach by voting narrowly to turn down a Rose Bowl invitation. Several reasons – academic as well as financial – apparently motivated the Council, but the primary cause seemed to be that many faculty members had simply grown tired of what they perceived to be an overemphasis upon football. On hearing the news just before addressing a group of

Figure 9.4 An out-of-control Woody Hayes ran into the middle of the field in a rage when the officials did not call pass interference on Michigan late in the 1971 game. Referee Jerry Markbreit assessed a 15 yard unsportsmanlike conduct penalty that sealed the Buckeyes' defeat 10–7. Hayes left the field only to break in half the sideline yard markers. Neither the Ohio State athletic director nor president reprimanded their coach. © Bettmann/CORBIS

boosters in Cleveland, a livid Hayes denounced the decision in his usual colorful manner. He launched an angry campaign against alumni director Jack Fullen, who helped orchestrate the decision. His attack was curious because Fullen had come to Hayes' defense during his first few seasons when cries for his scalp resonated across central Ohio. Fullen had even defended Hayes in 1956 when *Sports Illustrated* revealed that Hayes had provided modest, but definitely illegal, personal loans to several players, ostensibly because of dire personal circumstances. The conference and the NCAA disciplined the Buckeyes, but Fullen emphasized that Hayes was motivated merely to help needy students. The issue soon faded, overcome by a succession of winning seasons.

By 1961, however, Fullen had come to the realization that football at Ohio State under Hayes had become so important that it distorted essential academic and institutional integrity. The 1961 Buckeye team had gone undefeated, a tie with Texas Christian the only blemish on their record. This was a great team, led by wide receiver Paul Warfield and running back Matt Snell, both future professional stars (in fact, the entire offensive line would later play professionally). They ended the season on a high note, squashing Michigan 50–20. A trip to the Rose Bowl seemed a just reward for the team. Fullen, however, believed the time had come to rein in the football program and its head coach. He enjoyed job security because he was the employee of the independent alumni association and not the university. Ironically, he had created a booster group in the early 1940s called the Frontliners whose role was to support the football program. Now the program had become too powerful for Fullen's taste, and he and Hayes entered into a long and spiteful war of words.

Although Fullen was one of few Hayes critics in Columbus, he was not deterred. "The football tail is wagging the college dog," he famously wrote in an alumni magazine editorial entitled "Summa Cum Shame." He was embarrassed by Hayes' sideline antics and lamented that the administration did not discipline him. Most issues of the alumni magazine now carried a Fullen attack on Hayes and his "Football Machine" – hard-hitting editorials that were often highlighted by photographs of Hayes' irrational behavior during games. Woody gave as good as he got, accusing Fullen of "damned lies" and told an alumni meeting, "He's the greatest exponent of half-truths I've ever seen in my life."

According to University by-laws, even the incensed President Novice Fawcett could not overrule the council and he and Fullen became bitter enemies. In the days immediately after the decision, the *Columbus Citizen* published the names and home telephone numbers of the 28 faculty members who voted to reject the Rose Bowl invitation. Student protests and marches almost led to full-scale rioting. With his effigy hanging on the campus oval, Fullen reportedly left town for his own safety and police protection for his home was deemed prudent. The decision apparently affected Hayes' recruiting plans, with some top prospects for the next few years electing to play elsewhere after rival coaches gleefully told them that their faculty was not anti-football like at Ohio State. During the ensuing years Hayes' teams entered into a less-than-spectacular trough, losing two or three games each year, and even struggling to a 4–5 losing season in 1966. Hayes and his supporters angrily blamed the Faculty Council.

After that losing season in 1966, Hayes drove his assistant coaches and himself relentlessly, assembling his best ever recruiting class. In 1968, the "super sophomore" group led the resurgent Buckeyes to a 10–0 season. Having waltzed through the regular season, OSU routed Michigan by that embarrassing 50–14 score. This time around there was no question about a negative vote by the Faculty Council and the Buckeyes returned to the Rose Bowl for the first time since New Years Day of 1958. There they throttled Southern California and Heisman running back O. J. Simpson 27–16 to cap off a memorable season. The Buckeyes were voted national champions and Woody Hayes had returned to the top of the college football universe.

The situation in Ann Arbor was not so pleasant. Former star running back Bump Elliott had produced solid but unexciting teams. Attendance at the Big House had fallen precipitously – only 63,000 were on hand to witness the loss to Ohio State. New athletic director Don Canham, an administrator with a flair for promotion, got an early opportunity when Elliott resigned. When his overture to Penn State's Joe Paterno was rebuffed, Canham hired the relatively unknown Bo Schembechler. A native of Barberton, Ohio, the 39-year-old Schembechler had just completed his sixth successful season at Miami of Ohio, where he had compiled a 40–17–3 record. Schembechler had played tackle for Woody Hayes at Miami before graduating in 1950. After stints as an assistant coach at Presbyterian, Bowling Green, and Northwestern, he became an assistant to Hayes in 1958, coaching the offensive line for six years before taking the head job at his alma mater. During these tempestuous years, he and Hayes forged a close friendship based on mutual respect and a devotion to the game of football. They also argued loudly and profanely: in one special moment during a heated argument in a film session, Hayes threw a chair at his irate assistant, who promptly tossed it back.

Writers frequently called Schembechler "Little Woody" and there was some substance to that nickname. They did play the same brand of rock-'em, sock-'em football, but the similarities ended there. On the whole, Schembechler conducted himself with dignity and showed respect for the accepted tenets of coaching. He drove his players hard, but he did so with an effective leavening of good humor. And although his temper sometimes erupted along the sidelines, his behavior never crossed the boundary of professionalism, which frequently was the case with Hayes. He worked just as hard as his mentor and demanded as much from his coaching staff and players. During his initial spring practice in Ann Arbor, the physical and psychological pressures he put on his team stunned the players. Senior All-American offensive lineman Dan Dierdorf, only half in jest, told a reporter he was thinking of quitting football to join the track program: "The track team runs less than us. And their coach isn't so mean." Several veterans did quit the team that spring. In response, the new coach had a large sign posted in the locker room that read, "Those Who Stay Will Be Champions." One of his departing players scribbled in large letters on the bottom of the supposedly motivational banner, "And those who leave will be doctors, lawyers, and captains of industry." Schembechler reportedly enjoyed a good laugh at this example of insolence by an ex-player who would, according to legend, become a successful attorney.

From his first days on campus, Schembechler pointed toward the Ohio State game. Because the Buckeyes had 18 starters returning from their national championship season, the preseason hype not only awarded them another national crown, but also the presumptuous title "Greatest College Football Team of the Century." But, as Schembechler writes in his autobiography, "I had an advantage. I had worked at Ohio State for six years under Woody. I had played for Woody before that. I knew the way Woody worked, the way Woody taught, and I molded Michigan after his example. . . . Our goal was to beat him."

The first game in the Ten Year War between Schembechler and Hayes was arguably the best. The Wolverines had lost to highly ranked Missouri and were upset by neighboring rival Michigan State but went into the Ohio State game in Ann Arbor on a four game winning streak. The team had jelled and had run up large margins against Minnesota, Iowa, Illinois, and Wisconsin. The Ann Arbor campus, which had been roiled by anti-war protests and had become a haven for many radical movements of the tumultuous 1960s, found itself curiously coming together in support of the football team as the reviled Hayes – well known for his conservative politics and support of the Vietnam War – came calling with the most talented team of his career.

On game day, 103,878 spectators filled the Big House, much to Don Canham's delight. Ohio State was a 17 point favorite, but the Wolverines were still smarting about that two point conversion attempt a year earlier. Schembechler reminded them of that humiliation by having them wear T-shirts emblazoned with "50–14." Schembechler had indeed learned much from Hayes about motivating a team, and his efforts were rewarded with a shocking 21–12 half-time lead. In the second half the Wolverine defense stifled the famed OSU offense led by quarterback Rex Kern, and a Michigan field goal made the final score 24–12. As the fans stormed

Figure 9.5   Bo Schembechler and Woody Hayes chat at midfield before their first meeting at Ann Arbor in 1969. Michigan upset the top-ranked Buckeyes 24–12, a team that Hayes said was his best ever. Schembechler played for Hayes at Miami of Ohio and later served as a trusted assistant coach at Ohio State. [AP credit to be confirmed]

the field, the 225 pound Schembechler was carried off on the shoulders of his ecstatic team. As the coach dryly noted later, "Those who stayed were indeed champions." Hayes later told his protégé, "Goddamn you, Bo. You'll never win a bigger game." And he was right.

Schembechler had won his first Big Ten championship, but the trip to the Rose Bowl proved less than rewarding. Only hours before kickoff, he was rushed to a Pasadena hospital where he lay in intensive care with a coronary as his dispirited team lost narrowly to USC, 10–3. It was the beginning of a record-setting nine Rose Bowl appearances for Schembechler's teams, but it also set the template for the most frustrating part of his career. As he bluntly writes in his autobiography, "My bowl record stinks" (his account at Pasadena was a dreary 2–7). Although he naturally regretted several close losses to Pac-10 teams, he always said that his primary goal was to beat Ohio State and win the Conference: "Sure, I wanted to win those early Rose Bowls," he recalled, "but not as much as I wanted to beat Ohio State and Woody." He wryly notes that during the Ten Year War with Hayes, his adversary was just 1–4 at Pasadena. "So, he wasn't faring much better than me. We peaked for each other. Some years, we were so emotionally wrung out after that game, I'm surprised we had enough energy to board the plane."

Following his coronary, Schembechler recovered quickly and returned to his job with his usual enthusiasm. He put his unique stamp on the Michigan program, moving out of the shadow of his mentor. Like Hayes, Schembechler was often portrayed in the media during an emotional outburst, but he contends that such displays were for effect. "There is a method to my madness," he confessed after leaving coaching in 1989. "It's not temper, it's coaching." Many of his Woody-like sideline flare-ups were intended, he writes, to get the attention of an official in order to motivate his team and were mostly for show: "I'll let the [referee] know I'm there. It'll show my players that I'm 100 percent into the game and they had better be too." But then, he confesses, "Sometimes, I'm just mad as hell." Blessed with a good sense of humor, Bo would use that talent to defuse situations after he had roasted a player for a mistake. "Verbal, physical, emotional, or comical motivation is a beautiful thing when it works . . . Encouragement. Criticism. Screaming. Winking. Kicking. Yelling. Nodding. Ignoring. It's all part of coaching."

The Big Two and the Little Eight

Schembechler and Hayes – always friends but intensely competitive – turned the Big Game into something bigger than ever. The stakes were never higher than when their teams squared off at the end of the regular season: the Big Ten title and a trip to the Rose Bowl were always at stake. During their personal Ten Year War, the Big Ten Conference became, essentially, "The Big Two and the Little Eight," because one of the two schools won the conference championship each year.

The rivalry did not end for the year in November, but continued during the winter recruiting season. It got only hotter because Schembechler had the temerity to invade Ohio to recruit some of the state's best high school players. Hayes, relying on his strong in-state recruiting machine, which over the years he expanded to the East Coast and even on occasion to the Far West, generally refused to take any player from "that state up north." Michigan's rosters under Schembechler and his successors, however, normally included about one-third Ohioans.

The number of All-Americans who played in these games is too long to list, but the Ten Year War stands out for the play of two men. Ohio

State running back Archie Griffin (yet another Columbus product like Chic Harley and Howard Cassady) was such a complete player that Hayes discarded his famed "full house" T-formation to feature Griffin as the lone tailback in an I-formation. Griffin rushed for over 5,500 yards and scored 26 touchdowns during his career, and he still is the only player in history to start in four consecutive Rose Bowl games. He has the unique distinction of winning two consecutive Heisman Trophies, in 1974 and 1975. Michigan quarterback Rick Leach, a native of Ann Arbor, was a four year starter beginning in 1975. Ohio State defeated Leach's team as a freshman when he threw a pass interception that was run back for a touchdown to give the Buckeyes a 21–14 victory. Thereafter, the left-handed Leach, a natural athlete with an unquenchable desire to succeed, led Michigan to three straight victories over OSU. He enjoyed a record-setting career that saw him establish new school records for passing, touchdowns, and total offense. He was named All-Conference quarterback three times and All-American in his senior year.

After Leach led Michigan to a third consecutive win over Ohio State in 1978, the Ten Year War stood 5–4–1 in favor of Schembechler. Fans anticipated many more November confrontations between the two coaches, but such was not to be. At the Gator Bowl in December, Hayes' emotional eruptions on the sideline finally caught up with him. Late in the game, trailing Clemson 17–15, the Buckeyes' heralded freshman quarterback Art Schlichter tried to move his team down the field for a game-winning field goal attempt, but linebacker Charlie Bauman intercepted his pass and ran out of bounds in front of the Buckeye bench. The 65-year-old Hayes inexplicably rushed over and slugged Bauman on the jaw. He was given two unsportsmanlike conduct penalties, and Clemson ran out the clock. Schembechler recalls. "I was in the Rose Bowl that year, and I was sitting at the head table and [Big Ten Commissioner] Wayne Duke came up and said Woody had just hit a Clemson player. And I knew then, 'Geez, it's over.'" And indeed it was. The next day, OSU athletic director Hugh Hindman, a former Hayes assistant coach, had the unpleasant task of terminating the living legend. Hayes never coached again. He steadfastly refused to look at films of his behavior, never admitted that he had thumped Bauman or said sorry to him, and never apologized to the Ohio State fans for his inexcusable loss of control. Schembechler graciously attributed his action to deteriorating health caused by diabetes.

The Game Lives On

The spirited rivalry would go on without Hayes, of course, but it seemed to have lost a certain edge. Ohio State hired former Hayes assistant Earle Bruce, who had a long coaching resume in Ohio high school ranks (including Massillon, of course) and several winning seasons as head coach at Tampa and Iowa State. Bruce was expected to do the impossible: replace the legendary Woody Hayes, who still enjoyed widespread support among the true believers in Columbus. The paunchy Bruce did not cut a dapper figure along the sidelines, and his coaching portfolio apparently did not include refined public relations skills. Whereas Woody Hayes traveled across the state of Ohio to speak to anyone interested in OSU, Bruce tended to avoid the banquet circuit. Bruce never connected with the Buckeye faithful and was described by one insider as "whiny, grumpy, greedy, and petulant." Nonetheless, in his first season he led the team to a 10–0 regular season and lost the national championship when Southern California edged the Buckeyes in the Rose Bowl by one excruciating point. He never came that close again to a national championship. President Edward Jennings curiously terminated his employment on the eve of the 1987 Michigan game (which the Buckeyes nevertheless won 23–20 in Ann Arbor). His record was Hayes-like, winning 81 games with only 26 losses, claiming four Big Ten championships, and edging out Schembechler 5–4. During his nine years at Ohio State, Bruce had the best aggregate won–lost record of any Big Ten coach, but he had lost the support of Jennings who, apparently tired of hearing the many criticisms of his coach's public persona, seized upon a less-than-sterling but quite respectable 6–4–1 record as an excuse to "go in a different direction."

Following Hayes' dismissal, Schembechler coached for another 11 years and retired after the 1989 season with a record of 194–48–5. His record against Ohio State told the tale of just how close the rivalry was: 12–10–1. Late in his career, he began a stunning string of Michigan victories over the new Ohio State coach John Cooper, who was apparently moved to the head of the applicant line to replace Bruce after leading Arizona State to a victory over Michigan in the 1987 Rose Bowl. Cooper would win 111 games and claim three Big Ten co-championships during his 13 year stint at Columbus, but an unacceptable 2–10–1 record against

Michigan, coupled with a flow of negative news regarding academic and discipline problems, led to his termination in 2000.

Schembechler retired at age 60 after losing once more to USC in the 1990 Rose Bowl. In the years following his first heart attack, he underwent two bypass surgeries, the second coming after a second heart attack in 1987. As athletic director, he hired as his successor long-time assistant Gary Moeller, whose personal problems forced his resignation after five seasons. Moeller's teams, however, continued Schembechler's winning ways, compiling a 44–13–3 record while capturing two Big Ten titles. Another long-time Michigan assistant replaced him: Lloyd Carr continued in the Schembechler tradition, relying on a power-oriented offense and stout defenses. Carr's career record was impressive, 122–40, but even more impressive was his ability to cream Ohio State during his early years, beating John Cooper's Buckeyes in five out of six outings, producing howls of outrage in Columbus.

Carr probably wished Cooper had remained, because his fortunes in the Big Game turned sour after Jim Tressel took over at Ohio State in 2001. Tressel was a native of the Cleveland suburb of Mentor and had played quarterback for his father Lee both in high school and at Baldwin Wallace College. After graduation in 1974, he served as an assistant coach at Akron, Miami of Ohio, and Syracuse before becoming quarterback coach at Ohio State under Earle Bruce in 1983. He moved on in 1985 to Youngstown State as head coach and between 1989 and 1999 the Penguins made nine appearances in the postseason Division 1-AA tournament, winning the national championship four times.

In Tressel's first press conference after being selected, the new coach let everyone know that he understood the expectations, right down to the number of days before his first test against Michigan. "I can assure you that you will be proud of your young people in the classroom, in the community, and, most especially, 310 days from now in Ann Arbor, Michigan." Although some fans complained about his conservative approach to the game, they were thrilled by his five Big Ten championships, the 14–0 season of 2002 that ended with an upset double-overtime victory over the heavily favored Miami Hurricanes in the Bowl Championship Series title game, and an 83–18 record. Most importantly, he defeated Michigan in his first game and then went on to enjoy a sterling 8–1 record by the end of the 2009 season. Lloyd Carr's disappointing 1–6 record against Tressel was believed to have played a major role in his decision to retire at the age of 62 following a 14–3 drubbing before 106,000 spectators in the Big House.

Lloyd Carr's most disappointing defeat came the year before in Columbus when Ohio State squeezed out a narrow 42–39 victory in the Big Game of 2006. The defeat itself was bitter enough for Carr to handle, but he and the entire Michigan team had to deal with the news reports on the eve of the game that Bo Schembechler had died suddenly of a heart attack at age 77. The previous evening Schembechler had delivered his traditional talk to the team before its departure for Columbus. In typical form, he encouraged them to conduct themselves as proud "Michigan Men." That was, he told his rapt audience, much more important than winning any single game. Fifteen hours later he was dead.

The news stunned fans of both teams and dampened game day enthusiasm. Many Ohio State fans, however, complained that Schembechler had opted to depart this Earth on the eve of the Big Game in order to give the Wolverines a special extra motivation. It evidently did not work.

10 Enduring Baseball Rivals
The Red Sox and the Yankees

It's white hot. It's a rivalry on the field, it's a rivalry in the press, it's a rivalry in the front office, it's a rivalry among the fan base. It's as good and intense a rivalry as any you could have. (Larry Lucchino, President of Boston Red Sox)

Any rivalry that intense and productive over the last seven or eight decades is very healthy. I think it's the greatest rivalry in sports. (Bud Selig, Commissioner of Organized Baseball)

Even before it opened, it was called the "House that Ruth Built." The opening of the towering, triple-decked stadium on April 18, 1923, occurred amidst high expectations. The Yankees had won American League pennants in 1921 and 1922 only to lose the World Series both years to John McGraw's Giants. With slugger Babe Ruth leading the way, the future looked very bright. Sportswriter Fred Lieb wrote that Yankee Stadium "smelled of a newness of fresh paint, fresh plaster and fresh grass," and offered "a beautiful background for a ball game." The new stadium was, he gushed, "a masterpiece of baseball architecture," with "graceful pleasing lines," that rose "majestically" into the New York sky.

The opening of the stadium coincided with the rise of the New York Yankees to a dominant place in professional baseball. The Yankees, dressed in their "neat, new pinstriped uniforms," won the opening game against the Boston Red Sox on the strength of the first home run hit in the new park, a prodigious poke into the distant seats hit by, appropriately, right-fielder Babe Ruth. The Yankees proceeded to win their third consecutive American League pennant that season and captured their first World Series title by defeating McGraw's Giants. This would be the first of 26 World Series the Yankees would win in this magnificent stadium. As the decades rolled by, with the Red Sox repeatedly frustrated by their rivals from Gotham, Boston fans could only ask "What if?" What if the Babe – along with 13 other Red Sox stars – had not been sold or traded to the Yankees in the biggest fire sale of top talent in the history of the game? In 1990, looking back on one disappointment after another over seven decades, Boston sportswriter Dan Shaughnessy published a whimsical book suggesting that the sale of Ruth to the Yankees had placed a curse upon the Red Sox. The notion of a "Curse of the Bambino" might have provided an appealing rationale, but in reality the Red Sox were cursed by bad management and an extra large measure of bad luck.

The Curse

Yankees owner Colonel Jacob Ruppert's acquisition of The Babe signaled the beginning of a long and tortured era in Red Sox history. In fact, the fledgling Boson entry in the American League had won the initial World Series in 1903 and four more before the Red Sox sent Ruth to the Yankees in December of 1919. Lifelong Red Sox fan Cleveland Armory recalled the sense of foreboding he felt as a youngster when he heard the news of the sale: "From that moment on, being a Red Sox fan meant a life of sackcloth and ashes, a life of perpetual excuses, a life of misery, of sadness, of want and penury . . ." The Red Sox had enjoyed considerable success in their formative years. They moved into modern Fenway Park in 1912 and, led by centerfielder Tris Speaker, won the 1915 World Series. The young left-handed pitcher Babe Ruth emerged the following year as a pitching sensation when he won 23 games and posted a sparkling 1.75 ERA. When he wasn't on the mound, Manager Ed Barrow inserted Ruth into the lineup to take advantage of his powerful hitting. Ruth pitched and batted the Red Sox to the World Series title over Brooklyn in 1916, and the Sox repeated this success in 1918. In 1919, Ruth moved permanently to the outfield and hit a league record 29 home runs.

But all was not well in the team's front office. Owner Harry Frazee had purchased the team in 1915, but he had lost large sums making bad investments in Broadway musicals. He had also taken on an enormous debt when he bought Fenway Park. With his creditors putting on the squeeze, he had no choice but to sell the only major assets he possessed:

Figure 10.1   Young pitcher Babe Ruth poses before a game in 1919. His trade to the Yankees in December of that year sparked outrage among Red Sox fans since he was not only one of the premier left-handed pitchers in the American League, but also had established himself as a slugger, having set a new home run record for one season with 29. © Bettmann/CORBIS

the heart of his powerful ball club. Ruth was the first to go, but 13 others soon followed as Ruppert acquired a powerful team that could fill the seats in Yankee Stadium.

While the Yankees soared in the ensuing years, the Red Sox plummeted to the bottom of the American League. It would not be until 1934 that they managed to win half their games.

Murderer's Row

It would be misleading to suggest that anything akin to a rivalry existed between the Yankees and Red Sox from 1919 until after the Second World War. It takes two competitive teams to make a rivalry and the Red Sox did not live up to their part of the bargain. Between 1921 and 1964, however, the Yankees were masters of the baseball universe, winning 29 American League titles and 22 World Series championships. During that same period, the Red Sox won precisely one pennant.

The Yankees lineup during the 1920s was awe-inspiring to behold. After losing the World Series to the St Louis Cardinals in a classic seven game affair in 1926, the following season the Yankees won 110 games and ran away with the pennant as its famed Murderer's Row punished American League pitchers. The fearsome batting order ended the season with a remarkable .307 average; Ruth set the season home run record with 60; and first baseman Lou Gehrig slammed 47 four-baggers and drove in 175 runs. With their tally of 975 runs, they outscored their opponents by 376. The Yankees swept the Pittsburgh Pirates in four games in the World Series and easily dispatched the Cardinals the following year.

Revival in Boston

While the Yankees were riding high, the Boston club languished, averaging more than 100 defeats a season into the 1930s. Things began to change in 1933 when 30-year-old Tom Yawkey bought the Red Sox – a club that had just finished 64 games out of first place – for $1.5 million. Included in the deal was Fenway Park, but it was in need of serious renovation. Determined to produce a competitive team despite the limitations imposed by the Great Depression, Yawkey spent another $1.5 million to refurbish Fenway, including erecting the 60 foot high "Green Monster" in left field. He also authorized his front office to acquire quality players. Among the first to arrive were pitching ace Lefty Grove and power hitting first baseman Jimmy Foxx. In 1935, Yawkey paid $250,000 to Washington for hard-hitting shortstop Joe Cronin, who became a popular player-manager.

The Yankees won another world championship in 1932 although Ruth's level of play had begun to decline markedly. He had created major headlines as the Great Depression deepened in 1930 when he wheedled an $80,000 contract out of Ruppert. When a reporter inquired of the Babe how he could justify making more than President Herbert Hoover, Ruth famously replied, "Why not? I had a better year than he did." Ruth's last World Series came in 1932 against the Chicago Cubs in a year when the Depression produced a 70 percent decline in major league attendance.

The Yankee Clipper and The Kid

Before the start of the 1935 season, the Yankees traded the 40-year-old Babe Ruth to the Boston Braves, but 21-year-old Joe DiMaggio joined the team the next season. He more than lived up to the hype that accompanied his signing by leading the Yankees to another pennant (and a World Series triumph over the Giants) as he ran away with the Rookie of the Year Award, batting .323. It was the first of four consecutive World Series triumphs for manager Joe McCarthy's powerful team. DiMaggio was appropriately labeled "The Yankee Clipper."

An equally heralded rookie appeared in Boston in 1939. Ted Williams was tall and slender (6'3", 170 pounds), with a keenness of eyesight that made him the master of the strike zone. He almost never chased a bad pitch, and his tremendous line drive power was derived from his ability to whip the bat through pitches while generating force from the graceful turn of his hips. Williams hit .327 his rookie season, and one of his 31 home runs was the first in history to clear the second deck right field roof in Detroit's Briggs Stadium.

Baseball journalists had a field day comparing the relative merits of these two extraordinarily talented, but cantankerous stars. Until DiMaggio forced retirement, the personal duel between two of baseball's greatest players often overshadowed the rivalry between their teams. Williams was arguably the greatest pure hitter in the history of baseball, a distinction he intended to claim, but his fielding and base running skills were not compelling. DiMaggio was the better all-round player and, unlike Williams, focused less on individual achievement and more upon winning games. Williams elected to perfect his chosen role as pure hitter while DiMaggio took pride in his complete game: he ran the bases superbly, covered the vast expanses of Yankee Stadium's center field with majestic grace, possessed a rifle for a throwing arm, and batted for high average and above average power. He was especially dangerous with men on base, batting in 1,537 runs in 13 seasons.

Williams retired in 1960 after 17 seasons (he lost five seasons due to military service in two wars) with a lifetime batting average of .341, 521 home runs, and 1,839 runs batted in. DiMaggio, his career cut short by knee and foot ailments, retired after the 1951 season with a lifetime batting average of .325 and 361 home runs. In the end, Williams was widely considered to be baseball's greatest hitter, but as many critics in the Boston press corps never tired of reminding readers, he never helped produced one Red Sox World Series crown. DiMaggio, on the other hand, could claim ten world championships. In one revealing comment, DiMaggio once curtly dismissed Williams with, "Sure, he can hit. But he never won a thing."

The Yankee Hegemony, 1936-64

Between 1936 and 1964, the Yankees won 16 World Series titles and lost six others. The pre-war Yankees assembled by Ed Barrow have to be considered some of the most powerful teams in history. Beginning with DiMaggio's rookie season of 1936, they did something still unmatched in baseball history: they won four consecutive AL pennants by an average margin of 15 games and then clobbered the National League entries in the World Series by a stunning 16 games to three.

That streak, however, was tinged in sadness. In May of 1939, after having played in 2,130 consecutive games, the "Iron Horse" Lou Gehrig took himself out of the lineup because of the onset of a mysterious and terrifying disease. He would die two years later at the age of 37, victim of a rare condition that attacks the central nervous system: amyotrophic lateral sclerosis. It would become known simply as "Lou Gehrig's Disease." Gehrig's unfortunate departure, however, did not deter the Yankees from winning their fourth consecutive World Series in 1939 over the Cincinnati Reds. After they manhandled the Reds in four straight games, the NL president John Heydler complained, "Is this thing never going to change? No club can be as good as the Yankees have shown them-selves to be in recent Series against our teams."

In 1940, much to the relief of Yankee-haters everywhere, New York slipped to second place, but they reasserted themselves the next season as the winds of war swirled around the globe. Americans everywhere found

Figure 10.2 The Kid and Joltin' Joe. In the midst of a tight pennant race between their clubs, two of the greatest players in history enjoy a laugh before the 1949 All-Star game. Ted Williams is believed my many to have been the greatest pure hitter in the history of the game. Despite his heroics, however, the Red Sox played in only one World Series during his career, losing to the St Louis Cardinals in 1946. Joe DiMaggio, whom many believed to be the better all-round player, contributed to ten Yankee world championships.
© Bettmann/CORBIS

some relief from the ominous international news by following the sensational hitting streak of "Joltin' Joe" DiMaggio. On May 15, he singled off of White Sox pitcher Edgar Smith and continued to hit safely in each of the next 55 games. During this incredible steak, he struck out only seven times, while hitting 15 home runs and batting .408. As he extended his streak, press coverage intensified until it finally ended in Cleveland on the evening of July 17 when third baseman Ken Keltner made two backhand stabs of hot ground balls that seemed headed down the line for doubles. Undeterred, the next day DiMaggio launched another streak that lasted 16 games.

Not to be outdone, that same magical season Ted Williams also clubbed his way into the record books. He entered a double header in Philadelphia on the last day of the season, batting .39955, and proceeded to go six-for-eight to end the season with a .406 average. For an entire season, he reached base over half the time he came to bat! No batter has ever hit .400 since. Nonetheless, Williams' feat was not sufficient to win him the majority of votes by sports writers for the league's Most Valuable Player. They picked DiMaggio, whose hitting streak coupled with another Yankee World Series title apparently carried more weight.

Williams would never receive the benefit of the doubt from many sports writers. By 1941, his famous feud with the Boston press was already well underway. He had arrived at spring training in 1939 amidst a torrent of publicity. Boston's press proclaimed him the Red Sox's answer to Joe DiMaggio. Dubbed "Titanic Ted," he was, as *Boston Globe* columnist Gerry Moore predicted, "The Answer to a Sports Writer's Prayer." "Everything about Williams shuns the orthodox. His string bean physique, his inimitable nonchalance in fielding, his constant boyish chatter, seldom possessing any meaning, both on and off the field, and last, but by no means least, his frequent flair for committing eccentric or what is known in the baseball world as 'screwball' acts." Moore was correct.

By the end of his first season in 1939, Williams was widely perceived to be a spoiled brat, and when his play in left field seemed less-than-inspired, Boston fans began to boo their best hitter. Some fans took special glee in needling the aloof Williams, taking seats down the left field line just so he could hear their sharp barbs. Williams sometimes responded in kind, unleashing a stream of profanities for which he became famous. He eventually adopted a silent protest, going as far as refusing to tip his hat to the home crowd after hitting a home run. Boston's bevy of baseball writers began nit-picking over his every move. He responded furiously, telling a reporter that he did not like Boston or the people who lived there, complaining that his considerable salary (for the day) of $12,500 was "peanuts," and demanding to be traded. He panned the small army of Boston writers who covered the Sox, once calling them "human crows who perch on the rim of the ballpark and write typographical errors." For good measure, the 22-year-old budding star said of reporters, "I don't like 'em and I never will." In one typical response, a columnist wrote in 1940, "Ted Williams is a grown man with the mind of a juvenile." Once the battle between Williams and the Boston sports writers was joined, it would continue until he retired in 1960.

Williams was sharply denounced in 1942 for not following the example of boxer Joe Louis and baseball stars Bob Feller and Hank Greenberg and enlisting in the military. Williams drew withering criticism in Boston because he claimed a deferment as the sole support of his mother, but DiMaggio, who also played that season, received scant attention from the press. That year, DiMaggio led the Yankees to another World Series championship, batting .305 and winning another MVP award. Williams won the batting title with a .356 average, led the league in home runs (36) and RBIs (137), and predictably came in second in the MVP voting to the Yankee Clipper.

After that season, DiMaggio joined the Army Air Force and became a physical education instructor, which meant he spent the war largely playing exhibition games to entertain combat troops. Williams, on the other hand, went through the rigors of flight school and graduated with one of the highest ratings ever earned. During his training, the military learned why he was such a good hitter: his eyesight tested at 20/10, and he topped the charts for his reflex response, eye–hand coordination, and visual reaction time. He was deemed too good a pilot to send off to battle and spent the war as a Marines flight instructor at Bronson Field in Florida. He finally got his orders to report at Pearl Harbor for combat assignment in the Pacific, but those orders came 12 days after the second atomic bomb had been dropped on Japan. Like DiMaggio, the war had taken three years out of Williams' baseball career at an age when he would have been in his prime.

Continued Frustration In Boston

Bosox general manager Jimmy Collins had assembled a solid club for the 1946 season. In addition to Williams, there was the crackerjack double play combination of second baseman Bobby Doerr and shortstop Johnny Pesky. Joe DiMaggio's younger brother, the bespectacled Dominic, covered center field with aplomb, and veteran first baseman Rudy York could still hit for power. Pitcher David "Boo" Ferriss, at age 23, had won 21 games in 1945, and headed up a strong pitching staff that included Joe Dobson and Mickey Harris. Manager Joe Cronin's team led the league the entire season as Williams resumed his assault on American League pitching. On June 9, batting against the formidable Fred Hutchinson, Williams hit the dirt to avoid two high and inside fastballs. After dusting himself off, he responded to Hutchinson's challenge by hitting the longest home run in the history of Fenway Park. It landed atop a straw hat worn by Joe Boucher of Albany, New York, who was sitting in the 33rd row of the center field bleachers. Today a single red seat amidst a sea of green marks the site where the ball landed. With the Yankees floundering badly, by mid-September the Red Sox had wrapped up their pennant and Boston fans eagerly awaited their first World Series since 1918.

Early inklings of what would later be attributed to the Curse quickly surfaced. Williams was hit on the elbow in a practice game just before the Series began, and he played with a painfully swollen arm. He was frustrated by St Louis Cardinals manager Eddie Dyer, who utilized the famous "Williams Shift" in which he moved his shortstop well to the right of second base, stationed the second basemen in short right field and positioned third baseman Whitey Kurowski in the normal shortstop spot, openly daring Williams to bunt for a hit or to poke the ball into left field. Rising to the challenge, the headstrong Williams swung away and made only five hits (with no home runs) in the Series. His .200 average provided Boston writers with plenty of ammunition with which to label him as a good hitter who never came through in the clutch. The Cardinals, powered by the hitting of Stan Musial and the pitching of left-hander Harry "The Cat" Brecheen, battled the Red Sox into the seventh and final game at Sportsman's Park in St Louis.

The World Series turned on a daring play in Game Seven by the Cardinals' Enos Slaughter, who scored the winning run from first base on a single to center field with the score tied at 3–3. Slaughter's audacious move surprised shortstop Johnny Pesky, who hesitated for a crucial moment after receiving the ball from center fielder Leon Culbertson before making a futile throw to the plate. Williams went 0–4 in that game, and Brecheen got Williams to pop out in the ninth inning. It would be his last World Series appearance, but one his critics in the press box would never let him forget.

For the next five years, the Red Sox entered each season the pick of the experts to win the pennant. For five seasons, this collection of star players underachieved and somehow found imaginative ways to lose the pennant. As each pennant slipped away, the vilification that Boston writers heaped upon their favorite target increased. In 1947, the Red Sox and the Yankees fought for first place until Joe DiMaggio got hot and the Yankees went on a 19 game winning streak while the Sox folded, finishing 14 games behind their nemesis. The Sox stayed in the hunt in 1948 and won their final three games to tie the Cleveland Indians, only to lose a one game playoff 8–3 in Fenway. The 1949 season proved even more frustrating. After a tight pennant race, the Red Sox entered the final two games of the season at Yankee Stadium needing to win only one game to seal the deal. They lost both games and the Yankees went on to win another World Series over the Dodgers. In 1950, Williams went on the disabled list on July 11 with a broken bone in his elbow, but the Sox stayed close to the Yankees. When Williams finally returned in mid-September, the team promptly collapsed and finished four games behind New York.

By 1951, the star-studded cast that general manager Jimmy Collins had assembled at the end of the war began to show its age. The Red Sox were in first place in July, but then collapsed and finished a dismal 11 games behind the Yankees, who went on to defeat the Giants in the World Series. DiMaggio hit a double in the final game, but it would be his last major league hit. Emotionally and physically exhausted from a season plagued by nagging injuries, he retired.

The Yankees' Reign of Terror

After winning five consecutive world championships (1949–53), the Yankees continued their winning ways, capturing nine more AL pennants in the next 11 seasons. Meanwhile, the Red Sox tailed off into hapless mediocrity. The retirement of Joe DiMaggio was a major blow, but the Yankees never missed a beat, replacing him with their next superstar, Mickey Mantle. General manager George Weiss replaced aging veterans with talented youngsters who continued the winning tradition. When popular shortstop Phil Rizzuto reached the end of the line in 1956, Tony Kubek was ready to take over. Yogi Berra assumed the catching duties from Bill Dickey in 1946, and he in turn relinquished those duties to Elston

Figure 10.3 Roger Maris and Mickey Mantle pose before a game against the Baltimore Orioles in Yankee Stadium on July 30, 1961. At the time, both were in the hunt to surpass Babe Ruth's record of 60 home runs in a season. When Maris hit the record-breaking 61st home run on the last day of the season, Commissioner Ford Frick famously ordered an asterisk (*) be placed beside the record because the season was eight games longer than the 154 available to Ruth in 1927. © Bettmann/CORBIS

Howard in the early 1960s. And so it went throughout the lineup: second baseman Jerry Coleman gave way to Bobby Richardson, Moose Skowron turned over first base to Joe Pepitone, and in right field Roger Maris replaced the hard-hitting Hank Bauer. A bevy of top-flight pitchers, such as Don Larson, Bob Turley, Whitey Ford, Ralph Terry, Mel Stottlemyre, and Al Downing, kept the opponents at bay. From 1949 until they lost the World Series to Pittsburgh in 1960 (when Bill Mazeroski slugged his improbable ninth inning home run in Game Seven), the Yankees were managed by the cagy Casey Stengel. He apparently was not rehired for the unstated reason that he had turned 70 years of age. This prompted Stengel to affirm, "I'll never do that again."

Years of Mediocrity; Stains of Racism

In 1961, the former Giants shortstop and now their manager, Alvin Dark, commented, "You know why the National League is better. Because of the colored players." Tom Yawkey had long been known for his willing-ness to spend money for top talent, but that impulse did not to extend to African-American players. In April 1945, under considerable local polit-ical pressure, the Red Sox gave three star players from the Negro Leagues a tryout at Fenway Park. All three – Marv Williams, Sam Jethroe, and Jackie Robinson – relentlessly rattled line drives off the Green Monster, but they were not signed. A few years later, Joe Cronin, who moved into the general manager's position after the 1947 season, passed on an opportunity to sign the young star center fielder of the Birmingham Black Barons – Willie Mays – but so did the Yankees. The unwritten order to scouts of both teams was not to pursue blacks. In 1959, second base-man Pumpsie Green became the first African-American to appear in a Red Sox uniform. Pitcher Earl Wilson had been in their minor league system for several years and a scout's written report on him is instructive: "He is a well-mannered colored boy, not too black, pleasant to talk to, very good appearance, conducts himself as a gentleman." Wilson joined the Red Sox during the 1959 season and won 56 games before being traded to Detroit in 1966.

The Yankees' tally on the racial score card was not much better. Several good minor league prospects were traded before they reached the majors. Finally, the eminently talented Elston Howard made the roster in 1955 as an outfielder. Journalist David Halberstam effectively traces the sharp decline of the Yankees after their loss in the 1964 World Series to the St Louis Cardinals and the racism that pervaded the club's manage-ment. General manager George Weiss, Halberstam writes, "wanted his fans to be from the white middle class, and he most emphatically did not want black fans who came to cheer black players." In 1945, Weiss hired scout Tom Greenwade away from the Brooklyn organization. Greenwade had been intimately involved in Branch Rickey's search for the right black player to break baseball's color barrier. Weiss was adamant: "Now, Tom," he said in their first meeting, "I don't want you sneaking around down any back alleys and signing any niggers. We don't want them."

That the Yankees were headed in the wrong direction was evident by 1964: Mickey Mantle was hampered by bad knees, the power was leaking from Roger Maris's bat, and Tony Kubek had a debilitating hand injury. Manager Yogi Berra juggled his lineup and managed to squeeze by the Chicago White Sox by one game on the last day of the season, only to confront the surging St Louis Cardinals. The contrast between the two teams was stark. The Cardinals had three starting position players who were African-American – first baseman Bill White and outfielders Curt Flood and Lou Brock – and their dominant pitcher was hard-throwing Bob Gibson, who won three games and held off the Yankees with a complete game in Game Seven.

In August of that year, CBS purchased the Yankees and installed young Lee MacPhail as the new general manager. He fired Berra at the end of the season and announced that the Yankees needed a complete overhaul. The once-powerful Yankees promptly went into a prolonged slump, falling to under .500 for the season for the first time since 1925, and finished 25 games behind the Minnesota Twins. In 1966 they finished "a strong tenth." League expansion had increased the size of the league to ten teams. They did little better the next year when they barely managed to escape the cellar ahead of the woeful Kansas City Athletics. Twins manager Sam Mele said it well when asked to comment on the cellar-dwelling Yankees: "They never cried for us, and you can bet your tail we're not going to cry for them."

Impossible Dream in Boston

As the Yankees crashed, the Red Sox muddled along, overpaying for less-than-stellar "star" players. This changed suddenly in 1967 when feisty new manager Dick Williams conducted a demanding spring training that placed heavy emphasis on physical conditioning and the (re)learning of baseball fundamentals. No one held out any hope for a turnaround from a dreary 72–90 record in 1966. Less than 9,000 fans turned out for opening day at Fenway Park, but by season's end, attendance records were shattered as over 1,700,000 fans poured through the gates to watch Boston's "Impossible Dream." Powered by the hitting of three young outfielders – Tony Conigliaro, Reggie Smith, and Carl Yastrzemski – the Red Sox found themselves in a classic pennant race with the Twins, Tigers, and White Sox.

Even the tragedy that befell Conigliaro did not deter the Red Sox. On August 18, he was hit in the face by a fastball thrown by California's Jack Hamilton. The gut-wrenching "thud" of the ball silenced the crowd. The bright young star from nearby Lynn suffered a crushed cheekbone, fragments of which were driven into the eye socket, damaging the retina. On the final day of the season, the Twins and the Sox were tied at 91–70 when they took the field at Fenway. Yastrzemski and Ken Harrelson got key hits and ace Jim Lonborg went the distance for a 5–3 win. "Yaz" was voted the league's MVP with his batting average of .326, 44 home runs, and 121 runs batted in.

The heavily favored Cardinals, still propelled by the pitching of Bob Gibson, ran out to a 3–1 advantage in the World Series, but the Red Sox did not give up; they won Games Five and Six. Lonborg was asked to pitch the deciding Game Seven on two days' rest, but the Cardinals' bats were on fire and the Impossible Dream faded away 7–2 before Gibson's overpowering onslaught. After the game, Yastrzemski promised the Boston fans that, "We'll be back." It took eight years, but they did come back. By 1969 the Red Sox had been decimated by injuries and major player –manager confrontations that reduced Dick Williams to ranting and cursing at his sullen players. As Boston sportswriter Bob Ryan concluded, the Impossible Dream of 1967 "had been reduced to the Impossible Scream."

The Red Sox returned to top of the league in 1975. It was aging Tom Yawkey's last opportunity to win a World Series championship. Late in September, with the pennant within their grasp, the hard-hitting Jim Rice suffered a broken hand and was lost for the season. Despite his absence, the Red Sox swept triumphantly through the playoffs into the World Series, but their luck was such that they were matched against one of baseball's all-time great teams, the Big Red Machine of Cincinnati. This special team featured such stars as Johnny Bench, Ken Griffey, Pete Rose, George Foster, and Joe Morgan.

The Red Sox gave the powerful Reds all they could handle. Entering Game Six, the Red Sox were trailing in the series 3–2, but because of three consecutive rainouts, manager Darrell Johnson was able to insert pitching ace Luis Tiant into the starting lineup. The Reds pulled ahead 6–4, but Bernie Carbo tied the game for Boston with a home run in the bottom of the eighth. A sensational catch by right fielder Dwight Evans in the 11th inning off of a Joe Morgan line drive staved off a Reds victory. Then in the bottom of the 12th, Carleton Fisk hit a fly ball down the short left field line that began to curl towards foul territory. Fisk stood at the plate and waved frantically as if to will the ball to stay fair. It did – barely. It hit the foul pole atop the Green Monster and the Sox had triumphed in what many knowledgeable baseball men proclaimed the greatest World Series game ever played. As Fisk rounded the bases, the Fenway organist burst into the Hallelujah Chorus and thousands of frantic fans stormed the field in exhilaration.

The luck of the Red Sox, however, ran out one game short of redemption. Left-hander Bill "Spaceman" Lee nursed a 3–2 lead into the seventh inning, but a severe blister forced him to the bench and the normally reliable Red Sox bullpen was not able to contain the Reds, who won the game on a Morgan single in the eighth inning, giving them a 4–3 victory and the World Series. An estimated record 75 million Americans tuned in to watch that final game of what is considered the best World Series of all time. True to form, the Red Sox came up just short once more.

The Boss

Tom Yawkey owned the Red Sox for 43 years and, on his death in 1976, was remembered as a warm and kind man who never hesitated to spend his money to make his team better. He seldom meddled in the day-to-day affairs of the team. Some critics pointed to his slowness in firing inept front office personnel or field managers. The same could never have been said about the new owner of the Yankees, who arrived shortly before Yawkey departed. When he purchased the Yankees in 1973 for $10 million, Cleveland businessman George M. Steinbrenner hired seasoned baseball executive Gabe Paul to run the team and told the press that he would continue to operate his shipping company and let Paul run the ball club: "We plan absentee ownership, as far as running the Yankees is concerned," he told the New York media. "We're not going to pretend we're something we aren't. I'll stick to building ships."

Such was not to be. Steinbrenner became a headline-grabbing, micromanaging, impulsive owner whose angry outbursts and public feuds with his star players, managers, and members of the press became legendary. He could delegate responsibility but not authority. He second-guessed his executives, field managers, coaches, and players to the point of absurdity. Obsessed with winning, propelled by a domineering personality and a hair-trigger temper, he demanded immediate success. Over the three decades that Steinbrenner oversaw operations, his teams were usually competitive and managed to win more AL pennants and World Series flags than any other major league franchise. Nonetheless, a 15 year dearth of World Series appearances between 1981 and 1996 can be attributed to the shambles he made of his franchise.

Steinbrenner's preoccupation with winning added considerable fuel to the fires that stoked the Yankee–Red Sox rivalry. He absolutely loved to stick it to the Sox and their fans, and they in turn found him to be a man they could truly despise. It was a match made in heaven.

The Great Lakes shipping company that he took over from his father made Steinbrenner a wealthy man. Always attracted to sports, he purchased the Yankees in 1973. Shortly thereafter he pled guilty to felony charges for arranging illegal contributions to Richard Nixon's 1972 re-election campaign. Expert legal representation got him off with a small fine and probation, but baseball Commissioner Bowie Kuhn suspended him for two years. Unable to set foot in Yankee Stadium, he ran the club via the telephone. On January 19, 1989, in one of his last acts as president, Ronald Reagan granted Steinbrenner a full pardon. The Boss's detractors, especially *New York Times* columnist Red Smith, loved to refer to him as "a convicted felon."

Steinbrenner did not hesitate to spend large sums to produce a winning team, and when the Yankees came up short, he was not slow to change managers. By 1996, when he finally found in Joe Torre a manager he could live with, Steinbrenner had changed managers 21 times. At times his actions seemed bizarre. He hired and fired the tempestuous Billy Martin five times and dumped the highly respected Dick Howser after he won 103 games in 1980 because the Yankees lost to Kansas City in the play-offs. He even fired Gene Michael in September of 1981 after the Yankees had already clinched a playoff berth. Michael would later be rehired and fired again, then later appointed general manager. Hall of Fame pitcher Bob Lemon had two turns at running the club, as did Lou Piniella. Solid baseball men like Bill Virdon, Yogi Berra, Dallas Green, Stump Merrill, Bucky Dent, and Buck Showalter were limited to one brief managing opportunity.

Martin took the Yankees to the World Series in 1976 where they fell prey to the powerful Cincinnati Reds. In 1977, the manic manager drove his team relentlessly, often feuding publicly with his star players and his owner; however, he presented Steinbrenner with his first of six World Series titles after a 4–2 romp over the Los Angeles Dodgers. It was indeed time to celebrate: the Yankees had won their first championship since 1962.

The Yankees were the first team to take advantage of the new free agent market, and, much to the anger of fellow owners, Steinbrenner showed little reluctance to pay top dollar to stock his team with star players. When an arbiter declared future Hall of Fame pitcher Catfish Hunter of the Oakland A's a free agent in 1975, Steinbrenner did not hesitate: he signed

Figure 10.4 The Boss is in all his glory at spring training in 1983 as he announces the rehiring of Billie Martin as manager of the Yankees. A demanding, imperious owner, George Steinbrenner made 21 managerial changes as club president between 1973 and 1996, at which time he appointed the durable Joe Torre. The mercurial Martin held the record of five hirings and firings. © Bettmann/CORBIS

Hunter to a mind-boggling five year, $3.75 million deal. Two years later, with free agency now a part of baseball policy, Steinbrenner secured the services of another discontented Athletic, slugger Reggie Jackson. Jackson's clutch hitting in close pennant races and during postseason play earned him the sobriquet "Mr October."

In December of 1980, Steinbrenner continued to irritate money-conscious owners when he agreed to pay San Diego Padres outfielder Dave Winfield more than $21 million for a ten year deal. This stunning deal made the hard-hitting Winfield the highest paid player in baseball. Actually, Steinbrenner himself was not happy with that contract once he learned that Winfield's agent and lawyers had snookered him. Steinbrenner never appreciated being outsmarted in contract negotiations, but he had failed to notice that the contract contained a brief clause that included an annual adjustment to the initial salary figure to account for inflation, which meant that Winfield's income would actually come closer to $25 million. The incensed Boss subsequently launched a very public and petty feud with his high-priced outfielder that lasted for ten years and ultimately got Steinbrenner in more hot water.

Bucky @#$%@&! Dent

Boston began the 1978 season with high hopes under new manager Don Zimmer, while the Yankees looked toward a third consecutive AL title under Billy Martin. Zimmer commanded a powerful team led by veterans Yastrzemski, Fisk, Lynn, and Dwight Evans and had added pitchers Dennis Eckersley and Mike Torres to join Tiant and Lee in the rotation. The Sox broke away from the pack in April and by All-Star Break had an eight game lead on Minnesota. Meanwhile, the Yankees had stumbled badly, their clubhouse torn asunder by embittered acrimony between manager Billy Martin and superstar Reggie Jackson. By midseason, the Yankees had fallen 14 games off the pace. Never one to hesitate, Steinbrenner replaced Martin with the calming influence of Bob Lemon, and the Yankees started winning while the Red Sox fell into a funk. On September 7, the Yankees came to Fenway for a crucial four game series, having cut the Red Sox lead to just four games. The Yankees proceeded to sweep the series, outscoring and humiliating the Sox by a combined score of 42–9. The pressing Red Sox made an outrageous 11 errors in the series. The Boston press, as only it could do, excoriated Zimmer for questionable personnel and tactical decisions, blaming him for "The Second Boston Massacre."

However, the Red Sox regrouped and won eight straight games to end up tied with the Yankees at 99–63. A one game playoff was slated for Fenway. Having used most of his starters in the final days of the season, Zimmer had no choice but to start a Yankee castoff, Mike Torres. After a strong early season, Torres had tailed off badly, losing eight of his last nine starts. Nonetheless, Torres pitched scoreless ball through the sixth inning and took a 2–0 lead into the top of the seventh. Obviously tiring, he gave up two-out singles to Chris Chambliss and Roy White. Up came the "good field no hit" Yankee shortstop, Bucky Dent.

Dent was in a terrible slump and posed no power threat. Rather than go to the bullpen, Zimmer decided to permit Torres to pitch to Dent. Dent fouled a pitch off his foot, and limped around in pain until a trainer sprayed it with a painkiller. Torres' next pitch came in a tad high on the inside edge of the plate, and Dent lofted a high fly ball toward the Green

Monster in left field. It barely cleared the wall as it plopped into the protective netting while Dent gleefully circled the bases. In other ballparks it would have been a routine fly ball out. Before the Red Sox nightmare had ended, Thurman Munson had driven in another run and Jackson had homered. Although the Red Sox scored twice in the bottom of the eighth, they trailed 5–4 and fire-balling relief pitcher Goose Gossage got Yastrzemski to foul out with two runners on base to end the game. As stunned Boston fans slowly filed out of Fenway, everywhere the same angry comment could be heard: Bucky "bleeping" Dent!

Buckner's Blunder

The improbable saga of Bucky Dent drove a stake into the heart of the Red Sox and their fans. The team fell out of contention and remained there for several seasons. Star players like Carleton Fisk and Fred Lynn opted out via free agency, Yastrzemski retired, and another rebuilding program was launched.

By 1986, the Red Sox had rearmed themselves, building a contender around the overpowering right arm of young pitcher Roger Clemens and the hitting of Wade Boggs and Jim Rice. The Yankees made a late season run, but the Sox won the pennant by five games and defeated the California Angels in a stunning reversal of fortune after falling behind in the ALCS, 3–1. In the World Series they confronted the other New York team, the "Amazin' Mets."

Game Six arrived with the Red Sox standing on the brink of their first World Series title since 1918. Manager John McNamara had positioned his pitching staff so that Clemens was ready to seal the deal at Mets Stadium. However, a blister forced him to leave in the seventh inning with a 3–2 lead. Reliever Calvin Schiraldi gave up a sacrifice fly to Gary Carter in the bottom of the eighth and the game went into extra innings. In the top of the tenth, the Red Sox rallied for two runs, and Schiraldi went to the mound to clinch the Series. Attendants in the Red Sox locker room wheeled in the champagne and placed a T-shirt in each locker proclaiming the Red Sox "1986 World Champions."

They were a tad premature. With two outs, Gary Carter and Kevin Mitchell stroked singles, and Ray Knight singled to score Carter to make the score 5–4. McNamara brought in veteran Bob "Steamer" Stanley, but he threw a wild pitch that enabled Mitchell to score the tying run.

With two strikes on Mookie Wilson, Stanley fired a fastball that dribbled weakly off Wilson's bat toward first baseman Bill Buckner. Stanley and the Sox were apparently out of the inning, but the ball inexplicably skipped below Buckner's glove and through his legs as Knight scampered home with the winning run. In the clubhouse, the attendants feverishly hid the T-shirts and champagne before the bewildered Red Sox trooped in.

Game Seven was close until the eighth inning when the Red Sox pitching staff collapsed, and the Mets won Game Seven 8–5. Dan Shaughnessy addressed the heartbroken Red Sox fans the next day in the *Boston Globe*: "The Red Sox took you to the edge again. They made you fall in love and they broke your heart. Again." In just one play, the otherwise splendid career of Bill Buckner had become enshrined forever in the Red Sox hall of frustration.

Resurrection in the Bronx: The Torre Years

Following the disappointing loss to the Dodgers in 1981, George Steinbrenner became increasingly demanding. He turned repeatedly to the free agency market as the source of a quick fix rather than rely on his club's farm system. As one frustrating season followed another, he produced chaos in the clubhouse, firing third base coaches, pitching coaches, hitting coaches, even public relations staffers. Managers came and went with predictable frequency. As a result, Steinbrenner's ball club fell into disarray. His open checkbook no longer was sufficient to lure top free agents, who wanted no part of the Bronx Zoo. Despite the solid hitting of Dave Mattingly, who joined the team in 1984, the Yankees could not overcome the confusion that the owner had imposed upon his once-proud franchise. Steinbrenner's frenzy had created a disorder to which there seemed no end.

One constant during the 1980s was Steinbrenner's ongoing feud with Dave Winfield. Although Winfield played at a Hall of Fame level, he could never please his owner, who took notice of a temporary fall-off during the 1981 World Series and, in oblique reference to the "Mr October" moniker Reggie Jackson carried into retirement, sarcastically called Winfield "Mr May." At some point, Steinbrenner went over the line in his vendetta. He paid a gambler and small-time thug well known to New York City authorities, Howard Spira, $40,000 to dig up dirt on Winfield. The FBI heard of the scheme and arrested Spira in 1990, and Commissioner Fay

Vincent handed Steinbrenner a "lifetime" suspension, which lasted for all of two years. When Winfield entered the Hall of Fame in 1995, he did so as a San Diego Padre. An angry Steinbrenner attempted to get that decision reversed, but Winfield got the final word after all.

Once more, Steinbrenner was dispatched into exile. His quasi-suspension provided the Yankees with a time to regroup. With The Boss on ice, the front office under general manager Gene Michael drafted and traded intelligently. Promising minor league prospects were given a chance to develop, and a vanguard of young talent – Bernie Williams, Paul O'Neill, Jorge Posada, and Red Sox refugee Wade Boggs – set the stage for the arrival in 1996 of the next "Mr Yankee," shortstop Derek Jeter.

After falling in the 1995 playoffs to the Seattle Mariners – ironically managed by former, twice-fired, Yankee manager Lou Piniella – Steinbrenner hired a new manager with plenty of experience but whose credentials were suspect. In previous managerial stints Joe Torre had compiled a lackluster record of 894–1,003. But this native of New York City proved to be just the right person to lead the Yankees to another period of excellence. Torre exuded calmness under pressure and brought a wealth of experience to the job. He listened politely to his owner's rants and then went his own way. The result was the rejuvenation of a franchise that had become the laughing stock of baseball. Steinbrenner, however, did what he did best. He wrote lots of big checks to keep Torre's clubhouse stocked with top-notch talent. During his 12 years as manager, Torre had at his disposal an incredible array of pitchers that included David Cone, Roger Clemens, Andy Pettitte, Doc Gooden, David Wells, Orlando "El Duque" Hernandez, Randy Johnson, Mike Mussina, and super relief pitcher Mariano Rivera. Steinbrenner also brought in high-priced sluggers like Jason Giambi, Tino Martinez, and Gary Sheffield.

In Torre's first year at the helm, the Yankees finished atop the AL East, edged out the Baltimore Orioles in the ALCS, and handily defeated the Atlanta Braves in the World Series. It was their first championship in 18 years. The following year they lost to Cleveland in the playoffs, but in 1998 all of the pieces came together. The Yankees won 114 games in the regular season and swept past the San Diego Padres in the World Series.

By 1999, the Red Sox had regrouped once more, winning a wildcard berth in the postseason, but losing to the Yankees in the playoffs. The Yankees then went on beat the Atlanta Braves in four straight games for their third World Series championship in four years. The Yankees added a third straight title the next year in an all-New York classic, shutting down the Mets four games to one. This would be the last championship of Torre's 12 season run as Yankee manager. In the wake of the destruction of the World Trade Center on September 11, 2001, the Yankees rode an emotional wave of patriotic sentiment and rallied to win the pennant, only to lose in an emotional Game Seven of the World Series to the Arizona Diamondbacks. The usually reliable Rivera gave up a bloop single to Luis Gonzales in the bottom of the ninth for a 3–2 Diamondback victory.

Meanwhile, major changes were in the offing in Boston. The team was sold from the Yawkey trust to a consortium led by financier John Henry in 2001. The new ownership was determined to catch the Yankees and spent heavily to upgrade a team built around infielder Nomar Garciaparra, sluggers Manny Ramirez and David Ortiz, catcher Jason Varitek, leadoff batter Johnny Damon, and a formidable pitching staff headed by the incomparable Pedro Martinez. Club president Larry Lucchino hired the innovative 28-year-old Theo Epstein to run the ball club. Undeterred by his relative inexperience, Epstein boldly made key player trades and instituted innovations that included securing the services of baseball statistical guru Bill James to provide new perspectives on player evaluations and game strategies.

The much-improved Red Sox ended up in a dogfight in the ALCS in 2003 against the Yankees. The series went to the deciding seventh game. With Boston holding a 5–2 lead in the eighth inning, manager Grady Little opted not to replace tiring pitcher Pedro Martinez, who subsequently gave up three runs. The Red Sox then lost the game on a home run off knuckleball pitcher Tim Wakefield by light-hitting third baseman Aaron Boone in the bottom of the 11th inning. Once more the hopes of the Red Sox Nation had been snuffed out by the Yankees, whose supply of good fortune seemed endless.

Some fans grumbled about the Curse of the Bambino, but they grumbled much more loudly about Grady Little's judgment. Steinbrenner could not resist, taunting the Red Sox as their team bus departed Yankee Stadium: "Go back to Boston, boys. Goodbye. . . . We get the last laugh. . . . The Curse still lives!" Epstein replaced the embattled Little for the 2004 season with the experienced Terry Francona.

For the Red Sox, it was little solace that the Yankees lost the 2003 World Series to the Florida Marlins. No one knew it at the time, but it would be the last appearance Torre would make as Yankee manager in the World Series. Before the 2004 season, Steinbrenner became engaged in a highly publicized battle with the Red Sox to acquire the player widely perceived to be one of the greatest talents of all time, Alex Rodriguez. The hard-hitting shortstop had stunned the entire sports world in 2000 when he signed a ten year $252 million contract with the Texas Rangers, becoming the highest paid player in history. Rodriquez was voted the American League's Most Valuable Player in 2003, but the Rangers wanted to unload his enormous salary and thought they had a buyer in the Red Sox. The deal fell through when the players union refused to authorize a restructuring of the remaining seven years on Rodriguez' contract.

Meanwhile, the Yankees found themselves with a major hole at third base when Aaron Boone suffered a severe off-season knee injury. Steinbrenner saw an opening, one certain to irritate the Red Sox. He picked up Rodriguez's contract, and in deference to popular shortstop Derek Jeter, Rodriguez agreed to play third base. When the deal was announced, Red Sox owner John Henry was absolutely livid. He sent an email to reporters condemning the Yankees for excessive spending, which gave Steinbrenner an opening. He responded by observing that he was merely playing by existing rules, and that it was apparent to him that the Red Sox "chose not to go the extra distance for the fans in Boston." For good measure, he suggested Henry should "get on with life and forget the sour grapes." Several weeks later, he rubbed it in some more, blithely observing to reporters that, "We have made kind of a habit of handling them in tough spots."

Redemption in Boston

In 2004, the Sox and Yankees battled throughout the season before the Yankees pulled away to take the Eastern Division by three games. The Red Sox, however, claimed the wild card slot with 98 victories. They swept the California Angels to once more confront their historic nemesis. Epstein had added free agents Roberto Colon and Curt Schilling to the starting pitching corps and made several other moves at midseason that rejuvenated the team.

The playoff series with the Yankees did not go well for the long-tormented Red Sox fans. After losing two games in Yankee Stadium, the Red Sox limped back to Fenway only to be embarrassed by a 19–8 shel-lacking. No team had ever come back to win in a championship series after being down three games to none. Thus a disconsolate crowd assem-bled to watch the inevitable in Fenway Park. Their low expectations seemed to be justified as the home team limped into the bottom of the ninth of the game, trailing by one run as Torre brought in his super-closer, Mariano Rivera. But a walk, a stolen base and a clutch single by Bill Mueller tied the game, and the Red Sox won in the 12th inning on a David Ortiz home run. Game Five went an excruciating 14 innings before Ortiz singled in the winning run. Schilling shut down the Yankees in Game Six despite pitching on a painful ankle injury, setting up a showdown at Yankee Stadium.

In Game Seven, Johnny Damon slugged a grand slam home run in the second inning to set the stage for a 10–3 blowout behind the steady pitching of Derek Lowe. The rejuvenated Red Sox had deprived George Steinbrenner of another opportunity to gloat, and they demolished the St Louis Cardinals in the World Series, doing so in decisive fashion in a four game sweep. Given the 86 year hiatus, much was made in the media of the banishment of the Curse. After Derek Lowe and reliever Rick Foulke shut out the Cardinals 3–0 in Game Four at Busch Stadium, the Red Sox were greeted by a crowd estimated at 3.2 million people – all of who turned out for the long-awaited victory parade. Boston baseball writer Peter Gammons had long before written that the Curse of the Bambino was "a silly, mindless gimmick." Perhaps it was, but on the evening of October 27, 2004, some 86 years after a Babe Ruth-led Boston team had captured the 1918 World Series, the Red Sox once more stood atop of baseball. If there had been a Curse, it had been exorcised.

The Rivalry That Will Never End

The stunning season-ending comeback against the Yankees, followed by a four game annihilation of the exalted Cardinals, had swept away the fabled Curse. The Yankees no longer eclipsed the Red Sox on the field. The New Yorkers got the production from Rodriguez that perhaps justified his high salary as he won MVP honors in 2005 and 2007, but his diffident and inarticulate nature did not win him the love of Yankee fans or the admiration of many of his teammates. Meanwhile, Epstein did not hesitate to make major changes. He put together a revamped team that gave Red Sox Nation a second World Series title. Only six members of the Red Sox club that swept the Colorado Rockies in 2007 had been with the club in 2004. The Sox's renovated lineup featured several fresh faces, but holdovers David Ortiz and Manny Ramirez still provided the heavy lifting. The Red Sox had to deal with the increasingly bizarre behavior of Ramirez in 2008, eventually trading him and his powerful bat to the Los Angeles Dodgers in midseason. Nonetheless, the Red Sox finished a close second in the AL East to upstart Tampa Bay as the Yankees fell eight games off the pace.

Following another disappointing season in 2007, 78-year-old George Steinbrenner, in failing health, turned over the operation of his team to sons Hank and Hal. They quickly let the world know that, like their father, they would not shy away from controversy when they unceremoniously replaced the popular Joe Torre with former journeyman catcher Joe Girardi. Facing a substantial rebuilding effort of a team decimated by age, the young Steinbrenners opted to re-sign the multi-talented but perplexing 33-year-old Alex Rodriguez to a new ten year contact worth a staggering $275 million. His numbers perhaps justified such a commitment, but the contract meant that he had the Yankees on a most expensive hook until he turned 43 years of age. "A-Rod" had already hit 553 home runs in 13 major league seasons with a career batting average of .306. If his hitting prowess did not severely diminish by 2018, the Yankees new bosses calculated that he would provide plenty of future headlines and sell plenty of tickets when he approached the 773 career home run record held by Barry Bonds. But just as Bonds' claim as the greatest slugger of all time was called into question by allegations of steroid use, following the 2008 season Rodriguez admitted that he had used the powerful banned performance enhancing substance Dianabol between 2001 and 2003. Now his home run record and his future performance would become the subject of constant scrutiny.

As the 2009 season approached, the Yankees prepared to move into a stylish new 51,000-seat stadium located next to the abandoned House that Ruth Built. Opened at a cost of $1.5 billion, the opulent new Yankee Stadium offered a raft of customer-pleasing amenities aimed at an affluent clientele. Ticket prices were raised to astronomical levels, which was necessary to support an all-time high team payroll of $209 million, some $90 million more than their Boston rivals. The best team that money could buy rewarded management by sweeping through the Eastern Division and the league playoffs into the World Series against the Philadelphia Phillies. Just as Babe Ruth had powered the Yankees to a championship in the first year in the original Yankee Stadium in 1923, a rejuvenated Alex Rodriquez silenced his many critics by providing several clutch hits to cap off the first season in the new Yankee Stadium with the franchise's 27th World Series title.

The decision by the Yankees to abandon their historic stadium contrasted sharply with that of the Red Sox management to remain in Fenway Park. From time to time, construction of a new ballpark had been proposed, but instead they decided to remain in the 100-year-old Boston landmark that connects contemporary baseball fans to the rich legacy of a century of Red Sox baseball. New generations of the Red Sox Nation will be able to watch games played on the same field where the Babe, Teddy Ballgame, and Yaz once performed, but where the Curse no longer lurks.

Further Reading

Among the general histories of American sports are: Elliott J. Gorn and Warren Goldstein, *A Brief History of American Sports* (Urbana: University of Illinois Press, 1993, 2004); Benjamin G. Rader, *American Sports: From the Age of Folk Games to the Age of Televised Sports* (Upper Saddle River, NJ: Prentice Hall, fifth edition, 2005); and Richard O. Davies, *Sports in American Life: A History* (London and Boston: Blackwell Publishing, 2007).

My research included an extensive foray into newspaper and magazine accounts of many of the major events and issues examined in this book and I am indebted to the hundreds of journalists who enriched my narrative.

Chapter 1

Sources for the history of the Harvard–Yale rivalry are extensive. The place to start is with the authoritative history of early college sports written by Ronald A. Smith, *Sports and Freedom: The Rise of Big-Time College Athletics* (New York: Oxford University Press, 1988). See also, John Sayle Watterson, *College Football: History–Spectacle–Controversy* (Baltimore: Johns Hopkins University Press, 2000); Bernard M. Corbett and Paul Simpson, *The Only Game That Matters: The Harvard/Yale Rivalry* (New York: Three Rivers Press, 2004); Mark F. Bernstein, *Football: The Ivy League Origins of an American Obsession* (Philadelphia: University of Pennsylvania Press, 2001); Bernard M. Corbett, *Harvard Football* (Charleston, SC: Arcadia Publishing, 2002); Tim Cohane, *The Yale Football Story* (New York: G. P. Putnam's Sons, 1951); and Sam Rubin, *Yale Football: Images of Sports* (Charleston, SC: Arcadia Publishing, 2006).

Chapter 2

Two good general histories of baseball provide the context for this chapter: Charles C. Alexander, *Our Game: An American Baseball History* (New York: Henry Holt, 1991) and Benjamin Rader, *Baseball: A History of America's Game* (Lincoln: University of Nebraska Press, 1992).

In terms of both quality and quantity, the books that focus on the Giants are less compelling than those that explore the history of the Brooklyn phase of Dodger history. The major exceptions to this observation are two excellent studies: Frank Deford's *The Old Ball Game: How John McGraw, Christy Mathewson and the New York Giants Created Modern Baseball* (New York: Grove Press, 2005) and Charles C. Alexander's *John McGraw* (Lincoln: University of Nebraska Press, 1988). See also James D. Hardy, *The New York Giants Base Ball Club: The Growth of a Team and a Sport, 1870 to 1900* (Jefferson, NC: McFarland and Company, 1996) and Mark Fainaru-Wada and Lance Williams, *Game of Shadows: Barry Bonds, BALCO, and the Steroids Scandal that Rocked Professional Sports* (New York: Gotham Books, 2006).

For the Dodgers, see Jules Tygiel, *Baseball's Great Experiment: Jackie Robinson and His Legacy* (New York: Oxford University Press, 1983); Roger Kahn, *Boys of Summer* (New York: Harper & Row, 1971) and *The Era, 1947–1957: When the Yankees, the Giants, and the Dodgers Ruled the World* (Lincoln: University of Nebraska Press, 1993); Arnold Rampersad, *Jackie Robinson: A Biography* (New York: Alfred A. Knopf, 1997); Lee Lowenfish, *Branch Rickey: Baseball's Ferocious Gentleman* (Lincoln: University of Nebraska Press, 2007); Neil J. Sullivan, *The Dodgers Move West* (New York: Oxford University Press, 1987); and Michael D'Antonio, *True Blue: The True Story of Baseball's Most Controversial Owner, and the Dodgers of Brooklyn and Los Angeles* (New York: Riverhead Books, 2009).

The ugly dust-up between John Roseboro and Juan Marichal is examined by Larry R. Gerlach in "Crime and Punishment: The Marichal–Roseboro Incident," in *Nine: A Journal of Baseball History and Culture* (2004), pp. 1–28. Joshua Prager's artfully conceptualized and eloquently written book that revolves around one pitch in one game is baseball history at its best: *The Echoing Green: The Untold Story of Bobby Thomson, Ralph Branca, and the Shot Heard Round the World* (New York: Pantheon Books, 2006).

Chapter 3

The Duke–North Carolina basketball rivalry has produced its share of popular books. Art Chansky manages to overcome his North Carolina loyalties in *Blue Blood: Duke–Carolina, Inside the Most Storied Rivalry in College Hoops* (New York: St Martin's Press, 2006) but his *Dean's Domain: The Inside Story of Dean Smith and His College Basketball Empire* (Atlanta: Longstreet Publishing, 1999) is uncritical. So is Gregg Doyel's *Coach K: Building the Duke Dynasty* (Lenexa, Kansas: Addax Publishing Group, 1999).

Chapter 4

Two general books on the history of professional football provide a useful context for an examination of the Bears–Packers rivalry. Robert W. Peterson's *Pigskin: The Early Years of Pro Football* (New York: Oxford University Press, 1997) is useful for the formative years until the Second World War. For the period since 1940, the standard is Michael MacCambridge, *America's Game: The Epic Story of How Pro Football Captured a Nation* (New York: Random House, 2004). See also Stephen Fox's *Big Leagues: Professional Baseball, Football, and Basketball In National Memory* (New York: William Morrow, 1994). The detailed, if uncritical, biography by Jeff Davis, *Papa Bear: The Life and Legacy of George Halas* (New York: McGraw Hill, 2005), is comprehensive, while David Maraniss' *When Pride Still Mattered: A Life of Vince Lombardi* (New York: Simon and Schuster, 1999) is sports biography at its best.

Chapter 5

The primary source for this chapter is Ian O'Connor, *Arnie & Jack: Palmer, Nicklaus, and Golf's Greatest Rivalry* (Boston: Houghton Mifflin Company, 2008). Two autobiographies are well worth reading: Jack Nicklaus, with Ken Bowden, *Jack Nicklaus: My Story* (New York: Simon and Schuster, 1997); and Arnold Palmer with James Dodson, *A Golfer's Life* (New York: Ballantine Books, 1999). Also of interest is James Dobson's *Ben Hogan: An American Life* (New York: Doubleday, 2004).

Chapter 6

For an overview of the early years of professional basketball, see Stephen Fox, *Big Leagues: Professional Baseball, Football, and Basketball in National Memory* (New York: William Morrow, 1994).

For the Lakers, see Charley Rosen, *The Pivotal Season; How the 1971–72 Los Angeles Lakers Changed the NBA* (New York: St. Martin's Press, 2005); Scott Ostler and Steve Springer, *Winnin' Times: The Magical Journey of the Los Angeles Lakers* (New York: McMillan, 1986); Steven Travers, *The Good, the Bad, and the Ugly* (Chicago: Triumph Books, 2007); Jerry West with Bill Libby, *Mr. Clutch: The Jerry West Story* (Englewood, NJ: Prentice Hall, 1970); Phil Jackson and Charley Rosen, *More than a Game* (New York: Fireside Books, 2002); Elizabeth Kaye, *Ain't No Tomorrow* (Chicago: Contemporary Books, 2002); Roland Lazenby, *The Show: The Inside Story of the Spectacular Los Angeles Lakers in the Words of Those Who Lived It* (New York: McGraw-Hill, 2006); and Earvin "Magic" Johnson, *My Life* (New York: Fawcett Books, 1992).

For the Celtics, see Lew Freedman, *Dynasty: The Rise of the Boston Celtics* (Guilford, CT: Lyons Press, 2008); Dan Shaughnessy, *Ever Green: The Boston Celtics* (New York: St. Martin's Press, 1990); Arnold "Red" Auerbach and Joe Fitzgerald, *Red Auerbach: An Autobiography* (New York; Putnam, 1977); Dan Shaughnessy, *Seeing Red: The Red Auerbach Story* (Holbrook, MA: Adams Publishing, 1994); and John Feinstein and Red Auerbach, *Let Me Tell You a Story: A Lifetime in the Game* (New York: Bay Back Books, 2004).

Chapter 7

The context for this chapter is provided by Jeffrey Sammon's excellent history of boxing in the 20th century: *Beyond the Ring: The Role of Boxing in American Society* (Urbana: University of Illinois Press, 1988).

The best (albeit limited) source for the life of Joe Frazier is his autobiography as told to Phil Berger, *Smokin': The Autobiography of a Heavyweight Champion of the World, Smokin' Joe Frazier* (New York: Macmillan, 1996).

For Muhammad Ali, see Thomas Hauser, *Muhammad Ali: His Life and Times* (New York: Simon and Schuster, 1991), which is in fact a compilation of interviews conducted with a wide spectrum of individuals who knew him throughout his career. See also Elliott J. Gorn, ed., *Muhammad Ali: The People's Champ* (Urbana: University of Illinois Press, 1995) and Muhammad Ali's own ineffectual effort at an autobiography with Richard Durham, *The Greatest: My Own Story* (New York: Random House, 1975).

Also of interest are: Budd Schulberg, *Loser and Still Champion* (Garden City: Doubleday, 1972); Norman Mailer, *The Fight* (Boston: Little Brown, 1975); and David Zang, "The Greatest: Muhammad Ali's Confounding Character," in Patrick B. Miller and David K. Wiggins, *Sport and the Color Line* (New York: Routledge, 2004).

Chapter 8

For a detailed examination of this unique tennis rivalry, see Johnette Howard, *The Rivals: Chris Evert vs. Martina Navralilova; Their Epic Duels and Extraordinary Friendship* (New York: Broadway Books, 2005). See also, *Martina* (New York: Fawcett Crest, 1985) written by Navratilova with George Vecsey; R. R. Knudson, *Martina Navratilova: Tennis Power* (New York: Puffin Books, 1986); *Chrissie: My Own Story* (New York: Simon and Schuster, 1982) by Chris Evert with Neil Amdur; and Betty Lou Phillips, *Chris Evert: First Lady of Tennis* (New York: Simon and Schuster, 1977). For Navratilova's personal life, see Gilda Zerman, *Martina Navratilova* (New York: Chelsea House, 1995).

Chapter 9

For Ohio State football, see *Greatest Moments in Ohio State Football* (Chicago: Triumph Books, 1997); Bob Hunter, *Chic: The Extraordinary Rise of Ohio State Football and the Tragic Schoolboy Athlete Who Made It Happen* (Wilmington, OH: Orange Fraser Press, 2008); Andrew O'Toole, *Paul Brown: The Rise and Fall and Rise Again of Football's Most Innovative Coach* (Cincinnati: Clerisy Press, 2008); Robert Vare, *Buckeye: A Study of Coach Woody Hayes and the Ohio State Football Machine* (New York: Harpers Magazine Press, 1974); David Hyde, *1968: The Year that Saved Ohio State Football* (Wilmington, OH: Orange Fraser Press, 1988); Jerry Brondfield, *Woody Hayes and the 100-Yard War* (New York:

Random House, 1974); and John Lombardo, *A Fire to Win: The Life and Times of Woody Hayes* (New York: St Martin's Griffin, 2005).

For Michigan, see John U. Bacon, "Fielding Yost and Building a Sports Empire," *Michigan History Magazine* (September, 2000), pp. 29–33; "Robert Soderstrom, *The Big House: Fielding H. Yost and the Building of Michigan Stadium* (Ann Arbor: Huron River Press, 2005); Jim Brandstatter, *Tales from Michigan Stadium* (Champaign: Sports Publishing L. L. C., 2005); *Game Day: Michigan Football, the Greatest Games, Players, Coaches, and Teams in the Glorious Tradition of Wolverine Football* (Chicago: Triumph Books, 2006). Bo Schembechler with Mitch Albom, *Bo: Life, Laughs, and Lessons of a College Football Legend* (New York: Warner Books, 1989), is a cut above the usual sports autobiography.

Chapter 10

No two teams have produced more printed pages than the Boston Red Sox and New York Yankees. For an overview of their rivalry, see the combined work of several prominent baseball journalists in, *The Rivals: The Boston Red Sox vs. the New York Yankees* (New York: St. Martin's Press, 2004). See also Frederick Frommer and Harvey Frommer, *Yankees vs. Red Sox; Baseball's Greatest Rivalry* (New York: Sports Publishing L. L. C., 2005) and Richard Bradley, *The Greatest Game: The Yankees, the Red Sox, and the Playoff of '78* (New York: Free Press, 2008).

For the early years of baseball, see the standard biography of the architect of the American League by Eugene Murdock, *Ban Johnson: Czar of Baseball* (Westport CT: Greenwood Press, 1982).

For the Yankees, see the re-publication of the 1943 Frank Graham jewel, *The New York Yankees: An Informal History* (Carbondale: Southern Illinois University Press, 2002); Glenn Stout, *Yankees Century* (Boston and New York: Houghton Mifflin, 2002); Harvey Frommer, *A Yankee Century* (New York: Berkley Books, 2003); Daniel R. Levitt, *Ed Barrow: The Bulldog Who Built the Yankees' First Dynasty* (Lincoln: University of Nebraska Press, 2008); Robert W. Creamer, *Babe: A Legend Comes to Life* (New York: Simon and Schuster, 1974); Leigh Montville, *The Big Bam: The Life and Times of Babe Ruth* (New York: Broadway Books, 2006); Harvey Frommer, *Five O'Clock Lightning: Babe Ruth, Lou Gehrig, and the Greatest Team in Baseball* (New York: John Wiley & Sons, 2008); Richard J. Tofel, *A Legend in the Making: New York Yankees in 1939*

(Chicago: Ivan Dee, 2002); Richard Ben Cramer, *Joe DiMaggio: The Hero's Life* (New York: Simon and Schuster, 2000); Frank Strauss, *Dawn of a Dynasty: The Incredible and Improbable Story of the 1947 New York Yankees* (New York: iUniverse, Inc., 2008); Jack Mann, *The Decline and Fall of the New York Yankees* (New York: Simon and Schuster, 1967); Phil Bashe, *Dog Days: The New York Yankees' Fall from Grace and Return to Glory, 1964–1976* (San Jose: Authors Choice Press, 1994); David Halberstam, *October of '64* (New York: Fawcett, 1994); Maury Allen, *All Roads Lead to October: Boss Steinbrenner's 25-year Reign Over the New York Yankees* (New York: St. Martin's Press, 2000); and Joe Torre and Tom Verducci, *The Yankee Years* (New York: Doubleday, 2009).

For the Red Sox, see Peter Golenbock, *Red Sox Nation: An Unexpurgated History of the Red Sox* (Chicago: Triumph Books, 2005); Allan James Wood, *1918: Babe Ruth and the World Champion Boston Red Sox* (Lincoln: University of Nebraska Press, 2002); Leigh Montville, *Ted Williams: Biography of an American Hero* (New York: Broadway Books, 2004); John Updike, "Hub Fans Bid Kid Adieu," *New Yorker* (October 22, 1960); Dan Shaughnessy, *The Curse of the Bambino* (New York: Dutton, 1990) and *Reversing the Curse: Inside the 2004 Red Sox* (New York: Houghton Mifflin, 2005); Howard Bryant, *Shut Out: The Story of Race and Baseball in Boston* (Boston: Beacon Press, 2002); Bill Reynolds, *Lost Summer: The '67 Red Sox and the Impossible Dream* (New York: Warner Books, 1997); and Tony Massarotti, *Dynasty: The Inside Story on How the Red Sox Became a Baseball Powerhouse* (New York: St. Martin's Press, 2008).

Index